John Richard Houlding

Launching Away

Roger Larksway's Strange Mission

John Richard Houlding

Launching Away

Roger Larksway's Strange Mission

ISBN/EAN: 9783337167943

Printed in Europe, USA, Canada, Australia, Japan

Cover: Foto ©Thomas Meinert / pixelio.de

More available books at **www.hansebooks.com**

LAUNCHING AWAY;

OR,

Roger Larksway's Strange Mission.

EDITED BY

J. R. H. HAWTHORN,

Author of
"*The Pioneer of a Family; or, Adventures of a Young Governess,*" *etc.*

SECOND EDITION.

London:
HODDER AND STOUGHTON,
27, PATERNOSTER ROW.
MDCCCLXXXV.
All Rights Reserved.

BUTLER & TANNER,
THE SELWOOD PRINTING WORKS,
FROME AND LONDON.

CHAPTER I.

"Let us then be up and doing."—Longfellow.

I, ROGER LARKSWAY, at present of Melbourne, Victoria, was born near Greenwich Park, in a secluded dell full of rural beauty, although it was not far from the great busy city of London. As I now write, recollections of my early days come pleasantly waving over my fancy, like odours from a clover-field, or from buttercups and daisies in a newly-mown meadow. Our cottage was in an artificial wilderness of flowers and scented clinging plants, encircled with a hedgerow of hawthorn, woodbines, and sweet-brier. It was, indeed, a charming retreat, "the dearest spot on earth to me," and every flower which grew there seems to be still living in my memory, in perennial bloom and perfume. All the little birds around loved to hop about our garden, and they used to sing as cheerfully as if they were in the woods; for they seemed to know that there were no cruel boys to entrap them, and that our pet cat was stone blind.

The plaintive air to that dear old song, "Home, sweet home!" always seems to awaken in my breast echoes of the cuckoo clock in the hall of my birthplace, or the matutinal songs of the mavis in the lilac-tree under my bedroom window. I daresay many sensitive Englishmen, beside myself, have felt their hearts throb with home longings when they have heard that expressive song; and it would more tenderly touch their feelings if they were lonely wanderers in a foreign land—'tis then that they most thoroughly realize the sentiment, "There's no place like home!"

I stood on a rocky point in Sydney harbour near Wooloomooloo Bay, one summer evening a few years ago. It was a memorable occasion. Around me were thousands of persons on every available part of the shores, and tens of thousands more were afloat in steamers and yachts and ferry boats. We were all gazing at the fine steam frigate, *Galatea*, which was preparing to start for England. The rapid clank-clank of the windlass palls indicated that she was getting up her anchor by steam power, and there were other signs that the crew were having a busy time of it. On the bridge or platform amidships stood her royal captain, the Duke of Edinburgh; and I thought it was the proudest position that I had ever seen a young man occupy. In my opinion, nothing impresses one with the dignity and authority of a man more than to see him calmly stand and control or direct the working of a large steamship. No doubt the duke was conscious that he was the central object of attraction to many thousands of eyes; but he seemed quite self-possessed. Perhaps while the anchor was being hove up, he was thinking of the pleasant days he had spent in Australia's genial clime, and of the loyal attention and hospitality he had received from the colonists in general. There was no mistaking the looks of loving admiration of the multitude, and I daresay most of them thought, with me, that the duke looked very graceful in his undress uniform.

The sun was just sinking beyond the lofty range of blue mountains, when the stock of the *Galatea's* starboard anchor rose above water; at the same time the screw began to revolve, and the people cheered as heartily as ever British voices were heard in all time. His Royal Highness waved his cap, to signify "*Farewell!*" and then the brass band on board his ship struck up, in slow time, that sweetly simple little tune, "Home, sweet home!"

As the notes sounded across the still waters, they seemed to speak out the words, "sweet home!" with exquisite pathos, and I think my heart was never before more tenderly influenced by music. I should not care even to hint how much I was affected, only that there were other full-grown men around me, whose feelings were touched as softly as mine were; and hundreds of laced handkerchiefs, which had awhile before been waved with feminine hands towards the *Galatea*, were applied to the tearful eyes of the fair owners. Oh, how I did long to go home! I almost fancied that I could have swam off to the frigate and ridden home on her rudder chains. The gallant ship moved slowly ahead until she rounded the bluff rocks of Bradley, then full steam was put on, and away she sped on her long voyage to Old England. It is not likely that the *Galatea* will ever be seen in those waters again—at any rate, she will never again cause such general holiday excitement as marked her last memorable visit. Her royal captain has since had many important social and official duties to attend to; still he has, perhaps, not forgotten his final departure from Sydney harbour, in the gloaming of that calm evening years ago.

I said just now that the Duke of Edinburgh was in the proudest position that I ever saw a young man fill, when he stood at his post of duty as captain of the handsome frigate *Galatea;* but I was almost forgetting that I was with the applauding multitude which surrounded His Royal Highness when he stood patiently at the grand entrance to the Government House, Sydney, for several hours, while ten thousand or more of the children of various Sunday-schools, in the city and suburbs, were marched past him two or three abreast. Many Australian boys and girls went home that day rejoicing, to tell their parents that Prince Alfred, the son of the Queen of Great Britain, smiled and bowed to them as kindly as if he were their school teacher. They will never forget that honour; and some of them will no doubt tell their grandchildren about it by-and-by. That was the proudest position I ever saw a young man occupy, for he was voluntarily giving pleasure to many thousands of hearts. I overheard an old country woman in the crowd exclaim, with honest feeling, "May God bless the dear young prince! and bless his good mother, too!"

Writing of home recalled those pleasant events to my

memory, and I have been tempted to digress a little, almost at the beginning of my story.

My father was a seaman, and was at one time boatswain of H.M.S. *Terrier;* but he got injured in a gale off Lisbon, and disabled for sea service, so he was promoted to a snug berth in the naval school at Greenwich. He used jocosely to say he was "Professor of making knots and spunyarn." Whatever his work was, it was not troublesome to him, and his pay was satisfactory. But all his earthly duties are ended, and he is now where storm waves can never more disable him. My mother was one of the noblest of women. If she had a failing, I do not think either of her children knew of it. My only sister had our dear mother's loving nature, and she was as beautiful as she was amiable; but she died in the eighteenth year of her age. She passed away from us one sad evening, as gently as a bird. I loved her fondly, and she was equally attached to me. I cherish her memory in my inmost heart; it is a sort of talisman to me, a softening influence indissolubly linked with my life.

"He mourns the dead who live as they desire."

I had a pretty easy time of it, as far as books were concerned, until I was nine years of age, and then I was sent to a large boarding-school at Blackheath. Going from home was the first real trial I can remember, and I thought that nothing worse could befall me in life. There were several masters at the school, and my childish fancy pictured them in the grimmest colours as a race of savage men whose chief delight was to torture new boys. But my first week's experience dispelled all my gloomy ideas of the austerity of school life, and I really enjoyed it. Mr. Murray, the principal, was very genial and encouraging in his manner, and especially so with timid boys like myself; and the masters were gentlemen and accomplished scholars. Those school-days are amongst my happiest recollections, though I used occasionally to wish I were a man, that I could do as I pleased. It is natural, I suppose, for boys to think they will be more independent in long-tailed coats than they are in round jackets; and perhaps girls are almost as impatient as boys in their young spring days, for when they have given up doll's play, they soon wish to come out as women—with watches and chains and charms. They "had better bide a wee," as the song says.

My father was a cheery old man. His brusque manner was mere professional habit, for his heart was almost as tender as love itself. Though he had felt an average share of life's buffetings, they did not seem to ruffle him much, and I think very few persons ever heard him murmur at his lot. I have often wished I could realize his happy trustfulness and his uniform placidity of mind—it would be a comforting change for me. But I suppose there must be one of every sort of mind or disposition to make a complete variety in the great human family, and we are not alike blessed with constitutional robustness and moral philosophy. Father used to say to me sometimes, "You had better not be always dreading hurricanes on life's voyage, my boy, or you'll never have any peace or pleasure. Keep a sharp look out for squalls of temptation, and watch your moral barometer carefully; but don't always be fearing that you are going to founder. When you have fine weather, enjoy it as one of Heaven's kind gifts; but when rough weather comes, you may be sure it will answer some good purpose. Anyway, you can't alter it; so don't be fretful, but button up your monkey-jacket, and hope for a fine day to-morrow.

"Some days must be dark and dreary!"

I loved to go occasionally with father for a ramble in Greenwich Park, and to hear him and some of the old Naval College pensioners talk about storms and battles at sea; and I have wondered that old men, battered and bruised, and some of them with only half their limbs, could be so merry and talk so lightly about their bygone troubles or their present infirmities. One day, as father and I were sitting together on one of the park seats, I said to him, "Father, when I grow up to be a man, I should like to be the Astronomer Royal, and live in the Observatory on the hill yonder. It looks so snug and quiet among the trees, and the birds are always singing under the large windows. And I think that measuring the stars and looking out for comets must be very pleasant amusement." It was a childish whim of mine for the moment. I was even then a dear lover of quiet rural scenes, and the passion has grown with my age. Flowers and trees seem to me to be the only things in nature that can live together without quarrelling or eating each other, and they never make a disagreeable noise.

My father smiled at my simple remark, and said, "You are not a bad judge of a snug billet, Roger. No doubt yonder house must be a pleasant one to live in, especially in summer time; but I'm afraid the Astronomer Royal's trade would not suit your young constitution, so we won't 'prentice you to it. Star-gazing all night long for months on a stretch must be wearisome work for the body, though I dare say it is delightsome to the minds of gentlemen who have a fancy for it, and have gifts in that way. Suppose I try to get you a berth as organist at St. Paul's Cathedral, or Westminster Abbey? You might fill either of those posts as well as you could the Astronomer Royal's berth; and you would be quite as likely to get it."

I saw that father was only making fun of me in his pleasant way; so I said, "We will wait a bit, father; I am only ten years old, you know."

"Ay, ay, my lad, wait a bit. You can't think of two things at once nicely, though some lively boys fancy they can. Now is the time to brace up your thoughts to your school duties, to discipline your mind and qualify yourself for some useful part in life's great battle. We will think about the other thing in due time. It is not much good planning what voyage you will send a ship on while she is on the stocks."

I finished my schooling when I was about fifteen years of age, and then I went to spend a month at my

Uncle Robert's farm in Suffolk. That was perhaps the most pleasant holiday I ever enjoyed. A trip to the country is a real treat to a London schoolboy; and many persons whose school-days are over would vastly enjoy such an outing if they could afford it. If such annual holidays were practicable to the working townsfolk in general, much bodily suffering would be averted. Recollections of my delightful country rambles in Old England are still green in my heart, though so many years have intervened. I have often walked half a dozen miles, across fields and woods, to see an old water-mill down in a valley, "beside a shaded river," and to watch the sparkling water tumbling over the wheel. I would walk twice as far to-day for a similar treat. But where in Australia shall I find an old water-mill, I should like to know? There are plenty of high-pressure steam-mills to be seen everywhere; but there is no poetry in those puffing concerns, and I would rather hasten away from their noise and smoke, unless I was in want of flour.

About two months after I left school, I was apprenticed to my mother's brother, Mr. Jenner, who kept a chemist's shop in Greenwich. I need hardly say there had been a good deal of fireside discussion before that course was decided upon. My father thought it was a light indoor occupation, which would suit me very well, as I was not robust. My mother knew that I would be well cared for in her brother's family; and my sister was glad, because I would be pretty near to our home. I acquiesced in their views, for I was anxious to please them all; but in my heart I disliked the business, and would much sooner have been a farmer or a miller. I believe that to apprentice a lad to a trade that he has a distaste for, is almost as unpromising an act as planting sugar-canes or cocoanut trees in a frigid climate. It is a pity that my father did not have my head examined by a professional phrenologist before he apprenticed me.

Uncle Jenner was an easy-going old gentleman, more fond of his garden than he was of his business; in fact, he was a lazy man when in his shop. But it is said that "every man is as lazy as he can afford to be." I have heard uncle say that he ought to have been a nurseryman instead of a chemist. He did not try to make his business any larger than his father had made it before him; and I think that quite a fourth of his yearly profits was distributed to the sick and needy.

"That poor fellow wants mutton chops or beef steaks more than he wants physic!" I have heard uncle say, when some poverty-stricken customer has come to the shop with a prescription; and he would perhaps give him the physic for nothing, and a shilling from the till besides. He couldn't bear to see misery without trying to relieve it. In my youthful simplicity, I have often wondered why the Lord had not made my uncle and my mother very rich. They would certainly have done good with their money, to the poor and needy around them.

I tried my utmost to learn my business, and my uncle was always ready to answer any questions I put to him, in a kind, encouraging way. After my first year, I got more reconciled to it ; but it was tiresome drudgery, for the hours were cruelly long, and the night-bell was a regular nuisance, for almost every tipsy fellow who went past after midnight used to pull it, and of course that was equal to pulling me out of bed. It is no wonder that I was sometimes low-spirited. Every alternate Sunday I spent at home ; and oh ! how I used to enjoy those refreshing seasons of rest and family re-union. The bare remembrance of them is invigorating to me now. I always enjoyed a quiet Sunday.

There was an assistant in our shop, named Duncan Mackay, a young Scotchman. I learnt a good deal from him, for he was a clever fellow at his business, but sadly addicted to tippling. When uncle was absent, Mackay often went out to the tavern at the corner ; and at times I have been sorely puzzled, when prescriptions came in to be made up immediately. However, I never heard of a fatal mishap through my inexperience as a dispenser, which is more than every young fellow in my line can say for himself !

Why physicians so often write their prescriptions in a scrawling style has ever been a marvel to me. Common caution, I think, ought to impel them to write as legibly as possible, in order to guard against dangerous mistakes. I have sometimes been fairly bewildered when trying to make out a line in a prescription, which had no more the appearance of Latin words than a miniature picture of a New Zealand fence, or the photographic skeleton of a snake, would have. But when I was nonplussed, I used to give myself the benefit of the doubt, by substituting something which I knew to be perfectly harmless. That was perhaps the wisest course I could pursue, but I own it was not honest, either to the patient or to the doctor. It was better than poisoning good customers.

In our shop window there was a small glass frame, with the words, "Teeth Extracted," in letters fancifully made with decayed stumps: and we used to do a brisk trade in teeth-drawing during the prevalence of north-east winds. I had often seen my uncle draw a tooth, and he explained to me over and over again the method of the operation. I could now expound the same theory to any novice who liked to listen to it; but after all, I would not consent to his pulling out a tooth for me, as his first essay, for any moderate consideration I can think of. I am sure that practice is needful to make a skilful dentist.

"It's as simple as drawing a cork, mon!" said Mackay, when giving me his advice on the subject. "You must get a proper hold of the tooth with your key, that is the most particular part of the job; then put all your strength into your wrist for one steady w-r-rench, and out comes the tooth before the patient has time to squeak twice." I should mention that keys were the instruments then in general use; and clumsy things they were.

One day my uncle went to Shooter's Hill to collect some rare spiders and butterflies, for he was a bit of a naturalist; and at eleven o'clock, Mackay ran out to the tavern for a "wee drap o' whisky to cure his sair head." He had not been gone long, before a woman from the fish-market hurried into the shop, to have a tooth extracted. I told her that my uncle and the head assistant were both out, and I asked her to call again in an hour or so.

"Shure, thin, I'll not call agin! I'll have the thing out now; for sorra a morsel of rest have I had since Friday morning. Can't you pull it out for me, honey?"

"Oh, certainly, ma'am; I can take it out for you if you are in a hurry." My young professional pride would not let me decline the job.

"Then good luck to you, set about it quick, for it's ravin' mad I'm gettin' wid the pain."

I asked the woman to step behind a screen in the shop. She put a finger on the aching tooth, and I looked at it very knowingly; then I said, "At your age, ma'am, the loss of a tooth is a total loss. Nature will not replace it for you. This is a useful-looking tooth, although it has a hole in it; and I advise you to let my uncle stop it——"

"Tut! stop your talking, misther, and out wid the nuisance directly, or else let me rin down to t'other shop, fornint there, and see if they can do it."

Her allusion to the opposition shop, and the implied doubt as to my skill, stirred up all my mettle at once, and I felt plucky enough to have pulled out a wild boar's tusk. At my request, she seated herself in our easy chair and opened her mouth. I twisted a piece of lint round the key, in the exact way I had seen my uncle do it, and I fixed the formidable instrument on the tooth as tenderly as possible; then I gave a tremendous tug-wrench, and out flew the tooth, like a pellet from a popgun.

"Och, wirra!" groaned the patient, jumping up and looking very unlovingly at me. "Is it pulling the shoe off a cart horse you think you're doing?"

"It's all right, ma'am, the operation is over. Couldn't have been more quickly done. Here is your tooth, you see."

"Troth, ye've pretty nigh tugged the jaw off me, intirely; and ye've left a gap in me gums as big as the key-hole of a gaol door, so you have."

"The gum will heal up in a day or two, ma'am. Stop a minute, I will apply a little styptic to it."

"By Jerry, you'll put nothing more into my mouth, nor take nothing out of it agin. How much do you charge me for that ugly job?"

"One shilling only, ma'am."

The woman threw down the money, and I thought I heard her swear as she left the shop with her apron to her mouth. I was glad when she was out of my sight, for I felt rather nervous. I dare say it was the reaction of the enormous vital energy I had called into use, when iving the operating wrench. She had not been gone more than five minutes, and while I was examining the tooth with peculiar interest, in came Mackay half tipsy.

"I have just performed my first trick in dentistry!" I said exultingly, for I was as proud as a young soldier who had just shot somebody.

"I guessed as much, Roger; for I met a fish-wife away down the street, and she was telling another auld judy' that somebody had nearly tugged the head off her in this shop. But how many teeth did you draw for her?"

"Only one—a real grinder with three prongs, like the legs of a milking-stool. Here it is—she wouldn't take it away with her."

"Hech, mon! you have pulled out twa teeth, sure as death! Here is anither ane I picked up by the shop door as I came in. Woeful work that, Roger. A savage jerk you must have given, sure enow, to send the tooth dirling over the screen at that gait. You'll never please the women wi' such drawing as that, and ye'll ruin the trade a'thegether."

Whether that was another of Mackay's grim jokes, or whether I did actually make a double draw, remains an open question with me to this day, and it has caused me no end of uneasiness. Those two old teeth seemed to gnaw at my conscience by day, and to gnash at me in my dreams at night for many a month; and I have seldom since then taken a professional look into a patient's distended mouth, but I seemed to hear the re-echo of that poor fishwoman's wrathful wail, "Och, wirra! ye've killt me intirely!"

*   *   *   *   *

Reminiscences of my early days are precious to me; but I feel shy of printing them all, though I have the example of many great and good authors to encourage me. Often, in my lonely wanderings abroad, some tender part of my boyhood's history has suddenly come quavering up from memory's depths, and touched my feelings like the sweetly mournful music of distant evening bells. But they are not always happy memories, for thoughts of another sort will bubble up sometimes from my troubled conscience. One sultry day, when I was tramping from the Nonshicer diggings, and gaunt famine seemed to stare me in the face, I sadly remembered the roguish rhymes I once made, in dispraise of the suet dumplings that we used to have twice a week at school; and I was sorry enough for my sin in ridiculing substantial food. Gladly would I then have given half of the gold dust in my belt for one of those despised dumplings, even if it had been a year old and as hard as a frozen turnip. Yes, it is a stern fact, that on this great Australian continent, which official statistics prove to contain an enormous superabundance of sheep and cattle for the population, to say nothing of kangaroos, wild rabbits, and parrots, I have been on the verge of starvation. But let me state, for the credit of the country, that I was lost in the bush when I was in such desperately hungry straits. Assuredly there is plenty of food in Australia; and the fact may be comfortingly proved in a minute, by any man who has money in his pocket; and there is no danger of his famishing, even though all his pockets are empty, if he is within hail of a human being, for charity never grows dead cold in this sunny land. Hospitality is to be found in every shepherd's hut, and even in the bush camps of the poor aborigines.

A few words of explanation here are perhaps as needful to my story as the right key is to open a Chubb lock. The idea of printing my strange mission was first suggested to me by my Cousin Saul (of whom I shall have something more to say presently). I have long been waiting for the honest decision of a Chancery suit, which would make me rich ; and I have sufficiently proved that the mere anticipation of coming wealth is not sustaining to the corporeal man. When Saul first proposed that I should write a book, and demonstrated in his lively way that it would pay well, an uncommonly pleasing sort of illusion, as if I were shovelling up jewels in a dream, shimmered over my brain, and I half fancied that it was a partial arousing of intellectual gifts which I had never properly stirred up. I knew very well that my experience all the world over had been astonishingly varied, and costly too ; and though I had long ago estimated that it was all a dead loss to me, it now suddenly seemed easy for me to make some of it yield me a needful pecuniary return. Far more practical and homely than dreaming about jewels, it appeared to me—speaking figuratively—as if I had luckily struck a rich oil vein down in my own coal cellar, and all I had to do was to put down a handy pump, and work it manfully, to raise ready money in the smoothest way conceivable. It was an enticing prospect, but I tried to keep calm and humble, while Saul continued to urge his new scheme with the fluency of a Sandhurst share-broker, or a Sydney auctioneer. It would be amusing if I could remember all his fanciful arguments, and tell how glibly he sketched the most successful writers, past and present,—from Jeremy Taylor to Mark Twain,—in order to stimulate my hope and ambition. He also said that the fact of my having, years ago, passed a stiff examination for a dispensing chemist, was a proof that I had brains in my head, and it was possible there was literary virtue in them. It had been found in more unlikely-looking heads than mine. The idea of having an honourable and useful occupation, with fair pay for it, was as encouraging to me as flowers and sunshine are to working bees; so I soon yielded to Saul's persuasive eloquence, and promised to try what I could do.

After a few weeks' hard preliminary study, which had a rather subduing influence on my self-assurance, I took up my pen as an author, with a shrinking sort of misgiving, such as I suppose a young Indian juggler must feel when he first tries to swallow a sword. I have been going on cautiously with my task ever since. Saul is to have a share of my profits, on condition that he helps me with his literary oversight till the MS. is finished. He comes pretty often to inspect my work, but his criticisms are sharp as new cutlery, and I never can enjoy them. I certainly did feel the usefulness of a trustworthy helper when I was at the gold fields. I should have been badly off in working my deep mining claim, if I had not had a sober mate at the top of the shaft, to wind up the buckets of wash dirt, or to hoist me up at dinner time. And there are other occupations or duties in life where co-operative effort or action cannot be dispensed with: working a diving bell, for example, or playing a church organ, or getting married —and what not; but I hardly know what to say, just yet, about the value of a partner in the intellectual labour of making such a book as mine is going to be.

I told Saul, last night, that I should like to fill a chapter or two with reminiscences of my apprentice days, and to relate some of the incidents and accidents during my studies in chemistry, including the disastrous explosion when I was trying the effect of pure oxygen on phosphorus; but he said, with a discouraging grimace, that all my chemical experience would not be worth a dose of salts from a literary point of view, and he urged me to shut up shop at once, and launch out into the great universe. I must, however, state an occurrence in the last month of my shop practice, which was the mysterious means of turning the even course of my life's routine into the whirling current of adventure, and of sending me roving about the world like the "exile from home," in the old song that I have before tenderly referred to.

Mr. Mackay's visits to the tavern at the corner became so frequent that my patient uncle at last gave him a month's warning. Mac promised amendment, and gave up sipping whisky at a public tap, but he used to go slily to the tap of the spirits of wine in our cellar, which shows what a state of alcoholic toughness the coats of his stomach must have arrived at. On one of his evening visits to the cellar, the spirits caught fire, and the house narrowly escaped being burned down; so my uncle discharged him, and I took his place in the shop with two apprentices under me. I felt that my professional ability was expanding, and my natural diffidence was perhaps less noticeable. Success usually inspires a man with confidence in himself; it also helps to make his friends love him and respect his talents. One evening, when my uncle was at a vestry meeting, a smartly-dressed girl came into our shop, and in an excited manner asked me to go with her to see a person who was in a fit.

"You had better go for a doctor, ma'am. I am only a chemist," I replied, in a mildly condoling tone.

"I have been for Doctor Forbes, and he is gone to Chelsea. Do please come with me directly, sir. It is a serious case."

She said it so persuasively that I could not say nay again, and to tell the truth I felt rather glad to have an opportunity of perhaps distinguishing myself a little. So I off with my apron, and on with my hat and gloves, and was soon in the High Street walking by the girl's side, though at a modest distance from her, for she was quite a stranger to me. As we were passing the church door, the choristers came out after their usual week-night's practice. I was a member of the choir, but had not been able to attend practice that evening on account of my uncle's absence from the shop. I feared that there would be some quizzical remarks made to me on next Sunday about my bustling along beside a young girl at that late hour of the evening, so I stepped up to the choirmaster, and said in an undertone, "I am merely going with this young lady to visit a patient, Mr. Cleff."

He replied drily, "Ah—hem—just so! Take care of yourself, Roger. Mind you don't get lost among the trees."

I felt exceedingly nettled with Mr. Cleff. I was also vexed with myself that I had taken the pains to explain my errand to him. He evidently suspected that I was going for a walk in the park. His daughter Laura was beside him too, which made me feel doubly annoyed, for I would not have her suppose that I was given to that sort of evening pastime.

Since I have grown older, and perhaps a little wiser, I have decided that when I am in the ascertained path of duty, the best plan is to keep straight on, without stopping to convince everybody who is looking at me that I am not going wrong.

CHAPTER II.

"A man of pleasure is a man of pains."—*Young.*

WHEN my ruffled mind had calmed down a little, it occurred to me to ask the girl who was the sick person that I was going to see?

"He is my aunt's lodger," was her laconic reply, and just then she stopped at a house not far from the park gates. She opened the door with a latch-key, and bade me walk upstairs. I followed her into a room on the first floor, which was but scantily furnished, and by the dim light of a candle I saw a man lying on a sofa, and an elderly woman sitting on a stool beside him.

"Are you a doctor?" the woman asked in a raspy tone, which made the sick man writhe about as if he were terrified at it.

"No, madam; I am only a chemist and druggist."

"Ah, it doesn't matter. He is better now."

"What ails him, ma'am?"

"He has had another of his fits, that's all. I told him, three days ago, what he might expect; but I may as well talk to a born fool for any heed he pays to what I say."

The man muttered an execration which startled me, whereupon the woman remarked, "It is me he is cursing—not you, sir. That's the sort of abuse I get from morning till night."

I wished I was safely out of the house again, but I tried to look composed, and asked, "What do you want me to do for the unfortunate gentleman, ma'am?"

"I want you to throw that old woman out of the window, and then hand me a glass of gin," said the man, and he partially sat up and glared at me in a manner which plainly showed that he was suffering from *delirium tremens*. He was a man of robust build, and had a good-looking face, though it was terribly emaciated. By his dress and the superior jewellery he wore, I judged that he was a man of respectability and of some pecuniary means.

"I am sorry you are so ill, sir," I said in a sympathizing tone.

"So would you be ill if all your vitals had been on fire for six months," he muttered; and then he added, with a shudder, "Look at that old creature, and say if my life is worth a groat?"

I turned suddenly to the woman, and saw that she was making hideous grimaces at him; so I said to her reprovingly, "It is very wrong and cruel of you to excite the poor man in that way."

"The only way I can manage him is to make him afraid of me," she replied, sullenly. "You haven't seen him raving mad, as I have, or you wouldn't blame me for trying any means to make him lie still."

"If you will tell me what I can do for the gentleman, I will do it; otherwise I had better return to my shop."

"I don't know what you can do, unless you help me to tie him down to the sofa. He nearly scared the wits out of that girl half an hour ago. I wish you had been here then, and you'd have seen something."

I observed that the girl was seated near to the open doorway, ready to rush out if need be, and she still looked rather scared.

"Now, sir, let me beg of you to lie quietly. I will send a doctor to see you soon," I said, and I passed my hand gently across his hot forehead. He did not open his eyes, and seemed to be unconscious that I had spoken to him. Presently he said, in a sort of melodramatic tone, "'O thou spirit of wine! if thou hast a name to be known by, let us call thee Devil!' Aha, Shakespeare! you were a wonderfully sagacious fellow, no doubt; but you didn't know half as much as I know of the horrors of hard drinking."

I advised the woman to avoid doing or saying anything that might irritate the patient, and I promised to call on Dr. Forbes.

"He won't come if you call. He always gets out of the way when I send for him," said the old woman, fiercely. "He hasn't got any more feeling than this pair of tongs, and you may tell him Mrs. Jagg said so, if you like."

I left the scene of misery, and went direct to Dr. Forbes' house. He was at home, and I soon explained the purport of my visit.

"I am sorry to say I cannot do anything for the unfortunate man," said the doctor, feelingly. I have attended him for several weeks, and it is mere waste of time. He will not follow my directions, and he has thrown nearly all the medicine I have prescribed for him out of the window. I told him a month ago that he must inevitably die if he continued to drink to excess; but it is useless to advise him. No human skill can save him now, for his constitution is gone—burnt out of him with alcohol. If you could, however, manage to get him away from the house he is in, to a quiet, decent place, it would be an act of Christian charity."

"Do you know who he is, sir?"

"He says his name is Cameron, and that he came from Melbourne a few months ago. I believe he has been pursuing a course of dissipation ever since he landed in England, and the final result must soon be seen. He appears to be a well-educated man, and he must have some means, or he could not be living where he is. That is all I can tell you about him. I pity the poor mortal; but I cannot neglect my other patients to attend on a man who will neither follow my advice nor take my medicine."

My uncle had returned from the church meeting when I got back. I told him of the exciting scene I had just witnessed, and his sympathies were at once aroused.

"It is not right to leave the poor fellow in that miserable plight, without a hope either for this world or for the next. Send your mother to see him, Roger. Parson Blanche says she is the best sick visitor in his parish. She will speak tenderly to him, and who knows but that may do him good? Nothing in our shop would be half so soothing to a sick man as a few kind words from a good woman. As for that nagging old creature who is nursing him, I should have been cross enough to have turned her out of the house, if I had caught her making ugly faces to scare the poor delirious patient. Go and talk to your mother about it, Roger; and you can stop at home for the night if you like."

Accordingly I went home, which was only half a mile away. My father and mother listened attentively as I gave them an outline of the sad scene I had just witnessed, and it was plain that their sympathies were awakened. When I had finished, my father put down his pipe, and said,—

"I have seen a ship, when running under a press of sail in half a gale of wind, suddenly rounded to, and a lifeboat lowered to pick up an apprentice boy who had fallen overboard. Now, it seems to me that respectable folks on shore are not so smart in trying to save human life as common sailors are at sea. No, no, Roger; I don't mean to blame the doctor—far from it. He is a kind man, whatever that wicked old woman may say against him. He has a large practice to attend to, and many poor creatures to see every day without a fee. But surely there are some Christian men and women in Greenwich, who have time to spare to throw a life-line to a poor helpless wretch who is sinking into perdition!" Father paused for a minute, and looked at us all very seriously. Presently he cried, in his boatswain's style, "Man overboard! All hands on deck!" Then in a softer tone he asked, "Who will lend a hand to man a lifeboat to the rescue? You and I will make two at the oars, Roger; now, mother, what will you do?"

"I will do anything I can to help the poor man, my dear," said my mother; "but where shall we find quiet lodging for him?"

"Let us fetch him here, Janet. We have a spare room, and I can find time to look after him. I have had some experience with men in his condition, and I daresay I may be able to bring him round; any way, I am willing to try at it."

"But who is he, and what is he?" my mother asked, with very reasonable caution, for she did not want to have a dirty tramp in her house, kind-hearted as she was.

"Roger says the man looks respectable, and the doctor's report seems to confirm it; and his disorder is not contagious. But sailors would not stop to ask who is he and what is he, before they lowered a boat to pick up a drowning man. The poor chap is in distress—we are sure of that; so I say again, let us fetch him here, and we can find out who he is afterwards. What do you say to that, Janet?"

"It is very kind of you to propose it, Daniel, and I will help you to carry out the plan to-morrow."

"Let us get him here to-night. He may die before morning. Old boatswain Caulker will lend a hand, I'll warrant. He is always ready to put out in any weather when a soul is in danger. What say you, Roger; will you go and help us to bring the unhappy fellow home at once?"

I was quite willing, and I forthwith set out for the house to prepare the way; my father and Mr. Caulker (the sailors' missionary) followed in a cab. My mother and sister began to get our spare room ready for the expected guest.

On my telling Mrs. Jagg that I intended to remove Mr. Cameron to other lodgings, she became annoyed, and declared that he should not go out of her house till he was carried out in his coffin; but when my father came, his resolute manner subdued her temper in a minute.

"It is no use wasting time arguing with the cross old woman," said my father. "Off you go to the police station, Caulker, and ask Serjeant Smart to step up here directly. He'll soon decide it."

"Oh, you need not trouble to fetch a policeman to my house," whined Mrs. Jagg. "If you want the man, take him away as soon as you like; I shall be glad enough to get rid of a nuisance."

We had some difficulty in persuading Mr. Cameron to go with us; but eventually my father's ready tact prevailed, and he quietly allowed us to carry him downstairs and into the cab. Half an hour afterwards he was snugly tucked in the bed in our spare room, and my father was sitting beside him, keeping the first watch. At midnight father called me to relieve the watch, and said to me in a whisper, as I was entering the spare room, "He is quiet now, though he has had a hard time of it, poor fellow! He may get restless again; if so, you can give him half a glass of the soothing stuff in the bottle on the shelf. That will smooth him down for an hour or so."

"What is the mixture composed of, father?"

"It is merely gentian root, orange-peel, and gin. Essential oil of peppermint would perhaps have been better than gin, but I have not any in the house. That is the compound we used to give on board ship, to any of our crew who were suffering from the effects of a week's spree on shore. I have seen our chaps dreadfully bad sometimes."

"I will mix up something better than that for him to-morrow, father."

"Ay, ay, my son; I dare say you modern chemists have found out nicer remedies for the horrors, but that mixture used to answer pretty well in my day. Now you must keep your weather-eye open, Roger, for this gentleman is inclined to be tricky. He tried to give me the slip out of the window at about six bells. If he should shriek out that the devil is in the chimney corner, as he did awhile ago, don't you be scared, but take up this serving-mallet of mine and pretend to knock the devil's head off. You must humour him a bit, poor fellow! It is no use at all arguing with a man in his state. Kindly but firmly, that is your course, Roger. Now I'll go and turn in till four o'clock; but I will sleep with one eye open, and be with you in the turn of a log-glass if you sing out smartly."

I will not shock any one by giving a minute account of the scenes in that dreary room for three hours after my father left me. The patient soon began to be uneasy, then to be violently agitated. At one moment he would shriek out that there was a black snake coiled up in his blankets; by the time I had demolished that with my mallet, I had to pound away at a nest of centipedes, which he declared were under his pillow; and then I had to hunt a large iguana from the tester of his bed. During these make-believe operations of mine, the wretched man was trembling in every limb, and his eyes glared at me in a manner which showed how terribly real it all appeared to him. After a violent paroxysm, during which it took all my strength to keep him from knocking his head against the wall, he sank back in his bed exhausted. I gave him another dose of medicine from the bottle, and then he lay motionless for an hour —or so it seemed to me, but I dropped off to sleep while I was closely watching him. With shame I confess my negligence. Extreme weariness was my best excuse. I was aroused by my father, at five o'clock, and his first question was, "Where is the sick man, Roger?"

"Eh—ah—yes—there he is, father," said I, rubbing my eyes open and pointing to the bed. I soon, however, became conscious that my patient had made his exit through the open window, but where he had gone was to me a perplexing mystery.

It was one of my father's many sage qualities or virtues, that he never increased a disaster by getting cross about it; or in other words, he had a manly control over his temper. He used to say sometimes, "Get the ship upright first of all, and then talk to the lubberly helmsman who let her broach to." I was sorry indeed for my unwatchfulness, but my father did not add to my worry, and upset my sleepy intellect, by scolding me. "One thing at a time," was a frequent saying of his.

"Put on your monkey-jacket, Roger, and let us go and look for our patient," said my father good-humouredly. "It is likely enough he has gone to his old quarters; so we will go there first, and if he is not there, we must hunt about till we find him. Come, bear a hand, boy! Never mind stopping to comb your hair or cut your nails when the ship is on fire."

We went straightway to Mrs. Jagg's house, where we found Cameron, clad only in his night-gear, knocking furiously at the door, and the girl before noticed arguing with him from the balcony above, and trying to persuade him to go away. We took him home again and put him to bed, and my father resumed his watch and ward over him.

I do not wish to write any more about Cameron's sad experience than is really necessary. It will be seen, by those who may please to read on, that my falling in with him in the semi-tragical way I have described, has indirectly had a vast deal to do with my subsequent history, and my wanderings from home and kindred. His sufferings were very severe; but under the careful nursing of my good parents, aided by the professional advice of my Uncle Jenner, the poor fellow gradually recovered from *delirium tremens*, and in a month or two he was restored to his right mind. But his body was a mere wreck of a man, and a hacking cough forewarned us all that his days on earth were numbered.

CHAPTER III.

*" But I hate to be cheated, and never will buy
Long years of repentance with moments of joy."*
—*Montague.*

WHEN my term of apprenticeship expired, my uncle offered me a liberal salary if I chose to stay with him; but with his usual unselfish consideration, he said,—

"Though it would be to my interest to keep you, Roger, I don't think it will be well for you to remain here, for you have learnt all I can teach you. You are now twenty-one years of age, and you have hardly ever been out of Greenwich town. My business is comparatively a trumpery one; and I think it will be better for you to get a situation in some good house in London, to enlarge your professional knowledge, as well as to expand your ideas on things in general. But as you have not had a real holiday treat, except a day now and then, for several years, take a month or two now, my boy, and here is something to pay your holiday expenses." At the same time he put a purse containing twenty-five sovereigns into my hand. He was a generous uncle!

I had often sighed for a month's liberty, with a longing which chemists' assistants in general will thoroughly understand; but when I had it, I scarcely knew how to use it to the best advantage. It was not easy for me to make up my mind where to go to get the most enjoyment for my money, but I decided to spend a week at home before I went on my holiday excursion. I used to stroll out each day for an hour or two with Mr. Cameron, who had strength enough to walk a short distance leaning on my arm. He always enjoyed a seat under one of the oak trees in Greenwich Park; and I used to sit beside him and listen to tales of his travels, which were almost as interesting to me as Anson's or Cook's voyages round the world.

He had seen a good deal of bush life in Australia, and something of city life there also; but he did not like to say much about the latter. The manuscripts which I have in my possession, and the numerous drawings from his pen and pencil, evidence that he was a gifted man, and that he was a careful observer of the fauna, as well as of the general physical features, of the great continent of New Holland, and parts of New Zealand. I soon felt a growing desire to behold some of the grand mountain scenery which he described to me with a poet's fancy, while the animated expression of his face showed how much he loved the remembrance of his life in the bush. On my expressing, one day, a desire to emigrate, he said with earnestness,—

"A young man of your very steady habits and business ability could hardly fail to make his way in either of the Australian colonies. From a pretty close observation during several years rambling in town and country, I am of opinion that amongst the men of wealth and influence there is a greater number who worked their way up from comparatively obscure positions, than there is of men who arrived in the colonies with large capital. Mind you, Roger, I do not think there is a scarcity of young men in your own particular line of business in the colonies, and there are far more clerks there now than can find steady employment; but you seem to me to have a natural taste for rural pursuits, and if you choose to make agriculture or grazing your future life occupation and study, there is almost boundless scope for you in Australia, and I have no doubt you would succeed in making a comfortable independence. Ah me! I wish I could go back to that promising land and begin a new career! But my summer of life is past, and there is dreary winter in my soul. Well, I have had my day!" he presently added in a more cheerful tone, which I knew was assumed, by the tears which were rolling down his haggard cheeks.

At length I decided to spend my holiday at my uncle's house in Suffolk. When Mr. Cameron heard of it, he looked sad, and remarked, "When you are gone, Roger, I shall miss a cheerful escort in my rural walks." I felt my heart touched, and I resolved that I would defer my journey for a week or two, and would do all I could to cheer and comfort the poor invalid in the meantime.

For several days Cameron was confined to his room from excessive weakness, and my mother attended to him with unremitting care. She was not only a tender nurse, but she was an experienced spiritual adviser. When he got a little stronger, he went again one morning to the park. I noticed that he was in a thoughtful mood, for he scarcely spoke a word as we walked along. Soon after we were seated, he said, with a sort of pensive smile on his face,—

"Sydney Smith says, 'You may find people ready enough to do the Good Samaritan without the oil and the twopence.' He is right, Roger, as I have often found in my experience. But the ungrudging attention I have received from your family has done much to soften my views of the general selfishness of mankind. It is very kind of you to defer your excursion on my account. If I were likely to get better, I would not allow you to do it; but I shall not live many weeks, and I should like to have a little more of your company. I feel deeply grateful to your parents and to yourself for the kindness and care I have received from you all, —far more consideration than I have received from my own kith and kin. To your excellent mother, especially, I owe more thanks than I can express. Through her gentle teaching and her prayers, I have been led, a repentant, wandering prodigal, to my Almighty Father's arms. Miserable, despairing wretch that I was when you first carried me to your home! Yes; helpless as I was a few days ago, I feel no condemnation now. The fear of death is gone from my mind, and I have an expanding hope of rest for ever in the life beyond the grave. They are not tears of sorrow that I am now shedding, but tears of joy at the happy release my soul can anticipate. All my pains and troubles will soon be over!"

His voice became inarticulate with emotion. After a while he said, "If you will kindly bear with me, Roger, I will ease my mind of all that is now burdening it, and then I shall be at peace. I would have confided what I have to say, to your dear mother yesterday, but there were some things that I should find it hard to tell a lady, and I wish to be truthful. I can speak freely to you, and I trust you will not be impatient while I give you an outline of my dismal history."

I told him that I should feel honoured by his confidence, and that he need not fear of wearying me.

"Thank you, Roger. Now listen attentively. My name is John Cameron Campbell, though I have dropped the latter patronymic ever since I left my early home. I am descended from a good family in Scotland. I was educated for the medical profession. It was my father's rigid decision, but I had no taste for it. I knew that I was entitled to £7,000 at my maturity, under the will of a deceased aunt, and I dare say that indisposed me for the hard study which was necessary to qualify me for a physician. Mark you, in my youth I was neither a drunkard nor a gambler, nor otherwise openly vicious; but I was a careless student. I never really tried to acquire the necessary art of controlling and concentrating the powers of my mind for close analysis or for abstract subjects of any kind. I was passionately fond of field sports and wild adventure. I often absented myself from home for months together, and rambled unattended in various parts of my native country, which have been immortalized by that gifted novelist, Sir Walter Scott. Folks used to say I was a dreamer; and perhaps they were right, but I did not like to hear them say it.

"My only brother was the antithesis of myself,—a shrewd, calculating man; one, as Butler says,—

> 'Who could distinguish and divide
> A hair 'twixt south and south-west side.'

He is now very wealthy, for he succeeded to the family estates at my father's death. I have not received one shilling from them. I should have said before, that my mother died when I was very young, so I was deprived of that maternal care which is often the means of developing anything that is good and noble in the disposition of a child. I need not give details of our family feuds and petty disagreements. They were never healed up. Perhaps it was my fault, but I have only lately begun to think so. My father was very stern, and my brother was selfish. But I have said enough on that subject. I don't wish to use harsh language.

"About a month after I received my aunt's legacy, I sailed for Sydney in the ship *Dolphin*. I said my name was John Cameron. I did not acquaint any of my friends with my plans, and to this hour I presume they are ignorant of my whereabouts. I am not aware that they have troubled to search for me, and it is not likely they will ever do so. It is my wish that they shall remain in ignorance of my fate. Please to remember that, Roger.

"Clipper ships were not even dreamt of in those early days, and the *Dolphin*, which was 400 tons burden, was about the average size of vessels that traded to Australia. There were only two cabin passengers in the ship beside myself—an old soldier officer and his wife. In the steerage there were a man and his wife and a girl, whom they called their niece. This was her likeness," he added, as he took a gold locket from his breast-pocket, and showed it to me. "It is rather faded, for it has been long taken. What do you think of it, Roger?"

"A very lovely face," I remarked, and I gazed on the picture with admiration. "A blonde beauty!"

"Yes, she was indeed a beautiful girl. And what do you think of this one?" He showed me another picture on the obverse of the locket, and I noticed that his eyes were overflowing with tears.

"It is a remarkably handsome child!" I said, with almost rapturous earnestness. "She is not so perfectly beautiful as the other one, but there is more vivacity of expression in her face and more intelligence in her eyes. I admire this face most, if you wish for my candid opinion. They are sisters, I presume?"

"Mother and daughter," he replied, with a deep sigh. "These pictures were taken at different dates, as you will suppose. Dear Ella was eleven years of age when hers was taken. No doubt she is a handsome young woman now, if she is living."

"Who are the ladies, Mr. Cameron?"

"You shall hear presently, if you will kindly listen to my story. I found my life on shipboard intolerably dull. The captain was a rough, unsociable man, and the soldier officer and his wife seldom left their suite of stern cabins except at dinner time, and then they were so cold and stately in their bearing that I rarely ventured to speak to them. The first time I saw Clara Bond was about a fortnight after our ship left the land. She had been sea-sick, and did not come on deck till then. I was struck with her girlish face and figure the moment I first set eyes on her. I may say it was love at first sight, such as I have read of in old romances, but never expected to witness in real life. But love's shafts are as erratic as forked lightning. You smile, Roger, but I dare say you know it is true enough. There is no telling where Cupid's shafts may strike, and even old age and high intellect are not always reliable conductors to the befooling influence of his amatory smiting. With me it seems to have been a sort of half crazy infatuation, and I try to reason over it after twenty years' experience of its effects on my fortunes. I had rambled much about the highlands and lowlands of Scotland, as I before stated, and I had often met with pretty-faced damsels, and chatted with them in a merry, modest way, but I never felt my heart seriously smitten with the charms of even the finest of them; and, to tell the truth, I was rather concerned at my lack of appreciation of nature's loveliest works, and I was half afraid that conjugal longings did not run in our family constitution. My brother was as insensible to woman's attractions as a bronze soldier, and I believe he is still a moping old bachelor, 'loving himself alone.' Very few Scotch lads would have been deemed less likely to make a hasty match than myself. But I must get on with my narrative.

"Clara was sitting on the sunny side of the main deck when I first beheld her. I remember she was dressed in a loose print wrapper, and her flaxen curls were falling in charming negligence from beneath her gipsy hat. She glanced up at me as I was standing on the poop, and that look from her innocent blue eyes fascinated me. She was a mere girl; not much over sixteen years of age, and apparently very childish and simple in her ways. I think the first feeling I had for her was pity. She seemed to be so lonely, and I wished I were her brother, that I might sit down fondly beside her and cheer her up. Take heed, Roger! If pity ever comes to your heart in that equivocal guise, scout him off immediately, or he will make a dupe of you.

"I have had leisure since then to coolly reflect on —shall I say—the psychological features of my sudden attachment to that girl, and I believe that our isolated position, as it were, was an active cause of it. Had I seen Clara in a crowd on shore, she would have extorted a silent gasp of admiration, no doubt; a pretty female face will always draw that from the hardest man alive—unless he is mad; but I am almost certain I should not have been actually smitten by her, or not smitten hard enough to make me foolishly soft. Perhaps if there had been a score or so of girls on board the ship, besides herself, she would merely have come in for her share of the brotherly yearning I should have felt for them all round. But she was the only female on board, except her aunt and the soldier officer's wife, and they were both aged and plain. Clara was young and pretty—the only girl, perhaps, within a circuit of a thousand miles! I think that was the main cause of my very tender feeling for her, together with the palpable fact that all the officers and sailors almost worshipped the girl. The scarcity of an article usually stamps its value in the market. It may perhaps seem ungallant of me to use such a sordid figure, but you can see what I mean by it. If any one were to dig up a peck or two of large diamonds of the purest water, no doubt the famous Koh-i-noor would be far less attractive to the eyes of the world, and be less valued.

"It would weary you, Roger, if I were to tell all the tantalizing minutiæ of my love-making, if I may so call my silent adoration. It was next to impossible to secure a quiet interview, even for five minutes, when everybody on board seemed to be jealously or jeeringly watching the 'belle of the ship,' as Clara was called. Those hindrances further stimulated my passion for her. A tree laden with ripe rosy apples would be doubly enticing to a pilfering boy, if it were behind a high wall spiked with broken glass bottles. I did contrive to pass a few stolen moments with Clara, on two or three occasions, when she was on the main deck alone, and the few words I heard from her lisping tongue seemed to increase my longing for more of her company. When we were not far from Madeira, our ship was partially dismasted in a squall, and the captain resolved to make direct for the Cape of Good Hope, to refit. That was pleasant news to me, for I longed to get on shore somewhere for the chance of a quiet stroll with Clara, to unfold to her my simple tale of love.

"I had laid in a private store of luxuries for the voyage, for ships were not so well provisioned in those days as they are now; and it used to give me glowing satisfaction to launch out portions of my stock, every day or two, to Mrs. Badkin—Clara's aunt,—who always overloaded me with thanks, and said her little niece was glad of the things, and thought I was very kind indeed To be short, by the time the ship arrived in Table Bay, I was on intimate terms with Mrs. Badkin and her husband, and without any demur they accepted my offer to pay their expenses at an hotel in Cape Town, to save them the irksome alternative of living on board the ship while she lay in the port refitting.

"Selden says, 'Of all the actions of a man's life, his marriage does least concern other people; yet of all actions of our life it is most meddled with by other people.' That is true, Roger, as many unhappy wedded folks could testify, as well as I can."

CHAPTER IV.

"If you have tears, prepare to shed them now."—*Shakespeare*.

AFTER a short pause, during which I sat beside him in silence, Mr. Cameron thus resumed his story :—

"Soon after the *Dolphin* anchored in Table Bay, I went on shore to procure lodgings for myself and party. If I had been alone, I would have gone to one of the principal hotels in Cape Town, for I had always been accustomed to first-class accommodation when travelling; but I thought that my newly-found friends would prefer more homely quarters, so I secured three bedrooms and a sitting-room in an old-fashioned Dutch-built inn, not far from the military barracks.

"In the meantime a fierce south-easter sprang up, and I could not return to the ship. For three successive days it blew a hard gale, and Table Mountain was enveloped in white mist. Several ships in the roadstead dragged their anchors, and a signal of distress was flying on board the *Dolphin* for an anchor and cable; but no boatman would render the assistance for love or money, nor could I tempt them by any liberal offer to put me on board. My anxiety was intense. The *Dolphin* was riding to a single anchor, and my life's happiness seemed to depend on the tenacity of a chain cable, which might have been old and rust-eaten for aught I knew. If but one link broke, the ship would be driven out to sea; and in her crippled condition, there was no telling where she might drift to. Perhaps she would run to St. Helena to refit, and then it was not at all probable that she would put into Table Bay again to pick me up. There I should be left without money or even a change of clothing; and worse than all, Clara would be lost to me for life, for I did not doubt that she would have half a dozen offers of marriage before she had been in Sydney a month. Handsome girls, were comparatively scarce there in those rough days, and bachelors were lovingly watchful for new arrivals. Clara was not engaged to me, for I had not had an opportunity for saying half a dozen tender words to her on the subject of my heart's condition, so she was quite free so far as I was concerned—and free enough in other ways.

"We usually feel a strong attachment for an object that we are in danger of losing, and my passion for Clara seemed to increase with the gale which threatened to blow her away from me for ever. Bear in mind, Roger, I was but a little more than twenty-one years of age—a susceptible age, by the way, for any young man of mettle, but especially so for one in my position, and with a mind so ill-balanced as mine was. I seemed to be whirled to the conclusion that a union with Clara was positively essential to my peace of mind, and also to my physical health; indeed, it was an infatuation which completely mastered all my common-sense and judgment. I remember arguing with myself in some such silly boyish way as this: 'I am my own master, and I am independent as far so pecuniary means go. My family would certainly object to my marrying a girl of whose antecedents I know little or nothing; but what are my family's prideful opinions to me when my happiness is at stake? They have never been satisfied with anything I have done of late years, so I need not study their likes or dislikes. I have an undoubted right to please myself; so I will exercise that right, and get a companion to cheer my lonely existence—somebody to love, honour, and cherish me. Yes; if the ship weathers out this gale, and Clara gets safely on shore, I will ask her to marry me. If she consents, and her good uncle and aunt do not forbid the match, who in the world has a right to say nay to it?'

"Ah me! Roger, my lad, I was a young simpleton! Happy would it have been for me if the ship had been blown to St. Helena or anywhere else, even though it left me on shore penniless. I should have had a short season of misery, no doubt, but what of that? It would have been but like the momentary twinge of a dentist's forceps compared with months of torturing toothache. I will not bore you with any more of my sour reflections. Brief let me be. The gale abated. Clara landed safely, and looking prettier than ever, or so I thought. I wooed and won her in half an hour, and got her aunt and uncle's consent in half a minute. Two days afterwards we were married.

"I took apartments in a farmhouse on the road to Constantia, and there my young wife and I spent two weeks, which was the only time we really enjoyed together. In the confidential outpourings which usually occupy honeymoon seasons, Clara told me a little of her earlier history, which I need not trouble you with. Poor child! she had not received a good parental training; and she was almost as uncultured as one of our beautiful Australian bush flowers. But she was very fond and loving, if her conversational powers were defective; and love was all I looked for just then. We used to ramble about the bush (which very much resembles the bush of Australia), and we were happy together.

"I could not help blushing with pity when Clara tried to sign her name legibly in the marriage register; and I soon afterwards formed a quiet design of instructing her in the elementary branches of education. I had several of my old school books in my trunks, and I fancied how nicely it would relieve the tedium of ship life, to sit in the cabin and be tutor to my pretty young bride. But alas! that was another miscalculation of mine, Roger. At first Clara treated it as a mere joke, and used to make fun of everything I said, in her pretty childish way; but when I one evening with affectionate earnestness tried to show her the advantage it would be to the social standing of herself and me, if she would try to improve her education just a little, she quite startled me by the tartness with which she told me it was a pity I did not find out that she was such a dunce before I married her. I gave up the tuition scheme, for I could not bear to see her look sulky.

"Similar mistakes have been made perhaps a thousand times. I certainly have never met with more than one instance, in all my wanderings, where a young husband satisfactorily succeeded in educating his wife himself. I do not mean to infer that the fault was always on the woman's side; doubtless there was in some cases want of patience and perseverance in the husband. But it is usually a forlorn hope; that's all I wish to say about it.

"About three weeks after our marriage, the *Dolphin* was again ready for sea; and to my great chagrin, the captain sternly refused to allow my wife to go in the ship as a cabin passenger. I remonstrated with him on the injustice of such a refusal, and tried to show him that as Clara was my wife, she was entitled to equal respect as myself. Moreover, I showed our marriage certificate, to prove that there was no deception in that way, and I offered to pay double fare for her. The captain insultingly replied, that if I chose to make a fool of myself, he could not help it; but he could help having a *pair* of fools at his cuddy table, to annoy his other passengers. He said I might go in my cabin again if I liked, but my wife would have to keep in the steerage. Of course such a separation was not to be thought of, so I removed all my effects from my cabin into the steerage.

"I will venture only to hint at the miseries I experienced during our eight weeks' voyage from the Cape to Sydney. I soon found that the Badkins were exceedingly disagreeable companions (that is the mildest way I can describe them), and their vulgar familiarity was even more intolerable to me than the sly jokes of the other steerage passengers, or the occasional flirtations of the sailors with my over-petted, frolicsome young bride. If my infatuation had somewhat toned down before the end of the voyage, it is no wonder; still, I loved my little toy-wife, and whatever were my private thoughts, I never gave her reason to suppose that I regretted marrying her, and I seldom murmured at the inconveniences I had to bear in the grimy steerage of the *Dolphin*. When we arrived at Sydney, I hired a house and furnished it comfortably. At the tearful entreaties of my wife, I agreed to her aunt and uncle living in our house, providing they occupied the kitchen.

"My design in going to Australia was to embark in sheep-farming. It was an idea that I had entertained for years, and only waited till I received my capital to make a start. Several young countrymen of mine, who had gone to Australia some years before me, had written home such glowing accounts of the free and easy life of a squatter, and withal of the lucrativeness of sheep-farming, that I had become seized with the idea almost to an infatuation. My hasty marriage somewhat toned down my romantic views of life on a squattage; still I did not abandon the project. I resolved to take a tour through the northern districts of New South Wales for a few months, in order to determine the best locality to take up land for sheep, and also to get a little insight into my new vocation. On the recommendation of a stockbroker in Sydney, I invested £6,000 of my capital in Bank of Australia shares, which were then paying tempting dividends. I deposited £300 in another bank to the credit of my wife, and I had about £150 left to pay my own travelling expenses. I bought a good horse and necessary outfit, and set off on my travels.

"I went considerably beyond Moreton Bay (Queensland was not then a separate colony), and I saw a good deal of bush life, and became quite charmed with it. I was most hospitably received at every station I called at, and found that squatters and their families, as a class, were gentlefolks. I often reflected, with sorrow, on the difficulty I should experience in getting my wife to appreciate a quiet life in the bush, and I was troubled lest she should not be so cordially received by our neighbours as I desired.

"After seven months' absence, I returned to Sydney, and soon afterwards my wife presented me with a daughter. I was dotingly fond of my precious child— yes; and I love her now more tenderly than ever, for she is the only real tie my heart has to this world. I could give my poor dwindling life itself to hear that she is well and happy." Mr. Cameron again took the gold miniature frame from his pocket, and kissed his daughter's picture fondly. "Poor Ella!" he exclaimed, "you have lacked a father's care; but it was not my fault, darling! though you have been taught to believe otherwise. The bitterest sorrow I have now in my heart is the fear that

E

you, my only daughter, will ever remember me with unloving feelings, through misrepresentation."

I felt so full of sympathy for Mr. Cameron's distress, that I asked him to let me look at his daughter's picture again; and as I gazed at the lovely face of the dear girl, I could have kissed it with real enjoyment, but I did not like to take such a liberty before her grief-stricken father. In a little time he recovered his composure, and said,—

"I stayed in Sydney a few months after the birth of my child, and then I started again for New England, to buy a sheep station which had been offered me on easy terms. Before going, I drew the half-year's dividend on my bank stock, and paid it to the credit of my wife's bank account; and in the joy of my heart at the safe arrival of my treasured infant, I made Mr. and Mrs. Badkin a liberal present of money. I had, months before, candidly told my wife, that though I was willing for her relations to live with us while our home was in Sydney, I should object to their going with us to the country. She did not demur to my decision, and I thought she passively agreed to it. The Badkins seemed also to yield a sullen assent.

"I bought Glen Campbell station, with 13,000 sheep, for £9,000, which was considered a fair market price at that time. I soon returned to Sydney to arrange for two-thirds of the purchase money, according to agreement. Judge, if you can, of my concern when on arriving at home I found the house empty, and was told that my wife and her relatives had gone to New Zealand.

They had sold off my household effects, and taken the proceeds with them, together with other funds which they had raised in the neighbourhood on my credit. I also heard more than I like to repeat of the familiarity of my wife with a young officer of the *Dolphin*, which ship had again arrived in Sydney."

I said, "That must have been a great shock to you, Mr. Cameron?" I felt much moved at his sad story.

"Yes, it was indeed a shock, Roger. News of the death of my wife and child would not have been so heavy a blow to my heart. With ill-judged haste I resolved to go in search of the fugitives; not so much in the hope of reclaiming my misguided wife, as with the object of taking my child from her control; but I need not have been in such haste over it, for the poor infant was safer with its mother, for awhile, than she would have been under my care. It would have been a wise step if I had completed my bargain for the sheep station before I set out on such an uncertain errand. Glen Campbell station has increased in value four-fold or more, and I should probably be now a wealthy man. Heigho! what a wonderful difference it would make in the fortunes of some men, if they could at times get but a short glimpse into the future! One of my favourite authors says, 'For the sower of the seed is assuredly the author of the whole mischief.' The Badkins are mainly responsible for the crop of misery that has sprung from the seeds of discord they sowed around my domestic hearth. I do not exculpate my wife from blame, but I make much allowance for her defective training, and for the pernicious example of her unprincipled relatives. They were more blameable than she was; and I thought if I could remove her from their influence that she might be reclaimed to virtue. I felt that it was my duty to try to rescue her from ruin, even if I never took her to my home again; at any rate, I would recover my beloved child and take her under my own training. Accordingly I took a passage in the first ship that sailed to New Zealand, and a fortnight afterwards I landed at the Bay of Islands. There I learned that my wife and her friends had gone to Auckland. While I was waiting for a vessel to take me to that port, a terrible affray took place between the white inhabitants of the Bay and some native tribes. The town of Korrerareka was sacked and burnt. I escaped with my bare life to a ship then lying in the Bay, and was afterwards taken on with many other unfortunate refugees to Valparaiso. You see, Roger, I am giving you the barest outline of my history; the details would fill a big book, but it would be a very dreary book to write or to read.

"Luckily I had with me proofs that I owned bank stock in Sydney, so I was enabled to negotiate a loan to pay my current expenses and to procure a fresh outfit. After ten weeks' stay in Valparaiso, I returned to Sydney in a ship that was going to the colony with horses."

"Did you say horses, or did I misunderstand you, Mr. Cameron?"

"I don't wonder at your asking the question, Roger,

after the statistics I gave you last week of the horses and cattle in New South Wales. It is a fact, that in those days speculators in Sydney were importing shiploads of skin-and-bone horses from Valparaiso, and little rats of ponies from Timor Laut, an island to the north-west of New Holland. Now you may understand what I told you of bush horses sometimes having been sold in country pounds for half a crown a head.* On my return to Sydney, I learned to my great dismay, that owing to—

> 'Blest paper credit, last and best supply,
> That lends corruption lighter wings to fly;'

the Bank of Australia had recently failed, and not only was all my money lost, but I was liable also for the large claims of creditors to the bank, for it was not a limited liability company. To add to my weight of trouble, I was sued on my dishonoured draft to the Valparaiso Bank, and was put into Carter's barracks (the debtors' prison), from which I could only free myself by filing my schedule in the insolvency court."

Poor Cameron was so much affected by the recital of his varied losses and crosses, that I begged him to defer the remainder of his exciting disclosures to some other time. He willingly acquiesced, and we then slowly walked homeward, Cameron leaning on my arm, and apparently lost in his sorrowful recollections.

---

* I have been told, by a gentleman in whose word I have confidence, that a man at Braidwood once bought twenty wild bush horses for thirty shillings.—ED.

CHAPTER V.

> " Soon the shroud shall lap thee fast,
> And the sleep be on thee cast
> That shall ne'er know waking."—*Scott*.

FOR several days Cameron was too weak to leave his room. When he was somewhat better—for he had short intervals of ease—he wished to go again to his favourite retreat in the park; so I got a Bath chair and wheeled him there. When we were seated under the oak tree, he resumed his narrative :—

"The Insolvency Commissioners allowed me to retain my clothing and jewellery. I sold the whole to a dealer for £95; I dare say it cost me five times that sum. I bought a fresh outfit, consisting of a few slop shirts, coarse woollen jumpers, and corduroy trowsers; also blankets and sundry other articles which usually comprise 'a bushman's swag,' and I started on foot on a tour through the northern country. You may see, if you ever have patience enough to read my diary, that I travelled several thousands of miles, and met with some strange adventures. I suffered many privations, but upon the whole my life was an enjoyable one. I was shipwrecked when returning to Sydney from Wide Bay, and unfortunately lost many rare entomological specimens which I had collected; but my pencil sketches and my manuscripts I preserved. I had an idea at one time of writing an account of my bush rambles and researches for publication; but I shall never write another page—I shall die soon."

"I hope you will be spared for a long time yet, Mr. Cameron," I said, soothingly. "My mother thinks that if you persevere with the new medicine you have for your cough, you will get well again as the summer advances."

He shook his head, while a sort of sorrowful smile passed over his wan features, and he answered—

"No, Roger; I am beyond the healing power of physic. I may say I have prematurely worn out my constitution, and it cannot be renewed by human means. But I wish you to listen carefully to me this morning; and please to sit a little closer to me, for I cannot speak very loudly. The most important part of my communication is to come; but I will finish it as soon as I can, and then my mind will be more composed to prepare for the approaching finale. It is a solemn thing to feel one's self very near to the grave.

"My country rambles extended over three years without a break. I was sparing with my money, as you will suppose, for it to last me all that time. When it was spent, I took a situation as tutor in a squatter's family, not far from Toowoomba. I was treated kindly and paid liberally; but there were so many travellers calling at the station, that I became morbidly fearful of being recognised by some of them, so I left the place suddenly, and again took to bush travelling, or rambling, in the far north of the colony. I fell in with a gentleman, a sort of Robinson Crusoe, and we became very intimate. He was a kind-hearted, liberal Scotchman, one of the most unselfish men I ever met with, and a pleasant, intelligent companion. He was a thorough sportsman, and during the few months we were together, we might have made our shooting and fishing operations profitable; but my companion seemed to have a contempt for money, and I never had much love for it, so neither of us saved a shilling from the proceeds of our game bags. Poor Donald was drowned while trying to swim across a flooded creek.

"When I got back to New South Wales, I travelled over much of the southern and western districts. Then for three years I settled down as a shepherd at a station on the Murrumbidgee. You are right, Roger, it was a lonely life; but it was, I think, the most peaceful time I ever spent. My employer was a cultivated man, and of a kindly disposition. He occasionally spent an hour or two of an evening in my hut, and he several times invited me to his house. but I always declined the honour. He lent me many valuable books from his library; and I think I read more during that period than I ever did before, for I pretty carefully digested most of the works of Bacon, Macaulay, D'Aubigne, Paley, Cuvier, and some others of a similarly high character. My master once expressed his surprise that a man of my education should take to the humble

occupation of a shepherd ; but when he saw that his
remark caused me embarrassment, he, with gentlemanlike consideration, changed the subject, and he never
afterwards sought to know anything of my previous
history, more than I voluntarily told him. He was a
model master, Roger ; and it would be a happy thing
for shepherds if squatters in general were as considerate
for the moral and social welfare of the poor solitary
guardians of their flocks.

"When gold was first discovered near Bathurst, I set
off to Summer Hill diggings, and was pretty successful.
I was also at the Turon diggings, and afterwards at
the first Bendigo rush, in Victoria ; also at the Mount
Alexander, and other rich diggings. I daresay I might
have made a moderate fortune if I had continued at gold
digging, but it was a kind of life that I did not enjoy.
To me there was not half so much pleasurable excitement in digging for nuggets of gold, as there would be
in fishing with a deep-sea line ; besides, the companion-
ship was not always to my taste. I certainly met with
some diggers of refined habits and gentlemanly bearing,
but many others were of a different caste, and I could
not tolerate their roughness. Close reading or study
of any kind of an evening was out of the question in a
tent with three frolicsome mates, and surrounded on all
sides by noisy revelry. But after a while I fell in with
the current devices for killing time, and was soon in
a fair way of becoming a confirmed gambler and a
tippler. Previous to that time, let me say, I had never
been given to excess in drinking or eating, or in gross

sensuality of any other sort ; and my case shows how sadly possible it is for a man of mature years, whose previous life had been strictly temperate, to become a slave to the horrid vice of drunkenness, through yielding to the force of evil example.

"In order to break away from my mates, who I suspected were plotting to win all my savings from me, I started away to Melbourne, and thence to Sydney. I was previously aware that there were graziers on some of the poor coast runs, north of Sydney, who would gladly treat with a purchaser for their herds. I had a little more than £1,000 saved, and I invested it all in store cattle, which I bought at an average of twenty shillings a head. I hired stockmen, and drove my herds to Victoria. I was fortunate in losing very few cattle on the way, and also in finding a ready market. I cleared nearly £2,000 by that speculation, which only occupied me about nine months. I forthwith went to the agents of the Valparaiso Bank, and repaid the money they had advanced to me, with interest ; I also paid every tradesman in Sydney with whom my wife had contracted debts on my account. Thus I removed the horrid incubus which had weighted my heart for years, and made me hang down my head. I always dreaded debt far more than I dreaded poverty.

"Soon afterwards I determined to return to Scotland, to see if any of my relatives were living. I embarked in a fine clipper ship for London. We ran foul of an iceberg off Cape Horn, and had a narrow escape from foundering. There were two hundred passengers on board, many of whom were very intemperate, and a refreshment bar in the 'tween decks offered every facility for indulging our appetites to our hearts' content. With shame I confess to you, Roger, that I was not thoroughly sober at any time during the voyage. Drinking and gambling were my daily sports, and I lost about £400 at card playing. For three months or more I lived in London a round of dissipation, with several of my profligate fellow-voyagers. That period seems to me now like a horrible dream, and is full of bitter memories. In a half-demented state, I was lured to the house where you first saw me, and where I should doubtless have died miserably, if you had not rescued me. Thus you may see how a long indulgence in strong drink had blasted every good principle in my character. I cannot tell to what extent I have been plundered by Mrs. Jagg and her company, nor do I wish to say any more on the subject. It is hateful to me. You know the wretched condition I was in when you and your good father carried me from that den of vice, and you have witnessed much of my terrible sufferings since then. You now see me restored to my right mind, though I am tottering on the brink of the grave. Through the mercy of God my sins are pardoned ; still, the bitter memory of them will remain with me till death shall release me from all my troubles. Sin may be forgiven by God, but it can never be forgotten by the sinner. Try to remember that solemn fact, Roger, when you are tempted to do wrong; and pause ere you sow seeds for a harvest of pain and grief, such as I have suffered."

I told him that I would try to remember all he said to me; and I added, with a nervous consciousness that I was touching a painful subject, "I am anxious, sir, to know if you ever saw your wife again?"

"Yes, I have seen her, Roger," he answered with a sigh. "Better for my peace if I had never again beheld her. Six years ago I learned that she was living with a farmer at Illawarra, in New South Wales, and that my daughter was living with them. I at once journeyed to the place, and confronted my wife and her paramour. I will not go into the exciting particulars of that interview; suffice it to say, that I offered to leave them undisturbed, provided they gave me up my daughter. They sullenly agreed to the proposition, on condition that the girl was willing; but when dear Ella was brought into the room to see me, she shrank from my embrace, and tremblingly begged them not to allow me to take her away. That was the severest blow of all to my heart, for I knew that the poor child had been taught to loathe my name. Through the medium of a kind tradesman in that locality, I obtained a photograph of Ella. You have seen it twice. Ah me! poor girl! What would I not give to see her before I die? to tell her with my last breath how fondly I love her!

"I am weary, Roger," he said, after a violent outburst of grief. "We have stayed out too long for my strength. Let us go home, if you please. Do not speak to me any more just now, there's a dear fellow! I have told you all I wished to say on this sad subject; I hope you will remember it."

That same afternoon I went, at Cameron's request, for Mr. Martin, my uncle's solicitor, and he was closeted with the sick man for an hour or more. After the lawyer went away, Cameron bade me sit down beside his bed, as he had something else of importance to say to me. I obeyed, and he said in a feeble voice,—

"I have several times advised you to go to Australia, Roger. A firm belief that you would do better there than in England was the reason why I gave you that advice. I had no other motive then; but I have *now* a strong selfish desire that you should go, which I will perhaps explain to you. But tell me first, have you an idea of going there?"

I unhesitatingly replied, "Yes, I have, Mr. Cameron. I have thought over your kind advice, which coincided with my own inclination. My parents and my uncle, whom I have consulted, all think it may be a step in the right direction; in fact, my father merrily urges me to be off at once, and make my fortune before the gold is all scrambled up."

"I am extremely glad to hear it. Will you undertake a responsible commission for me, Roger? You see I am testing your friendship sorely."

"I will do anything in my power to serve you, sir."

"Thank you, thank you, my boy! I believe you will. You have always been kind to me, and I am grateful. I wish you to find my poor, misguided wife, and tell her that with my dying breath I forgive her for all the unhappiness and loss she has caused me. I shall surely be dead before you go away. Tell her that I died at peace with God, and at peace with all the world. But especially I wish you to find my beloved daughter. Take her these articles of jewellery, and give them into her own hands. I will seal them in a small packet presently. Please to avoid, if possible, saying anything that may tend to prejudice Ella against her mother; but I wish her to know that her father was not such a thoroughly depraved character as I fear she believes him to have been. I will leave you to explain it in the way that your feelings towards me suggest. Give my fondest love to dear Ella, and tell her to follow me to the home above, where our eternal fellowship will never be beclouded by mistrust. My darling girl! Oh that I could see her, for one minute only! Do find her if you can, Roger, and the blessing of a dying father will follow you on your way."

It was most painful for me to witness the poor man's emotion and his severe physical sufferings. I begged of him not to say any more on the distressing subject, and again I solemnly promised that I would spare no effort to find his daughter, and would say all I could to make her revere his memory; and I would also try to find his wife, and tell her all the comforting things I could concerning him.

"I thank you, Roger," he said, and he pressed my hands convulsively. "Now I feel my mind at ease, and I am ready to die whenever God shall see fit to call me. I have instructed Mr. Martin to draw up my will, and to ask your good uncle to be my executor. I am not sure what is the amount of my balance in the bank, for I have drawn cheques in a reckless way without making any entry of them ; but I am sure there is ample to pay the costs of my funeral, and to cover the expenses you may incur in your search for my wife and daughter in Australia. I have a section of land in Victoria. It is not worth much now, but it is sure to become valuable a few years hence. That I leave to my darling Ella : it may be a little fortune for her. The title deeds are in my writing desk. You will also find a paper in the desk which will give you a clue to the whereabouts of my poor wife. All the other private papers in my desk you can look over at your leisure, and you may do what you please with them. I have no wish that you should put a stone over my grave, Roger ; but if you should choose to do so, please call me simply—John Cameron. I leave it to your judgment whether to tell Ella my real name or not. I fear it would be no advantage to her, poor girl, to know of her proud relatives in Scotland. I forgot to say before that I have not had any communication with my family on this side of the globe since my return. They do not know that I am in England. Perhaps they have long ago forgotten that I was ever in existence. Now I have said all I wish to say about my affairs. I hope you will not speak to me again of them. I have done with the world. Please to sit a little closer to my bed, Roger, and read to me again about Jesus, the sinner's Friend."

* * * * *

Poor Cameron lingered for a fortnight longer ; but he never again alluded to his temporal concerns. I was frequently at his bedside, and he was glad to hear me read from the New Testament, but he did not seem inclined for conversation. Our good pastor visited him several times, and read and prayed with him. On the evening of his decease I was sitting quietly by his bed, watching while my mother went to rest for an hour or two, when suddenly he said in feeble accents, "Give me your hand, Roger. I think I am going; but do not call your mother yet—she must be weary, poor dear lady! Hear my last request. Do try to find my poor, unhappy wife, in Australia, and tell her that with my dying breath I prayed for her. I forgive her for all the wretchedness she has caused me. And, Roger, my dear boy! speak kindly of me to my darling Ella; and if you can help her in any way, do it for my sake." His tongue faltered: not another word could it utter. About midnight he died.

We buried him in Greenwich churchyard, and placed a stone over his grave, upon which was the simple inscription:

Sacred to the Memory of

JOHN CAMERON,

Aged 39 Years.

If the reader will follow the course of my strange story, he may see that my promise to Mr. Cameron, to seek and find his wife and daughter, was not very easy to perform.

CHAPTER VI.

"I will a round, unvarnished tale deliver
Of my whole course of love."—*Shakespeare.*

THE balance in the London bank to the credit of the late Mr. Cameron was £595. It would have been a much smaller sum if all his cheques had been duly honoured; but payment of some of them was refused on account of the illegibility of the signatures, and the persons who presented them did not trouble the bank again, which was conclusive evidence that the cheques were not given for honest value received.

Cameron's will directed that fifty pounds should be paid to my parents, in grateful acknowledgment of their kind care of him in his illness; and after payment of his funeral and testamentary expenses, the residue of his estate and effects was bequeathed to me, all except the section of land before alluded to, and his jewellery, which he bequeathed to his daughter. He had a large stock of good clothes, which fitted my father to a nicety; so for his generous attention to a helpless man in a time of extreme need, he received a handsome pecuniary recompense (though he had not counted upon receiving anything), and a supply of clothing enough to last him as long as he lived.

I soon began to prepare for my voyage to Australia. Getting my outfit ready was a sorrowful duty for my mother and sister; but my father was as cheerful over it as if I were only going to Battersea, which is a few miles above London Bridge, on the river Thames.

"Come, cheer up, my darlings!" said my hopeful sire, stepping into the workroom one day, where my mother and sister were mending all my old garments and marking my new ones. "I declare, any one would think, from the looks of you two sorrowing ones, that Roger was going to be blown from a gun's muzzle to-morrow morning. My stars! I only wish I were a young fellow again, or that I stood in Roger's sea boots, and had his chance of making my way to fortune with wind and tide in my favour! When I first set out from under my mother's lee, to go as an apprentice boy on board of a collier, I could have stowed all my effects in the pockets of my monkey-jacket; and I dare say you will have tight squeezing to get Roger's outfit into two sea-chests. Surely the boys and girls of this age are a wonderful deal better off than their fathers and mothers were. 'So they ought to be,' you say, Emmy? Well, no doubt you are right, my girl, for the world is progressing; and I dare say I was much better off as a boy than my forefathers were, if I go down to the time when they lived in caves, and used blue paint instead of blue cloth for jackets and trowsers."

After much pressing, I induced my sister to accept of £50 as a parting present; but my mother, in her conscientious way, objected to it, and wished Emily to give it back to me. "I do not think, my dear Roger, that in strict justice you have a right to apply poor Mr. Cameron's money to any other purpose than paying your own lawful expenses. You will perhaps have some trouble to find his wife and child, for Australia is a wide place, I am told, and you may want all the money you have. Besides, it is possible that you may find them in poverty, and if so, you will like to be able to relieve them. Do, my dear, ever remember your sacred promise to the poor dying man, and try your utmost to fulfil it faithfully."

"Mother, dear!" I replied, in a somewhat touchy tone, for which I have since been rather sorry. "Mother! I have no more idea of breaking my promise in that matter, than I have of trying to break your heart by any other departure from right principle. No doubt I shall have some trouble in finding poor Mr. Cameron's relatives; and surely I have a right to pay myself for my time. Do let Emma keep the £50, or I shall be sorely grieved." My father came up at the time, and said cheerily, "Pocket the money, my girl, and buy yourself a new outfit." That settled the little controversy, for my mother always had a sensible respect for my father's authority.

I was informed that just then some of the best ships of the day were laid on for Melbourne, so I secured an intermediate berth in a fine new clipper ship, called the *Stormberg*. She was specially recommended to me as being one of the largest sailing ships that had ever crossed the sea to Australia ; and her captain was noted for making quick passages. My father and mother and sister accompanied me to Liverpool, to inspect my accommodation, and to see me start off for the land of gold, as it was poetically called at that time. After paying for my passage and outfit, I had £20 in ready cash, besides a bank draft for £400. I confess that I felt some pride in being the possessor of so much capital.

I may as well spare myself the task of describing the tender parting scene on the deck of the *Stormberg*, between my dear relatives and myself. It was the first separation we had ever experienced since my father left off going to sea, and we all felt it very much; but it is not likely that strangers will care to know anything about it.

My voyage across the ocean was a very rapid one for a sailing ship. I had never been to sea before, so I was in comfortable ignorance of the peculiar perils and dangers which ever beset passengers in a clipper ship, with a captain who ambitiously aims at beating everything afloat, at all hazards. When the *Stormberg* was plunging along with her fore-yard almost scooping the water, and making the masts and yards crack again, I thought it was all right, and that ships were built to sail on their broadsides. And when the lighter sails and spars were carried away occasionally, and the split canvas flapped about the eyes and ears of the sailors who were trying to secure it, I used to smile at the fun, until I one day overheard the old boatswain mutter to himself, that "carrying on sail till it blew away was wilful murdering work for the crew"; and then I saw that there was more risk to human life and limb than the honour of making an extra smart passage was worth. I have since observed, that when the newspapers report a remarkably quick trip of a favourite ship, they usually praise the smartness of the captain and officers, but the broken bones of the common sailors are not worth mentioning.

Our voyage ended a day sooner than any of us anticipated ; that is to say, instead of entering Port Phillip Heads with flying colours and with dry clothes on our backs, as we might have done if every man on board had done his duty, we ran on shore near Cape Otway, and the *Stormberg* became a total wreck. That fine, new clipper ship never floated again, except in fragments of firewood. Fortunately no lives were lost, and I daresay the owners were satisfactorily insured, so that there was not much stir made over it. No doubt there was negligence somewhere, but I am not sailor enough to explain exactly how the mishap occurred ; and lest I should put the blame on an innocent head, I will say no more about it, save that it scared me very much, and made me pray more solemnly than I ever prayed before, and perhaps more earnestly than I shall pray in future, until death again stares me in the face. The immediate prospect of a violent death will make the most careless wretch tremble ; and the man whose whole life has been devoted to sport and conviviality will look serious if he is in a sinking ship. However much blasphemous talk and tipsy jocularity I witnessed throughout the voyage, there was not much of that sort of fun to be heard or seen when the ship lay wallowing in those frightful breakers, and the rocks were grinding her bottom into pulp. That was a time to weep, rather than a time to laugh. Never shall I forget that awful night, until I forget the world altogether.

I cannot easily describe my first ideas of the Victorians. Upon the whole they favourably impressed me, though there certainly was much strange freedom about some of them, similar to what I have read of in American story books. When I landed at Sandridge from the tug steamer which brought me up from the wreck, I was received by a crowd of well-dressed persons on the pier, with most exciting demonstrations of attention, if not respect. I might have fancied that I had fallen in with a host of old neighbours in a strange land, and that they were all glad to see me. It did not strike me that my having been wrecked the previous night in a new clipper ship, at the very doorway of my home, as it were, and the general curiosity to hear the details of the mishap from my lips, were the circumstances which stirred up that pleasing display of fraternal feeling. By the way, it is a curious fact, which I have since had leisure to reflect upon, that the condolence a shipwrecked man usually meets with, is, to a marked extent, regulated by the size and class of the vessel in which he was cast ashore. I have a shrewd impression, that if I had been wrecked in an old collier schooner, or even in a brig laden with Warrnambool potatoes, I might have landed at Sandridge without much recognition, save from some of the sailors on the pier, or a few lodging-house touters

—stay, I will qualify that speculative sentence, by adding that I have no doubt the zealous chaplain of the "Sailors' Church," or some good friend from the "Sailors' Home," would have been on the look out for me. I was, however, too much excited when I stepped on shore to ponder over the many fitful phases of human sympathy, and I received the greetings of the crowd with more gratitude than the people really deserved.

Some gentlemen in the railway car in which I took my seat for Melbourne, were eager to know more than I could tell them about the wreck. My story was simply as follows : " I was suddenly awakened by being jerked out of my berth on to the sharp edge of my sea-chest. I hastened on deck, and saw white breaking waves all around me and dark clouds above me. The ship's timbers were crunching, her masts were falling, and her sails were flapping into rags. Confusion seemed to be ruling everywhere, and my head was distracted. Soon afterwards I found myself on the rocks ; but how I got there, I cannot exactly say, for my senses were temporarily scared away. The only visible personal damage I sustained was a small bruise on my left leg."

That certainly was a short report of a great catastrophe, but I could not honestly make any more of it. Some of my hearers did not seem half satisfied with it, and they cross-questioned me to a perplexing extent, as if they fully believed that I knew who was to blame for the disaster. At length I told them, with polite firmness, that I could not give them any more information on the subject, and they had better wait till some official report was printed. One queer-looking little man then asked me if I had any objection to show them the bruise on my leg? Of course I knew that was only common chaff, and I treated it with dignified contempt; but every one else in the carriage laughed like a flock of bush kookoo-burras.

When I got out of the train at Flinders Street station, I again received some public notice; and at the hotel where I lunched that day, I was an object of marked attention. I could almost have swam in "shandy-gaff," and other American beverages of a stimulating nature, which were pressed on me by many fraternizing strangers; and if I had not possessed sober virtue, I should assuredly have been drunk that morning, and then I daresay I might have given a comical account of my shipwreck, and my dear friends at home would have been astonished when they read it in print two or three months afterwards.

But my popularity was not durable; it never is in such cases. In a few days the wreck of the *Stormberg* ceased to be talked of at *café* tables, and I only received an occasional nod of recognition from some person who had more leisure than his busy neighbours, or a verbal salute from others, whose familiarity closely bordered on contempt.

I recovered my baggage from the wreck. It was a little moistened by sea water, but was otherwise all correct. The temptation to spend a month or so in seeing the many objects of attraction in and around

Melbourne was hard to overcome; but I was firm in my resolution to fulfil my promise to Cameron before I attended to my own pleasure or minor interests, so I prepared to go to New South Wales, and there to begin my search for his wife and daughter. The next steamer for Sydney was called the *Columbus*. But as I did not hear a very favourable character of the ship, I went by rail to Sandridge to look at her and judge for myself. In those "golden days" many old steamers were sent to Melbourne and Sydney for sale, and they were bought up, at almost fabulous prices, for the intercolonial passenger trade. The *Columbus* was one of those top-heavy looking steamers that are specially built for navigating the American lakes, and in my judgment it was not a very trustworthy vessel for ocean service. I am not sure that I would have trusted myself and luggage in her for the short trip to Sydney, only that one of her owners was going as a passenger. He looked like a man who knew how to take care of himself, so I resolved to chance it. By the way, that short phrase, "chance it," is very common with colonial boys,—and with their fathers too, sometimes.

After securing my berth, I left the ship and strolled along the Sandridge beach, reflecting as I went that I had passed through more stirring scenes during the last ten weeks, than I had experienced in the whole course of my previous life. Only a few months before, I was dispensing medicine in my uncle's old-fashioned shop in Greenwich High Street, and had no more idea of going to Australia than I had of going to Greenland. I could hardly realize that I was at the warm antipodes, though the fact was being dinned into my ears by myriads of trumpeting mosquitoes. Presently I tried to draw a mental panorama of all my old Greenwich friends standing on their heads, and their houses and churches turned topsy-turvy. I was just picturing a general smash of uncle's physic bottles and gallipots, when my comical fancy was checked by a shrill screaming, the cause of which I will explain in one paragraph.

There is perhaps nothing very romantic or picturesque in the town of Sandridge, though it is a busy place, and one of the principal shipping ports of Victoria. Being less than three miles from Melbourne, and only about five minutes' run by railway, some of the citizens like to go there on warm afternoons for an hour or two, to escape from the dust of the busy metropolis, and to enjoy the sight and scent of the wide waters of Hobson's Bay. The beaches at St. Kilda and Brighton are more enticing and more popular than Sandridge beach; but tastes vary in Melbourne, and some of the folks prefer the latter place. I think I shall always retain a veneration for Sandridge. But to go on with my narrative. As I was strolling along the western beach, I saw a group of little girls in charge of a nursemaid, who was sitting on a log knitting, while the children were gambolling about in innocent merriment. Some of them were building castles in the sand for the waves to wash down, and others were capering, like young naiads, on the top of an old rusty boiler, which once belonged to a steamship with a curious history. Soon after I had passed the playful group, I heard cries of distress, and on looking round I saw that a little girl had fallen off the old boiler into the sea. There was a commotion among the children, and the nursemaid had dropped her knitting bag and was running to the rescue with all speed; but I was there before her, and stepping into the water, I clutched the struggling child and carried her on shore. The nurse seemed too much flurried to utter a word of thanks to me for the timely service. Indeed, I did not wait half a minute. I knew that the child had not suffered, except from fright and a thorough wetting, and as I was wet half-way up to my neck, I hastened to a cab-stand, and drove direct to my lodgings. I did not mention the incident to my landlady, though I could see that she was longing to know how I had got so wet on a fine sunny day. I had before noticed that she was an inquisitive old dame, and I did not choose to humour her taste for news that did not concern herself.

Since that day I have many times heard my friends say it was a lucky chance that I was close at hand to save the dear child; but I do not believe that mere luck or chance had anything to do with it. I shall have some more to tell about the occurrence in the course of my story.

CHAPTER VII.

"Here's a pretty lot of us
Nice young maidens!"—*Old song*.

ON the morning after the foregoing incident, I read a paragraph in one of the Melbourne newspapers, headed "Heroic Act!" It highly applauded the courage and humanity of a gentleman, whose name could not be ascertained, in saving the life of a little girl who had fallen into the sea at Sandridge. It occupied seventeen lines of brevier type.

I could not help smiling as I reflected how little I had done to merit such flattering commendation. The water was about three feet in depth, and the child could not have been drowned if she had felt for the bottom with her feet, which she would naturally have done if I had given her time to do it. I simply ran into the sea, not quite up to my watch-pocket, and carried the screaming little child on shore. That was all, and I would have done almost as much to save a chicken. My first impulse was to write to the newspaper and modestly disclaim some of the praise that was lavished upon me; but upon reflection, I thought it was better not to notice it. The paragraph was perhaps written by a grateful parent; but I might be suspected of having had a hand in it myself, in order to revive my short-lived popularity. Schemes as paltry as that have been resorted to by men who are greedy for public favour, and who can accept of unlimited eulogy with as much complacent relish as a petted elephant swallows currant buns.

After getting ready to start by the 2.30 train for Sandridge, I sauntered into a Melbourne restaurant, from the hidden recesses of which issued an exhilarating odour, that pleasingly reminded me of the *Stormberg's* galley on Sundays, on which days there were special dainties cooked for the intermediate passengers. I took a seat just inside the doorway, behind a small table which was meant to accommodate four guests. My motive for getting into an out-of-the-way corner was to avoid perchance meeting with any of the facetious gentlemen who had interviewed me when I first landed from the wreck. No one enjoys a pleasant joke more than I do, but too much of that sort of thing is nauseating, and I had grown almost disgusted at being so often hailed in public places, " Hallo, Stormberg! How is your bad leg?"

Soon after the city clocks had struck one, a rapid human torrent poured into the dining-hall, and the score or more of little tables were occupied in less than three minutes by gentlemen, the majority of whom seemed to me to be employés in mercantile offices or warehouses. There were printed bills of fare on each table, or long lists of edibles to be had on demand, and I observed that the said bills were eagerly clutched at by some of the guests before they had time to take their hats off. Of course I concluded that they were ravenously hungry; indeed one youth—notwithstanding his chubby face—might have been supposed to be actually starving, by the clamorous way he shouted, "Ox tail here! Look sharp, Sarah!" In general, however, the company were as well behaved as any similar gathering that I had seen in London, only there were more sporting and mining topics discussed than I had ever heard at the restaurant in Cheapside where I used sometimes to dine; and the frequent calls for "A nobbler of *P.B.*," was a local demand quite as new to my ears as the shandy-gaff before alluded to. There were no "small beer" customers at these tables!

I soon discovered that my seat, in an extreme corner, was a badly chosen one in reference to my chance of being served with any food while the joints were in good cut and smoking hot, for I seemed to be quite out of the tide-way of victuals. I beguiled the time I had to wait in watching the waltz-like gyrations of the waitresses, and wondering how in the world they contrived to pass and repass each other so rapidly, on the centre floor—laden double-handed as they were—without colliding and upsetting dinner upon dinner. But not a single mishap of the kind did I witness, although I did not take my eyes off the girls for a moment. The amusing exhibition softened down my rising impatience for food.

There were a dozen, or perhaps more, of those active

maidens; and I could not but approve of the taste and sagacity of the owner of the restaurant, in providing such agreeable substitutes for the male waiters that I had been accustomed to see in London. For my part, I thought, I would not mind paying a few pence extra for my dinner, to have the comfort of gazing at so many pleasing faces and figures while I was eating. It would naturally assist digestion.

Most of the girls were good-looking and were all neatly dressed, and their hair was tidily arranged according to their respective fancies; indeed, it is reasonable to suppose that they all looked as pretty as they could conveniently make themselves look, under present circumstances. A few of them were favourites, as I could see by the special calls that were made on their services; but their work seemed like play to them, for they were always smiling over it. I particularly noticed a fair-haired damsel, whose movements were as graceful as my sister Emma's, which is saying as much as poetry itself could say for her. I could easily tell that her name was Bella, for she was often shouted for by several customers at once; but she seemed to attend to them all in their turn, as pleasantly as if she were feeding pet rabbits.

No doubt girls will be girls everywhere, in about the same degree or proportion that "boys will be boys," according to the old adage; and I certainly noticed coquettish glances now and then directed to some of the smart young sparks seated at the tables; but the girls had not too much to say in reply to the compliments which were freely bestowed on them, and I concluded that they were all lasses of good character.

After waiting more than a reasonable time, I thought I had better speak up for myself, or the provisions might all be eaten before my share came to me ; so I made bold to shout, "Bella!" in close imitation of the friendly style of some of the regular diners. My call was promptly answered by the damsel appealed to, who, in a voice as musical as a blackbird's, asked, "What can I get for you, sir?"

"I will take a Scotch pie, Bella, if you please," I said ; and as she gracefully tripped away to supply my demand, I felt struck all at once with a notion that I had seen her face before. Yes, it was more than a notion, for I was certain that I had seen her in Greenwich ; I would have solemnly declared to it if necessary. There was no mistaking her pretty face among a million of faces.

"Who can she be?" was the question I put to myself, and which puzzled me beyond measure. Was she one of Miss Gibbins' daily boarders, that I used to peep at every afternoon through the blue show-bottle in my uncle's shop window? or did she serve at the pastry-cook's round the High Street corner? Was she one of Madame Trim's millinery apprentices? or did she belong to the charity-school choristers that used to sing in our parish church? Had I on some bank holiday got an impressive view of her handsome figure, as she was running down one of the grassy knolls in Greenwich park? Somewhere in that locality I *had* seen her, I was sure, and I resolved on the instant to ask her all about it; for the fact of meeting with any one—especially with a beautiful maiden — who had trodden, as it were, on the very threshold of my beloved home, touched my feelings like a soft hand. I state it as a remarkable fact, that no living girl had ever before affected me so suddenly, and I could only account for it by the charming notion I had that she was born in or near to my own native town. My cousin Saul has just twittingly remarked that a paving stone from the old mouldy town of Greenwich would be more attractive to my fancy than the great Bendigo gold nugget which everybody is talking of. I calmly retorted that I feared he had no more veneration or tender feeling for *his* early home than one of those cast-iron lamp-posts in Collins Street had for its native foundry in Glasgow. A good moral rub like that, now and then, may benefit him!

It may seem rather mysterious to some stoical minds, but it is nevertheless true, that there are loving mothers in this land who would set far more value on one of their lost baby's little old shoes, than they would on a whole shipment of the newest fashioned boots. I have in a secret drawer in my desk a single leaf, which was sent to me, years ago, in the last letter I received from my dear deceased sister. It was plucked by her hand from the honeysuckle that we together planted in our garden at home on her tenth birthday. Dry and withered and intrinsically useless as that leaf is now, I would not exchange it for a chest of curly

G

leaf pekoe tea from the best plantation in China. And the moss-rose bud that I received by the last English mail from my beloved mother, though it is faded and scentless, and flat as an old bone button, has more value in my eyes than the gorgeous bouquet which I saw on the centre table in St. George's Hall, Melbourne, at the tea meeting last Friday night. There is certainly less commercial spirit than sentimentalism in all that; still they are some of the soft phases of human fancy that cannot easily be argued away.

Bella was not gone more than a minute for my pie. I thought I had never before seen a girl carry a little dish with such modest grace. When she placed the steaming hot dainty before me, I asked,—

"I say, Bella, do you know Greenwich?"

I used the most insinuating tone I could affect, and I looked as softly persuasive as a shopman selling bonnets; but the girl evidently thought I was beginning to joke with her, after the common way of some of the ruder *habitués* of the saloon, for she only responded by a slight toss of the head, and away she tripped to attend on some other customer. At the same time, I was quick enough to observe that there was something in her look which she meant to signify, "I must not gossip at dinner-time." Such was my own interpretation of the sparkle in her lovely eyes, and I was encouraged to hope that after the bustle of dinner was over, she would not mind having a little chat with me about our dear old town far away; so I sat and ruminated over my Scotch pie until nearly all the other guests had finished their meal and had gone away to resume their sterner duties.

The slow way my teeth were working against time almost lulled me to sleep; but at length the last man laid down his knife and fork and departed. I was glad. I thought a convenient time was now come for me to have a little innocent, homely gossip with Bella, and I kept a watchful eye all over the room; but I could not see her, which made me anxious lest she should have knocked herself up with her exertions in waiting on so many hungry men. Very soon the staff of waitresses (their duties being over for the day) seated themselves in a group at a table just in front of mine, and as near as possible to the snug corner I occupied for the sake of seclusion; and then, without apparently noticing me, they exercised their tongues while they rested their limbs. Truly their chatting powers were astounding, and it was clear to me that they had no arbitrary rules to restrict their freedom of debate, for they all seemed to be speaking together. I might have heard many little love secrets if I had chosen to listen attentively. I confess that I did hear *some* soft things that had been said to them at dinner-time by amorous customers, but they will remain locked in my breast with other secrets that were revealed to me in professional confidence. Presently, however, the conversation seemed to me to be too confidential for my ears, and my honour prompted me to make the girls aware of my presence; so I said in my mildest way, "Young ladies, will you please to tell me where is Bella?"

The girls whose backs had been towards me, whirled round simultaneously, and more than a dozen pairs of laughing eyes seemed to be piercing me all over like silver skewers. I was naturally embarrassed, though I tried my utmost to appear self-possessed. Thinking that they did not hear my question, I repeated it, "Pray where is Bella?"

"Bella is upstairs. Can I get you anything, sir?" said a smirky-faced waitress with mock servility.

"N-no, thank you, I have had my dinner."

The quizzical looks of the girls excited me; indeed, I should like to know what modest youth would not have felt discomposed in such a case. I wished I were out in the street, but I kept my seat like a man.

"I will call Bella down to you, sir," said another roguish-looking maid, and away she ran to a staircase and shouted, or rather screamed, "Bella! Bella! come down directly! Here is a young gentleman wants to see you particularly."

Four minutes passed: a trying time for me as I sat in silence, looking at the last mouthful of pie, which I had kept on my plate as an excuse for lingering at the table. I was conscious that the girls were gazing at me, and their partially suppressed giggles did not help to steady my fluttering nerves. At last Bella came tripping down the stairs, looking more beautiful than ever, for she was flushed and excited.

"Here, Bell, make haste!" cried the previous screamer; "this gentleman has been waiting to see you ever so long."

"Do you want me, sir?" asked Bella, in a rather sharp tone for a girl with such soft-looking lips.

"I—I merely wish to ask you if you came from Greenwich, miss?" I said, in the blandest way I could affect.

I think I shall never forget the scorching look she gave me as an answer to my question. "Why did you call me down to be trifled with, Maria?" she asked, with a flush of anger at the laughing screamer; and then she hurried upstairs without deigning to look at me again.

I paid for my pie, and out of the saloon I marched, less happy than I was when I entered it, although I had eaten a good dinner. I forgot my umbrella till I was outside; but if I had not been in a hurry, I doubt if I would have gone back for it and faced those girls, who were all laughing as if they were tickling each other. I hastened to the railway station, and was only just in time to catch the train for Sandridge, and to reach the steamer before she started.

If it were easy for me to express my feelings verbally, I doubt if any business man of the world would care to read my synopsis; and men of calm natures will sympathise enough with my mental perplexity if I do not add a word of comment to the foregoing plain statement. What the maids in the saloon thought of me I shall never exactly know, but I can guess it quite near enough for my peace. Australian girls are little rogues —in a poetic sense—when they get together for a frolic. No doubt those waitresses had many a good laugh at me and my umbrella; but I have tried to cheer myself with the reflection that they would perhaps have laughed just as much if I had been the son and heir of the greatest man in the land, for it is as natural for girls to laugh as it is for kangaroos to jump. No bye-law or rule, civil or social, could stop a company of lively girls from making fun of a sedate-looking youth, like myself, any more than it could stop a family of young kittens from playing frisky antics with a cotton reel or a ball of worsted.

The *Columbus* was three days on the passage to Sydney, so I had ample time to reflect on the exciting incident; and as the weather was rainy, I could not fail to remember that I had unluckily lost my umbrella. I was ungenerous enough at intervals to think almost spitefully of poor Bella's treatment of me, though my brotherly feelings ought to have suggested that the girl had acted just as I would wish my sister to have done if she were accosted in the same familiar way by a stranger. Nothing could shake my belief that I had seen the girl in Greenwich, and the only reason I could assign for her being ashamed to confess it was not a very creditable one to her. But notwithstanding I tried to make up my mind that I had been fortunate in escaping a conference with a doubtful character, I could not help thinking of her modest-looking face and her symmetrical figure. A little while before the passengers landed at Sydney, a sickly-looking young man, who had shared my cabin, remarked to me in a sort of drowsy, jocular strain, that he had not slept much on our first night at sea, because I so often shouted "Bella!"

His remark vexed me exceedingly, especially as there were several other passengers and the mate standing by laughing. I lost my usual control over my temper, and said in a vengeful tone, "Sir, you are a comparative stranger to me, and I decline to take your statement as a joke, whoever may choose to laugh at it. You either believe what you say, or you do not: if you do believe it, allow me to say that you mistook your own bellow for my voice, for you were roaring with sea-sickness or snoring all through the voyage. But if you do not believe your assertion, you are an impudent fellow, and if you presume to annoy me again with your wretched jokes, I will punish you on the spot."

He was completely cowed. He could not fail to see that I was more than a match for him, physically, for he was a small man; and I daresay I looked cross enough to do him bodily harm; so he picked up his carpet-bag and walked ashore without saying another word.

After I had cooled down a little, I felt grieved that I had allowed myself to be mastered by ill-temper, and of course had made myself look contemptible to my fellow-voyagers. My conscience also cuttingly asked me what I would have done or said if the stranger had been a big, strong man? That would have been a touching question if it had come from any other quarter outside of my own breast, and I might have given an evasive answer; I could not, however, but honestly confess to myself that, in such a case, I should have spared my pompous syllogism, and my savage threat of summary punishment as well. My secret opinion *now* is, that the poor little man was right, and that I really did shout "Bella!" in my dreams; but I would have been put into the boiler of the donkey-engine sooner than have confessed to it when I was in a pet.

*   *   *   *   *

Saul has just proposed to me that I should, in a fresh chapter, notice one or two other establishments that exist in Melbourne, by way of showing a sensational contrast to the pie shop, which he says I have described in such a pleasant style that I shall perhaps be suspected of having been feed for puffing it. He offered to be my *cicerone* on an evening visit to certain places, with which he seems to be too well acquainted. Without a moment's hesitation, I replied,—

"Cousin Saul, ask me not to go with you in the way that leads to infamy!"

"A-ha! you have borrowed old Parson Blanche's pulpit whine," sneered Saul; and he put on his hat to go out.

"I am glad you remember our kind pastor's voice so well," I said. "Perhaps you also remember the text of the last sermon you heard him preach? If you do not, I can tell it you, for I was with you that night, you know: 'There is a way that seemeth right unto a man, but the end thereof are the ways of death.'"

My cousin, Saul Jackson, is the only relative I have in Victoria. He is clever, but very erratic in his ideas and unsteady in his habits; that is the mildest way I can describe his characteristics. He took honours at his college in England; but I am sorry to say he has not gained much honour for himself in this part of the world, though he is a remarkably handsome young fellow, and a most amusing companion when he is quite sober. He brought a nice useful capital (£2,000) with him to Melbourne three years ago, and he lost it on the turf in about nine months. But his gambling operations have nothing to do with my story, and they are quite out of my line. Since he has lost all his money, he has tried various means for regaining it speedily, but hitherto he has been unsuccessful. He is naturally a sanguine young man, and it has often needed all my dead weight of caution to keep my head from being upset by his flighty schemes for making money without working for it. He has tried his luck in fossicking—as he calls it— at several of the gold-fields, but with very poor success. Settling into actual work as a mining labourer is what he cannot make up his mind to; and the days are gone by when inexperienced men can pan out gold dust from almost any blind creek. Since Saul's return from his last unsuccessful rush to Barren Gully diggings, he has lost much of his bombastic manner, and at times he looks as subdued as a wounded bushranger. It is a gratifying change to me, though I fear it is not a permanent reform in him, but merely a temporary dulling down of his spirits through poor diet. He causes me a good deal of worry at times. I would almost as soon be locked in a railway car with a mad soldier as have

Saul in my room when he is tipsy; still, I do not like to close my door against him. I heartily wish I could induce him to turn steady.

It is saddening to reflect that there are many men in this land who, like my cousin, have had thousands of pounds spent on their education, and who brought capital to Australia, but who squandered it in riotous living, and now they are almost destitute; and some of the poor fellows have neither the energy nor the necessary physical strength for steady work, even though they could meet with any one who would show confidence enough in them to offer them employment.

CHAPTER VIII.

"Small habits, well pursued, betimes
May reach the dignity of crimes."—*Hannah More.*

LOW indeed were my spirits when I arrived at the steamers' wharf, in Sydney, in the dusk of a drizzling evening. I had never felt such a chilling sense of loneliness since I left my home-roof, not even when I was sitting on the weedy rock near Cape Otway, after my shipwreck; for then the soft edges of my susceptibility were rasped off by terror. My fellow-voyagers from Melbourne, most of whom had been sociable enough on the passage up, suddenly became selfish, and were wholly absorbed in the care of themselves or their personal baggage. The stewards, too, who had hitherto been attentive and civil to everybody, began to feel that they were no longer at the beck and call of passengers who had paid their scores; their bustling efforts to straighten up their several departments seemed to imply that the sooner their customers went on shore the better, and their general demeanour resembled that of a fidgety family with whom I had overstayed my welcome to their hospitality.

In a deprecatory tone I asked the under-steward (to

whom I had shortly before given a fee) if he would be so good as to take charge of my luggage while I went to look for lodgings. He replied, smartly,—

"All right, sir. I shall be on board till eight o'clock. It is Saturday night, remember, sir."

"I will be sure to fetch my things before you go away, steward," I said; and then I walked on to the wet wharf. I was immediately beset by a crowd of boarding-house keepers or their agents, and I might have secured comfortable quarters easily enough—that is to say, if the qualities of each lodging-place corresponded with the pleasant description given by the respective owner or agent. Bearing in mind my mother's frequent injunction, "Be cautious, Roger!" I declined committing myself to either of the pressing canvassers any further than by taking a card of the address of their several happy homes.

I should have before stated that I had in my possession credentials from my good uncle, which, if they were properly estimated, might have gained for me the confidence of any one who wanted a competent young chemist and druggist. I had also a testimonial from the excellent pastor of the church to which I was attached in Greenwich, and a short note from the organist of the same church, certifying that I was the most energetic bass singer in his choir. I made a good use of my respected pastor's document when I was in Melbourne, and I was favoured by a minister there with a letter of introduction to a brother minister in Sydney.

Though I have heard some persons speak slightingly

of introductory letters in general, I here most confidently recommend any young man who may read this story to carry testimonials with him from his pastor or Sunday-school superintendent, if he is going abroad. Introductory letters to the secretaries of Young Men's Christian Associations would also be very useful in either of the Australian colonies.

I soon found Mr. Brightman, the clergyman, to whom my letter was addressed; and although he was busy preparing a special sermon for the next morning, he dropped his pen, shook hands with me, and cordially welcomed me to Australia. He then gave me some very useful advice, and in an encouraging tone bade me tell him if he could assist me in any way, as I was a "stranger in a strange land."

I thanked him for his kindness, and told him that I wanted to find comfortable lodgings as soon as possible, in order to remove my luggage before the ship was locked up for the night; whereupon he put on his hat and off he went with me to the residence of a member of his church, a nice motherly old lady, he said, who would study my comfort in every way. I found that she lived in a large, ancient-looking house, but it was in one of the quietest streets in Sydney. Mr. Brightman introduced me to Mrs. Dyke; and having ascertained that she had a vacancy for one boarder, he bade me adieu, and hastened away to finish his sermon, leaving me to make my own terms with my new landlady for board and lodging.

Mr. Brightman was on many subsequent occasions of

service to me, both as a spiritual pastor and as a trusty adviser in matters relating to my temporal concerns. He was one of the most diligent men that I met with in Australia. He was always usefully employed, and yet he was never in a hurry or a flurry; and go to him whenever I would, he was always willing to listen to anything I had to say to him, and to give me his advice, which I often needed. I used to wish I had his happy, systematic way of working; and I one day modestly asked him how it was that he managed to do so much. He answered, with his usual kind smile, "It is by doing one thing at a time, Mr. Larksway, and keeping to my work. I never *waste* time."

Making a bargain with Mrs. Dyke was easy enough, for she was evidently a fair-dealing old lady; the only misgiving I felt was on account of my having to share a bedroom with Master Dyke, a youth of fifteen years of age; but his mother gave him an excellent character, and I tried to appear satisfied with the arrangement.

Mrs. Dyke was a widow, about fifty years of age; and I was quite taken with her simple, unaffected kindness of manner,—too much taken with her, in fact, for while I sat pleasantly chatting with her about my home-life, and some of the troubles I had encountered since I left my parental roof, I forgot how time was flying, until I suddenly remembered my luggage. So I seized my hat, and after a few words of apology, I hastened down to the steamers' wharf. But, alas! I was too late. The steward's staff had left the ship, and the second mate, who was in charge of everything, would not let me even look at my luggage. I certainly felt vexed with myself that I had gossiped so long with my new landlady; however, I fell back on one of my dear father's trite sayings, "All's for the best!" There is plenty of comfort in that maxim if one can only draw it out, and I often try at it when I am in straits which seem to have no outlet.

Sunday is a day on which I specially like to put on a clean shirt. I can hardly account for the tenacity of that fancy, unless it be from the force of habit. Sunday has always been a clean shirt day with me, ever since I first dressed myself, and it has become like a part of my religion. If any one should sneer at this simple admission, or call it a heathenish whim, let me remind him that there are forms and ceremonies now-a-days, in some religious sects, less rational than putting on a clean shirt. 'Tis true I had changed my under-clothing when the *Columbus* was off Mount Dromedary, two days before, so I was not in a bad condition; and if my piety had been up to the right standard, I should have buttoned up my vest and gone to church, without a scruple about the purity of my linen. That absurd crotchet of mine clearly shows how easily a man may find an excuse for the non-performance of a duty that he has a lazy desire to shirk. With shame I now confess that my shirt had little or nothing to do with my stopping away from church that morning; but the plain fact is, that the free-and-easy sort of life on shipboard had dulled down my religious feelings to a hazardous extent. I believe that a ship life has sometimes had a like dissipating effect on better men than myself. Mrs. Dyke's pressing invitation to me to share her pew could not move me a tittle; and without explaining my reason for declining it, I moodily replied that I did not mean to stir out of doors that day, whereupon the good old lady looked almost as much shocked as if I had plainly declared myself to be a pagan.

"You will go with us, Mr. Burney, I suppose?" said the widow, kindly addressing another of her boarders, who was lolling on a sofa toying with his eye-glass.

"Aw—I don't think I shall show out this morning, Mrs. Dyke. The fact is, I bought a pair of boots last night, and they are so awfully tight I can't breathe in them. Yes, ma'am—thanks—I am aware that I have some old boots upstairs; but I shall stay at home this forenoon. I'll do the hospitable to Mr. Larksway. Horrid things tight boots are," he added, throwing one of his legs up over an arm of the sofa, and looking at me. I thought he expected me to say something, so I said he had better take his tight boots off and put on easy ones.

"Yes—that's the idea—aw—but I don't want to go to church," muttered Mr. Burney, and he made a grimace behind Mrs. Dyke, and winked at me. I thought he was very ill-mannered, though he dressed like a gentleman.

"Well, *you* come with me to church, Robert. Get your books, dear." Mrs. Dyke was evidently a little ruffled, by the way she spoke to her son, and at the same time she cast a reproving look at her two Sabbath-breaking lodgers.

"O ma! I wish you would let me stay at home this morning," whined the boy. "I think it will rain, and I left my umbrella at the office yesterday. Besides, I want to ask Mr. Larksway to tell me some more about his shipwreck."

"I insist upon your coming to church with me, sir," responded his mother, peremptorily. Master Bob saw that his plea would not do, so he clutched his hymn-book, as if he had a spite against it, then slouched his hat down over his eyes and sullenly obeyed. His sisters did not look cheerful, and I thought it was because their mother was rather upset.

"Aw—they look like real miserable sinners!" drawled Mr. Burney, when the family had left the room. "She is not a bad old woman, but rather too strict in some things. Now, for my part I don't see why a fellow should be bored to go to church if he has a mind to stay away. One of the poets, I forget his name, says,—
'A man may cry 'Church! church!' at every word,
  With no more piety than other people;
A daw's not reckoned a religious bird
  Because it keeps a-cawing from the steeple.'"

"Tom Hood wrote that witty rhyme to satirize 'Cant,'" I replied. "I do not think it is fair to quote it against Mrs. Dyke. It was certainly very kind and motherly of her to invite me to go to church with her family, but I had a reason why I thought fit to stop at home."

"Just so—that's exactly what I say—aw. But what are you going to do with yourself all the morning, Larksway?"

I said, "I am going to sit in my bedroom and read."

"Oh, are you? I would have gone to church with the girls if you had told me that before. I thought I should have had a nice chat with you about holiday fun in Greenwich Park, and other sunny memories of the old country; but if you are going to read, I shall practice a little. I suppose you don't object to music?"

"Oh no, I am fond of it; I mean to say, I like to hear sacred music on Sundays."

"Aw—yes, it's very nice; but we shall get enough of that sort of entertainment this afternoon from Selina and Annie. I am going to practice a piece or two from the 'Night Dancers.' Splendid opera that! Did you ever hear it?"

"No, I never did."

"Ah, you would like it. There are some charming airs in it. This is a song from it, that I sang at a party last week,

'Wild is the spirit that fills me now,
It sits on my brain, it burns on my brow.'

How do you like that air, Larksway?"

"It is pretty enough," I replied, "but I do not care for secular music on Sundays; I have never been accustomed to hear it."

"Then you and Dame Dyke will get on delightfully together. I can't even strike a lively chord on Sundays when she is at home. Aw—absurd idea! as if it mattered a bit to her old piano what is played on it at any time. By the way, would you like a brandy and soda, or a glass of pale ale; say the word, and I will get it round the corner by the back way."

"No, thank you; I would rather not take any," I said. Soon afterwards I went to my bedroom, leaving Mr. Burney strumming away on the piano, in a style which must have pleased any of the neighbours around, who approved of a bold touch.

I sat at my bedroom window and listened to the chiming of the church bells in the city. They ceased when the clock struck eleven; and then in fancy I could see my late revered pastor, at Greenwich, ascending his pulpit stairs to begin Divine service. Just then a quotation in a kind letter I received from him at parting, rushed into my mind,—

> "Think that day lost whose low descending sun
> Views from thy hand no noble action done."

It seemed to arouse my conscience in a way that I had never before experienced, though I had often felt some severe twinges when on board ship. Through giving way to an absurd whim, or more reprehensible lazy feeling, I had on my first Sunday in a new land neglected a religious duty which I had been taught from my childhood sacredly to observe. Moreover, I had pained the mind of poor Mrs. Dyke and her daughters; I had by my example almost influenced her young son to absent himself from church; I had certainly kept Mr. Burney at home, and there was no saying how many quiet households in the neighbourhood he was disturbing with his noisy practice on the piano.

"A bad beginning, Roger," nagged my conscience, over and over again, and I could not get away from the silent impeachment. In vain I tried to console myself with the plea that I was not worse than other persons I had seen since I came to Australia, some of whom I thought had not so much excuse as I had for neglecting public worship. I could get no comfort from any such reasoning; and on that bright Sunday morning, my first Sabbath in Sydney, I was as joyless as a skylark locked up in a coal cellar.

"Do you feel better, Mr. Larksway?" kindly asked Mrs. Dyke, soon after she returned from church.

"I thank you for your inquiry, ma'am, but I have not been unwell," I replied, with a slight embarrassment.

"Oh dear! then I have made an unfortunate mistake. Mr. Brightman asked me how you were, as we were coming out of church, and I told him I thought you were poorly. He said he was very sorry to hear it, and he will call and see you to-morrow. I am vexed that I should have misinformed him, sir."

"Pray do not distress yourself, Mrs. Dyke. The fault is mine; and I will explain it to Mr. Brightman when he calls on me."

"We have had such a nice, instructive, and comforting sermon, Mr. Larksway; I do wish you had heard it."

"I wish I had, ma'am," I replied, with a suppressed sigh.

"One of Mr. Brightman's figures, or illustrations, I

am sure you would have felt specially interested in, because it was something about a shipwreck, and I thought of you as he was speaking. I cannot remember all of it exactly; but he said, in alluding to the common error of deferring religious decision to a more fitting time, 'If any of you were in a sinking ship, you would not lose a moment in escaping from it if a lifeboat were alongside; and I venture to say that not a man of you would wait to arrange his necktie or to get his boots polished.' That was something like what he said, Mr. Larksway."

I thought it was a solemn coincidence that Mr. Brightman should have used that nautical illustration; and my conscience was increasingly sore. Mr. Burney laughed derisively, and remarked to me when Mrs. Dyke went upstairs to take her bonnet off, that the old lady had invented the touching little bit about the boots, just to frighten him into piety; but he was too knowing a bird to be caught with that sort of chaff. I did not reply to his foolish remark.

In the evening I buttoned up and went to church. I was soon very glad that I had resisted the lazy desire to stay at home, lolling on a sofa, for the service was as refreshing to my heart as a spring shower is to a thirsty meadow.

Though it will be digressing again from my story, I feel constrained to notice, in a few sentences, how my young friend Frank Wellby spent his first Sunday in Sydney, as it will show a cheering contrast to my own humiliating experience.

The ship in which Frank sailed from England, dropped anchor in Port Jackson one Saturday evening. He was ready dressed in his shore-going clothes, and he got into the first waterman's boat that came alongside. He had letters of introduction to a well-known minister in Sydney, so he went direct to the parsonage and presented his credentials. The minister received him cordially, and recommended him to suitable lodgings, and also invited him to take a class in the Sunday-school attached to his church. The next morning, punctual to time, Frank was at the school. He had been accustomed to useful work of that sort in England, and he was delighted to begin at it again. He had a "glorious day," to quote his own happy expression. At the boarding-house which he had made his home, there were several young men who were not very steady in their habits, but the influence of Frank's example on them was soon noticeable. I was told by the good old lady who kept the house, that the change in the behaviour of those gay youths was really wonderful, and she hoped that they were thoroughly reformed. She could hardly have believed it possible for any one to influence some of her young boarders to attend religious services in the house; but Frank, in his winning, loving way, had succeeded, and he persuaded the whole of them to begin to lead "godly, righteous, and sober lives." As long as he lived, my staunch friend, Frank Wellby, held on his consistent Christian course; and certainly godliness was profitable to him, even in his temporal affairs, for he became a very prosperous man. No doubt Frank had a religious training under his parental roof, and before he set out from home, he was specially warned against that subtle enticement, the intoxicating cup, which has been fatal to so many bright youths soon after they were launched out upon the ocean of life.

CHAPTER IX.

"With spots of sunny openings, and with nooks
To lie and read in, sloping into brooks."
—*Leigh Hunt.*

DURING my voyage to Melbourne, I had carefully examined the contents of Mr. Cameron's writing-desk; but amongst the various memoranda, I could not find any that would tell me the name and address of Mrs. Cameron's paramour, and I concluded that Cameron had, in some moment of jealous excitement, destroyed the document which he told me I should find in his desk. I advertised in the leading Sydney newspapers for Mrs. Cameron, and also for Miss Ella Cameron; and I waited for a fortnight in the hope of receiving replies. In the meantime I amused myself in strolling about the city of Sydney or the Botanic Gardens by day, and in listening to the musical performances of Selina and Annie Dyke in the evening. All that was pleasant enough; but I could not, with justice to my mission, indulge very long in such pastime, so as I did not receive any answers to the advertisements, I shook off the listlessness which a long release from any settled duties had induced, and prepared to begin an energetic search for Mrs. Cameron and her daughter. The only clue I had to their whereabouts, was that poor Cameron told me of their living with a farmer at Illawarra ; and it appeared to me almost as hopeless to find them in such an extensive district, as it would be to catch silver eels in a large pond, without a line or a spear. Nevertheless, I was bent upon trying my utmost to fulfil my important errand; so I started one night by steamer for Wollongong, a seaport town about forty miles south from Sydney Heads.

It was on the eve of the Wollongong races, so there was an unusual number of passengers on board the steamer, many of whom, including myself, could not find sleeping accommodation below. When I first descended to the saloon, an altercation was going on between an old man who was lying in one of the berths, and a tall, handsome gentleman who was sitting on a sofa. The old man and his little son had gone on board in good time, and turned into one of the vacant berths, without consulting the steward or looking at the list on the cabin table to see if the berth had been previously engaged, as honest and reasonable people usually do in coasting steamers. When the gentleman came below to turn in for the night, he found his bed occupied, so he politely told the old man that he had made a mistake in taking that berth.

"No mistake at all, mister," replied the man in an offensive tone. "I found the berth empty, so I put my boy into it, and turned in after him ; and here we mean to lie till we choose to turn out again."

"Steward! please to come and explain to this person that the berth he is in belongs to me," said the gentleman; "my name is on the list, you can see,—berth number ten."

"I don't care a copper whose name is on the list; I am in the berth, and I defy any man on board to turn me out."

"Here's the man who will do it in a twinkling," vociferated the steward, bustling up to the impudent intruder. "Out you come, daddy, or I'll haul you out heels first, and the boy after you, and walk you off to the fore-cabin." Suiting the action to the word, the steward seized the man by the legs, and, despite his kicking, in half a minute more he would have been lying on the floor, for the steward was an able man but the gentleman interposed, and said calmly,—

"Leave him alone, steward. The little boy is asleep, so don't disturb him. I will take a shakedown on deck, as it is a fine night."

"You had better not disturb him, governor," said the man, in the same offensive strain. "If you do, you'll soon feel my kangaroo-skin boots."

"Now listen to me, old man, whoever you are," responded the gentleman: "if I were so inclined, I could take you by the neck and heels, and toss you on deck through the skylight. You deserve to be turned out of the saloon, for you don't know how to behave properly; but for the sake of the sleeping boy beside you, I will let you stay in my berth." He then took his travelling rug, and went on deck to lie down.

I thought I had seldom before seen a more pleasing instance of forbearance—such a triumph of a strong man over a weak one. It made me blush, as I remembered how I had used my towering strength to cow down the little sick passenger in the *Columbus*, who had simply told me the unpalatable truth, that I had shouted "Bella!" in my dreams. I felt far more respect for that patient gentleman's courage than I should have felt if he had taken the impudent old man in his powerful grasp, and tossed him under the saloon table or through the skylight. Of course I don't mean to record every little incident of my travels, but I feel constrained to notice this one for the sake of the wholesome lesson it taught me, on a generous forbearance or self-control. I shall try to remember it.

At Wollongong I put up at an inn not very stylish in its outward appearance; but it was almost as comfortable as my Aunt Sarah's farmhouse in Suffolk. I never had any previous experience of inn life, and I imagined that as I was but a poor customer for the tap, I should not be much cared for. But I was comfortingly mistaken. The landlady was attentive and motherly, and I was glad that my first experience removed the libellous notion that had been put into my head by Mr. Burney, that all innkeepers in the country appreciate their guests only in proportion to their drinking tendencies. I have since then stopped at other inns of a similar home-like character; but I must in fairness add, that I have also had at times to put up at bush grog-shops, where my board and lodging were as rough as I should expect to find it in a greasy old whaling brig.

My first day in Wollongong was spent in strolling through the town, peeping into shop windows in search of photographic specimens, and hoping that I might see the pictures of Ella and her mother, whom I was sure I could recognise from a whole gallery full of portraits. But my search in that way was in vain. I may here mention, that the locket with the portraits of Ella and her mother was in the sealed packet with the other jewellery, and was addressed to Ella. Doubtless it would have helped me in my search if I had had those portraits in my pocket, but I felt it would be a breach of trust to open the parcel which Cameron himself had sealed up. I inquired of several persons, including my landlady, during the day, if they knew a family in the neighbourhood, of which the mother and her daughter were fair-haired and rosy-faced, and I was informed that there was a family named Kelly who a short time before lived in a little farm on the Dapto road. Mrs. Kelly and her girl had light hair; but that they had lately sold their farm and left the district.

Though there was not much to encourage me in the information, I determined to make a beginning, and see what it would lead to. The next forenoon I set out on foot from my inn. I was soon out of the town, for it is not a large one, and then my senses were enraptured with the varied landscape beauties around me:

"Creation's grandest charms were there combined."

It was a bright, cloudless morning, and the dewdrops in the flowers which bespangled the meadows glistened like myriads of jewels. I sat on a stone by the side of a wild raspberry bush, which served my fancy for an English blackberry hedge, and tried to imagine myself at home again. Yes; before me, to the north-west, was Greenwich Park, though expanded to ten times its old dimensions; and by a vigorous effort of imagination, I could make Mounts Keira and Kembla do for Flamstead Hill and One-Tree Hill, only they had grown amazingly in a few months. If the bush trees were not so symmetrical as the oaks and chestnut-trees of the park, there were ten times more of them to be seen, to say nothing of the sweet-scented mimosa, and other smaller trees and shrubs, which no one ever saw in Greenwich Park, or anywhere else out of doors in that latitude. Thousands of birds were chirping among the trees (as if to convince me that somebody had misinformed me when he said that there were no singing birds in Australia), the wild notes of the magpie being predominant; and my heart seemed to dance within me at the gladdening music—more inspiriting to me than thousands of fiddles.[1]

"This is certainly a lovely prospect, worth coming all the way across the sea to behold!" I exclaimed with rapture. "Mrs. Cameron must have some taste,

---

[1] For beautiful descriptions of Illawarra scenery, I would commend some of the "Lyrics" of Henry Kendall, an Australian poet.

after all, to locate herself in such a charming district." By a natural association of beautiful objects, I then thought of Ella as I had seen her face in the locket, and I said to myself, "If at eleven years of age that girl's face was so exquisitely pretty, what a fascinating creature she must be now that she is developed into the maturity of eighteen!" That exciting reflection almost made me forget the fine landscape; and I know not to what length or height my fancy would have flown in that new direction, if I had not been aroused from my delicious reverie by a passing cart carrying pigs and kegs of butter to market. I started up and resumed my walk, singing cheerily,—

"As I view these scenes so charming!"

I continued to stroll along the road, each turn of which brought changes in the prospect, which was still lovely and sunny and flowery, and the air seemed full of perfume and bird music. Presently I came in sight of a cottage, a few roods from the high-road. It was a humble-looking dwelling, but it charmed me more than my first look at the Governor's house in Sydney had done. It was literally smothered in flowering creepers and climbers, and it reminded me tenderly of my own dear native home, and seemed to carry me back in a moment to—

"Sweet childish days, that were as long
As twenty days are now."

I was smitten with a strong desire to see the inside of the cottage; so I opened the garden gate, half expecting Ella to come tripping out to meet me. Suddenly, however, I received a shock, which put all my romantic fancies to the rout, like a flock of cockatoos at the discharge of a gun. I was stopping in the middle of the pathway admiring a double wall-flower, when I saw an enormous bull-dog shuffle up from beneath a rustic seat and trot towards me. I have a horror of dogs of that ferocious breed, for I know it is their nature to bite hard. It was impossible for me to escape from the beast by flight, and quite as hopeless to fight him without a deadly weapon of some kind ; so I stood and trembled, and the dog stopped and looked at me very sullenly, and smelt my boots, but did not open his mouth. After a while I took courage and walked up to the cottage, closely followed by the watchful animal. A man opened the door after I rapped, and my first words to him were, " Please to call your dog inside ; I am afraid of him."

" He is all right, sir. He won't bite you so long as you don't touch anything in the garden. Go away, Bully ! "

" Oh dear ! " I sighed ; " he has scared me very much. He is such a powerful brute ; his bite would break my leg."

" Yes, I daresay it might, if he got a fair hold of it," said the man coolly. " He would only just nip you if you merely picked a flower ; but if you were walking off with a plant, he would pin you down in a minute, and he would never let go till I spoke to him."

"It is very hazardous to let such a vicious dog go at large," I said, with a shudder at the remembrance of the close proximity of his teeth to my legs.

"Not at all hazardous to honest people, sir. That dog is as knowing as a policeman. I trained him up from a pup to mind my garden, and I think he takes as much pride in it as I do. I never knew him to hurt anybody unless they were picking and stealing; and then it serves them right to get a nip. The people about here know Bully, and my flowers are as safe as my money in the bank."

"He is a wonderfully sagacious animal, though he looks so stupidly savage," I said. "I think it would be well if there were a few such discriminating dogs kept in the Botanic Gardens, Sydney; for I have several times seen persons picking flowers and seeds when the gardeners were out of sight."

"More shame for them to do it, sir. I only wish my Bully were there to see them at it; he'd soon let them feel his teeth. You can hardly expect youngsters to keep their hands off flowers, unless they are looked after, but grown-up folks ought to have more honest sense. It is very annoying to a man who takes a pride in his garden, to see people picking and fingering his choicest flowers and plants; and such shabby rogues usually take the best of everything. It does me good when I see old Bully give any stranger a nip for picking my flowers."

I saw that the man was one of the loquacious sort, who would have talked all day about the wrongs of florists, and the peculiar virtues of his bull-dog, so I turned him off by asking him if he knew a family in that locality named Kelly.

"The Kellys lived in the next farm you come to up the road; but they sold off a while ago, and I don't know where they went."

"Does any one live on the farm now?"

"Yes; a man named Rafferty lives there, and he'll pretty soon die there of starvation, I reckon, unless he has some money saved up in his sea chest. He bought the farm from Kelly, and he has found out before now that he made a bad bargain. A thorough farmer might perhaps get a living off it; but Paddy Rafferty knows no more about raising crops than my Bully does about clockwork, though he may be a good seaman for all I can say."

"I suppose it is not often that sailors turn farmers, Mr. Gardener?"

"Any sort of fellows can turn farmers in this country, or they think they can, and that is the reason why so many find that it doesn't pay, and we hear so much grumbling now-a-days in these parts. Nobody could stop things from growing years ago, when the land was new and as fat as chocolate; but now that the strength of it is pretty well exhausted, through double cropping year after year, and never giving it muck, or change of crop, or any chance at all, it isn't easy for slap-dash farmers to make a tidy living off a bit of arable land, and they are beginning to find that out. 'Every man to his trade,' is an old saying that I always stick to."

I

"I suppose Mr. Rafferty would agree to that maxim?"

"No doubt he is sorry he bought that farm; though I never heard him grumble much over his bad luck. Ha, ha! he is a real character! I should like you to see him driving his spring cart to church on Sundays, with one rein in each hand, as if he were holding the tiller ropes, and his wife sitting beside him holding the whip for him!"

"Has Rafferty been captain of a ship?"

"Not he! He came to Sydney a few years ago, as a sort of under-steward in a fine crack steamer, and he had better have stuck to his berth, for he says he is as much out of his element now as a porpoise in a pig-stye. He won't earn steward's wages at growing potatoes or making butter off his farm, I'll engage. But most sailors like to try their luck on dry land, by way of a change."

"And some of them have found it a lucky change. I drove past a fine mansion, not far from Sydney, fit for a nobleman to live in, and I was told that it belonged to a gentleman who some years ago was captain of a whaling ship. He left off going to sea and turned merchant, and made a large fortune."

"Yes; that's very likely. Anybody with common sense might have made money at trading years ago, when I first came to the colony; and it didn't matter whether they were trained to business or not. I often wish I had set up a shop in some line or other, instead of keeping to my own calling, though I don't know that I should be a bit happier if I had ever so much money."

"I would much rather be a gardener than a shop-keeper," I said. "Cultivating flowers and fruit-trees must be almost as interesting an occupation as keeping a school, and training up boys or girls to be useful men or women." After chatting a little while longer with the man, and eating some fresh fruit from his orchard, I bade him good day. The bull dog followed me to the gate, and I was careful to avoid even brushing a flower with my coat tails, lest it should provoke him to give me an admonitory nip. I determined that I would call on Mr. Rafferty, and try to find out what he knew of the Kelly family.

CHAPTER X.

"I love the sailor—his eventful life—
His generous spirit—his contempt of danger."
—*Cotton.*

FOLLOWING the gardener's directions, I kept along the Dapto road until I came to a gate on which was written in rude letters, "Calabash Farm." I went through the gateway, and presently I saw a man ploughing with two bullocks in a small paddock to the right of me. By the eccentric way he held the plough, I thought he was tipsy; but I soon found that his staggering gait was owing to his want of practice in ploughing over rough, stumpy land; and I fancied how my Uncle Robert's expert Suffolk ploughmen would have stared, had they seen him wasting his strength and bruising his hips in that fashion. As I approached the man, I could tell by his rich brogue what part of the world he came from. He was scolding, or rather arguing with his bullocks, which seemed to be an obstinate pair of workers, in their master's opinion.

"Gee, Boxer! Gee, Baldy! Bad manners to ye for a pair of contrary bastes! Can't ye see ye're making the furrow as crooked as an ould scythe-stick, forbye knocking all the wind out of me intirely? Arrah! come hither again, Baldy! Where are ye going to now, at all? Ye're allers yawing too much to one side or t'other. Hallo! here's another big tree buried alive! Whoa, waa, whoa, I say! Be aisy, or ye'll smash the machine an break yer necks, soh! Ye can't pull that root up, so ye needn't try."

I was then close behind the man, so I said, "Good morning to you, Master Farmer." He turned hastily round and said, "Oh, good morning, sir. It's a rale warrm day this."

"It is refreshing weather to me. But you seem to be having some warm, troublesome work in ploughing up this stumpy land."

"Troth, you may say that, mister. It's rale hot work for me, and it bates me intirely, so it does. The gossoon that I kape to drive the bullocks for me went to Dapto yesterday to see his sick mother, and he hasn't come back yit; so I thought I'd try my hand at ploughing a bit widout a driver, for I like to be independent; but I can't make any headway at all, as the lighterman said when the keel of his craft got foul of the punt-rope. The stem of my machine has got jammed in a big root underground, you see, and I don't know how I'll get it out again; anyway, it will have to stop here till I get more breath in my body."

"Are you Mr. Rafferty?"

"Timothy Rafferty is me name, sir."

"I wish to ask you a few questions about the family that occupied this farm before you came to it."

"Troth thin, I wish that same family was in it now,

so I do, or else that I had niver come anigh it—one or t'other. But will you walk up to the house forenint there, and sit down? I'll be wid you in two minutes, for I want a bit of a rest. But I must put a stern line on to these crathers, or they'll be slewing round to horn one another while I am away, and they'll be certain to break the bows or the yokes." He then took a piece of spun yarn from his pocket, and deliberately lashed the bullocks' tails together. "Now they are fast head and stern, and I'll engage they'll stop there till I come back, for they can't drag the plough from under that stump, any more nor a gunboat could drag with a frigate's best bower anchor ahead of her."

We were met at the door of the house by a portly, good-tempered looking woman, whom Mr. Rafferty introduced to me as his wife. She bade me welcome, and placed a cushioned chair for me to sit upon.

"Bring a jug o' milk, Sally, honey; for I'm nigh choking wid dry dust in me throat. Maybe the gintleman wud like a cup of tay."

"No, thank you; I would prefer milk, if you can spare it."

"We have lashins of it. Dhrink as much as you like, and ye're welcome to twice as much, sir. You were axing me just now about the Kellys."

"Yes. There was a family of that name on this farm not long ago, I believe. Can you tell me where they are now, Mr. Rafferty?"

"They did live here awhile agone, and I bought the place from them, more fool me for doing it; for sure enough I'm no more fit for a farmer nor I am for a soger or a horse-doctor. As for where they are now, that's more nor I can tell you. They went out of this to a place called Windsor, and I think they meant to open a grogshop, more luck to them."

"Pray where is Windsor? I am a stranger in this country."

"Dear knows where it is. Somewhere away to the westward of Sydney. I can't direct you half a point nearer nor that to it, sir."

"I understand the Kellys had a daughter about eighteen years old. Can you tell me the name of the girl, Mr. Rafferty?"

"Yes, I can tell you that. Her name was Nelly; sometimes they called her Nell."

I reflected for a minute that Nelly would very likely be substituted for Ella by common people; besides, it rhymed so naturally to Kelly: "Nelly Kelly." I did not fancy the name as I muttered it to myself, still I felt somewhat encouraged to hope that I was on the right track, so I asked, "Had Miss Kelly fair hair?"

"She had so—a rale heavy crop of ginger, and as tangled as a dry swab."

"Had her mother fair hair also, may I ask?"

"Yes, sir; her head was as fair as a snowball or the inside of a flour bag."

"That is certainly not flaxen hair," I mentally reasoned; "still, she may have grown prematurely grey. Many persons get grey before they are forty years old; and conscience—in her case—may have had something to do with turning her hair." After a little further consideration, I said, " Mr. Rafferty, you look like a man that I can speak to confidentially. I have an important reason for wishing to find that family, but I am not at liberty to explain it to you at present. May I presume to ask if you think that Mr. and Mrs. Kelly are legally married? And do you think that Nelly is Mr. Kelly's daughter? These are delicate questions, and I hope you will pardon me for asking them in the presence of your good wife."

I could see that Mr. Rafferty was puzzled, by the comical way he scratched his head. Presently he said, "Kelly and his wife were legally married, sure enough; and Nelly calls old Kelly her dad, and he calls the gal his darter. It's true I did not see the ould pair married by either priest or parson; still an all I'm as sartain sure they are legally spliced as if I had seen the thing done wid me own eyes. Cos why? they used to quarrel and fight almost every day of their lives, and, depend on it, that if they were not yoked up as tightly as my two working bullocks yonder, they would have been off different ways long agone, for there isn't a haporth of love between 'em—that any stranger could see. That has been my strongest argument against the new Bigamy Bill they have just made a law of the land."

"The Divorce Bill you mean, Tim," said his wife, softly.

"True for you, Sally. Divorce Bill I mane, sir, though it's pretty much the same thing afther all. I used to say afore the bill passed, if the lawyers make it aisy for married pairs to slip clear of the wedding knot, they'll have no end of work of that paying sort, and a reglar confusion there'll be among families growing up. The most loving couple in the world no doubt have a little tiff now and again, about nothing at all; and the divil, who is always wide awake for roguery of every sort, would be certain to stir them up to have a rale shindy, and then before they had time to cool down agin or to think twice over it, they'd find themselves legally single agin, and free to go courting anybody else as soon as they liked. But when they know that they are yoked hard and fast together for life, common sense itself tells 'em they had better forget their quarrels and pull along quietly the one way, bekase they can't lawfully get away from the yoke, and the more they kick and struggle, the more they will get galled, and nobody in the world will pity 'em a haporth."

"I believe your view is a sensible one, Mr. Rafferty."

"It's raysonably natural, sir, anyhow. Just look at my ould bullocks now for an example. There they stand, quietly munching away at nothing, in the identical spot where I left them awhile agone. Sorra an inch have they budged. Now, do you suppose they would have stood there so lovingly quiet if they didn't know they were made fast together head and tail? Not a bit of it! Likely enough they'd have had a horning match or a kicking bout, and then have scudded off at full trot to different ends of the farrm. I know their cranky ways, and mankind is pretty much like bastes in some things."

"But some men unluckily have wives, and some women have husbands, with whom it would be impossible to live quietly," I remarked.

"That's true enough, worse luck. Still an all, I think it wad be better to let 'em do the best they can with their bad bargains, than to make a law to unmarry 'em; bekase it will cause no end of botheration in the land, to make that job as easy as getting your tooth out or your hair cut. The poor unlucky crathers would have the liberty of taking all the comfort they cud draw out of the belief that they are serving as beacons or bell-buoys, to warn other soft-hearted simpletons from rushing into matrimony in a red-hot hurry, and maybe without thinking more about it beforehand than they would do about buying a monkey-jacket or a straw bonnet."

"You did not think long about it, Tim," said Mrs. Rafferty, with a merry chuckle.

"Ye're right, Sally, me darlint! But thin any fellow that wasn't silly would see in a twinkling that there was no mistake in your honest face. A sensible man wudn't be long taking your measure, honey!"

A little playful banter ensued between the lively couple, which was as amusing to me as the vagaries of Punch and Judy. After a while I asked Mr. Rafferty how he came to turn farmer?

"Shure, it was a mad notion my wife put into my head. About a year agone she came down here from Sydney, to see a cousin of hers who kapes a dairy farrm at Wallandoola Creek—fornint there; and she got so fond of the birds and the green bushes, and the flowery meadows and the swate fresh air, and the pretty scenery all about this part, that when I came down to fitch her home again, she coaxed me to buy this farrm and come and live aisily for life. But dear knows, it's a mighty hard sort of aisy life to me—so it is."

"I judged that you had not been long used to farming work, Mr. Rafferty."

"Ha, ha! I supposed you thought so whin you seed me awhile agone steering the plough among the roots and stumps yonder, and yawing about like an ould bumboat in a tide ripple? Well, ye're right, sir. I haven't been a farmer long; but I've been a sailor ever since I was a boy. I left my ship a few years ago in Sydney, to look after a young fellow who hadn't brains enough to look after himself; and whin my wife and I put him all right and straight; I made up my mind to stop on shore for good; so I got a berth as waiter in one of the big club-houses in Sydney. It was a good billet of the sort, and not bad pay, but shure the work was everlasting, from sunrise to midnight and after it; and Sunday was just the same as Monday to me, for there wasn't many of the gintlemen that came there who seemed to care much about the souls of the servants. So last of all I said to myself, This won't do at all. There's no luck in working on Sundays, when I am not forced to do it to get the ship out of danger; so I gave up my berth and took to dealing a bit, but that game wouldn't suit me a morsel."

"Surely dealing was not hard work!" I remarked.

"Tut! not at all. That wasn't why I hated it; but this was it, sir; I seed no end of great big fellows, strong as bullocks, going about wid baskets same as I was, and I got ashamed of myself. So I said to my missus, after I had been at the game about a fortnight, 'I won't go on that tack any longer, Sally! There are hosts of poor old men and women who are too feeble to work, and I think they ought to have the hawking trade left to them,—anyway, they shall have my share of it. Nobody shan't catch me skulking about wid a basket agin, selling small wares, because I don't believe it's fair and raysonable of me to do it, so long as I can work for a living.' So next day I sold my basket and my stock of whim-whams to an old blind man, and a rale bargain he got. A week or two afterwards I got a letther wid a bank draft in it for £300! So wid that lucky lump, and what my wife and I had saved up before, we bought this farm—more's the pity."

I said, "Is it fair of me to ask who made you such a nice present?"

"I'll tell you, sir, and glad to do it. It was the young gintleman that I tould you about just now, that Sally and I put on his legs agin. He wint home after his father, ould Misther Cockle, died, to receive a fortune; and as soon as he got his money, he remembered his old shipmate, Tim. I believe he is now on his way out to Sydney agin, wid a wife under his arm—good luck to him; and it's plased enough I shall be to see him, soh."

I might have got a good deal of information on

things in general from the talkative Irishman, if I could have spared time to draw him out. Both Mr. and Mrs. Rafferty were pressing for me to stay and dine with them ; but I felt sanguine that I had the right clue to the whereabouts of Mrs. and Miss Cameron, and I was anxious to follow it up. I returned to Wollongong early enough to catch the afternoon's steamer for Sydney, and at night I was at Mrs. Dyke's house again.

The following day I started for Windsor. It was a singularly lucky omen, I thought, that the very first inn I saw at the outskirts of the town had the name Patrick Kelly painted on the sign-board, under the figure of a black bull. I went inside and ordered luncheon. The landlord was an elderly man, and my first glance at him made me pity his wife. His manner indicated that his liquors had not an enlivening influence on him, for he looked as sullen as the painted animal on his sign-board. While a man-servant was preparing the table for my meal, I walked into the bar and asked the host if Mrs. and Miss Kelly were at home ?

"No. They have gone to Wilberforce. I expect them back soon," he replied. His sharp tone and suspicious looks seemed to ask, "What do you want with them ?" I merely said, " I will wait till they return." I never can get very confidential with a surly-looking man.

The afternoon was wet ; so I beguiled the wearisome time indoors listening to two half-tipsy customers in the tap-room. I could not be charged with eavesdropping, for their conversation might have been heard on the opposite side of the street. I learnt some dreary particulars of a recent flood, which had done much damage to the farms in that district, and wrecked many homesteads. I also overheard the wisdom and justice of a flood relief committee fiercely condemned; and it seemed clear to me that the two men had not received from the relief fund all the pecuniary help they wished to get. I have subsequently learnt that discontented ones were not scarce in other parts of the colony which suffered from flood waters; and that, as a rule, such grumblers got more than their fair share of relief, to the injury of more severe sufferers, many of whom got no relief at all, because they were too modest to ask for it, or to press their claims.

About dusk, I heard a cart driven into the inn yard, and the host began to scold his wife and daughter for their prolonged stay.

"Bah! What's the good of scolding us, Kelly? You ought to be glad to see us back again safe and sound! We couldn't come home while it was showering hailstones like cobs of corn." That was the reply of a crisp feminine voice, which I guessed was owned by Mrs. Kelly.

"There is a young fellow in the parlour—been waiting nearly all day to see you and Nell."

"Who is he? and what does he want with us?"

"How should I know? Go and ask him."

In another minute I heard footsteps of two persons approaching, and I naturally felt a little embarrassed, for the woman's voice had not favourably impressed me; on he contrary, it made me feel half scared.

"Did you want to see us?" asked a gaunt old woman; at the same time she dragged a shy-looking girl from behind her.

A single glance at the two faces assured me that I had made a mistake. Nelly Kelly no more resembled the picture I had seen of Ella Cameron, than a moulting magpie resembles a satin bird; and Mrs. Kelly was nearly sixty years of age, and very plain in face and figure. My first impulse was to rush out of the house; and if I had seen a fair chance of getting out alive, I should have started, and the consequences might have been serious to me, for there is no telling what crime I might have been suspected of plotting. At that crisis a helpful idea came into my head, and I said, with as pleasant a look as I could assume, "Mrs. Kelly, I am sorry to say I have made a mistake in coming here. I came from England on purpose to look for two ladies, a mother and her daughter, who once lived at Illawarra. I have seen the picture of the ladies—very handsome women they are. At Wollongong I heard of you and your daughter; and from the description given of you both, I thought you were the ladies I want. I went to your old farm to look for you, and was directed to this place; but I find that though you and Miss Kelly in some respects resemble the ladies, you are not the ones I am in search of. Will you please to accept this explanation, and pardon my unlucky blundering, for which I am sorry on account of the loss of time to myself."

Mrs. Kelly and Nelly giggled, and looked pleased

rather than cross with me. I could see that my sophistical allusion to the resemblance they bore to the two handsome ladies, whose pictures I had seen, touched their nature, and all fear of being personally assaulted left me in a moment. Conscience twitched me a bit for my wheedling hypocrisy, but I mentally argued that Nelly certainly did resemble Ella in point of age, and Mrs. Kelly no doubt resembled Mrs. Cameron in her vulgarity of speech and lack of reverence for her husband. Furthermore, I held that I was justified in using a little soft policy, to save myself from personal damage.

The following reproof to affected honesty, from one of Sterne's sermons, cropped up from my memory's store as I was taking my tea :—" Look out of your door ; take notice of that man ; see what disquieting, intriguing, and shifting he is content to go through, merely to be thought a man of plain dealing. Three grains of honesty would save him all this trouble ; alas! he has them not."

CHAPTER XI.

"All's for the best, if a man would but know it."—*Tupper*.

AFTER tea, I resolved to get all the information I could from my host and hostess. They doubtless knew many folks in Illawarra, and they might know the very persons I was in search of. I walked into the bar, and, to my agreeable surprise, Mr. Kelly looked quite cheerful; perhaps the return of his wife and daughter had raised his spirits. Mrs. Kelly, too, seemed in good humour, and she invited me into the bar parlour. After awhile, Mr. Kelly came in to smoke his pipe by the fireside, and Nelly was sent to mind the bar. Everything seemed to favour me, and I grew very hopeful. On my first arrival, the host had perhaps fancied I was a junior member of the detective corps; but that damaging impression had been removed by my polite little address to his wife and daughter, of which no doubt they had told him.

Mr. and Mrs. Kelly soon became as communicative as I could wish; more so, in fact, for I did not care to hear their slangy description of the schemes they had used to beguile simple Tim Rafferty into buying their barren farm, and seven old cows as lean as a blackfellow's dogs ; nor could I enjoy the uproarious mirth of Mrs. Kelly, as she told of the rare bargain she had made with Mrs. Rafferty for the rotten churn and butter tubs, and other dairy utensils. However, I let them talk, because I did not know how to check them without perhaps making them sulky ; and presently, by the exercise of my tact in questioning them, I learnt that a man named Joe Winkle had lived on a little farm at Lake Illawarra, but when butter got down to sevenpence a pound, he gave up his farm, and went to work at the Belambi jetty. He had a woman living with him whom the neighbours called " Lovely Clara," and she had a daughter nicknamed the " Lyre Bird."

"Was that because the daughter was so very beautiful?" I asked.

"No ; it was because she was so proud and grand in her way."

"She wasn't wild, or a vicious girl, I hope ?"

"I never had much to do with her, sir, at any time, for she was so extra superfine, she thought none of us was good enough to speak to."

"She was very pretty, I believe."

"Y-yes, so they say ; but I don't think she came up to our Nell. It was all through her that Bill Whackly got into trouble."

"In what way was she blamable for it ?" I asked ; for anything that was at all connected with Ella was interesting to me.

"Why, Bill was half crazy about her long before she was out of her short frocks ; and her mother encouraged him, for he had a few head of cattle of his own in the bush. But my lady wouldn't speak to him, and the poor fellow got quite thin with fretting about it. One day Bill and young Sam Gork were splitting shingles t'other side of Mount Keira, when Sam began to joke him about Ella Cameron."

"Yes—that is the name. I beg pardon for interrupting you, Mrs. Kelly. Please to go on; I want to know what Bill Whackly did."

"Well, he couldn't stand joking on that subject; and when Sam said that Ella winked at him in church one Sunday night, and that he meant to court her, Bill hit him a crack on the head with a shingle, and half killed him. For that little mistake, Bill got two years in Berrima gaol; and everybody was sorry for him except Ella."

"Do you think that Ella cared much for Sam Gork?"

"Tut! not she, indeed! Didn't I tell you before that she thought everybody dirt beside her? Why, when young Royson, who was the son of a great man in the land, came down our way for a spree, and hunted her out, she wouldn't even look at him."

"If she was so proud and high principled, I wonder that she lived in Winkle's house, knowing that her mother and he were not married," I remarked, musingly.

"She didn't live with them after she was fifteen years old. Joe wouldn't have her there because she was always showing off her proud airs, and quarrelling with her mother.

"Where is she now, Mrs. Kelly?"

"That's more than I can tell you; but I think she went as a school teacher somewhere. Her uncle sadly wanted her to go and live with him to serve in his bar; but she was a rare sight too grand for that sort of work, and she vexed the old fellow terribly because she wouldn't go. My word! how he did rave about her when he called at our house on his way home."

"What was her uncle's name?"

"Badkin. He kept an inn somewhere at Maneroo."

"Yes, that is his name," I said. "Did you know him?"

"I believe I did know him, worse luck!" chimed in Mr. Kelly. "He sold me a gig horse, and warranted him as quiet as an old cow; but he turned out the worst bolter in the district, and I had to send him to Sydney, and sell him for just what he would fetch. Badkin told me he only parted with the horse because he was rather too fast for him."

No doubt I might have heard more about Mr. Badkin's trading peculiarities if I had cared to listen; but I had got the information I so much wanted, so I soon retired to my bedroom. But I was too much excited to sleep. Pleasing thoughts of my sagacity in so nicely finding the clue to the whereabouts of Ella and her mother kept me wakeful. I have sometimes wondered how detective officers can sleep at all; but then their work, exciting as it must be, has not so much heart exercise in it as mine had.

The next morning I was off to Sydney betimes. At

night I again went by steamer to Wollongong, and on the morning following I reached Calabash Farm, just as Mr. and Mrs. Rafferty were sitting down to breakfast.

"Come in, and welcome, sir. Glad to see ye again!" was Mr. Rafferty's cheering salute when I rapped at his open door. There was such a heartiness in his tones, and such a good-natured smile on his wife's face, that I went in and sat down at the breakfast table with as much confidence as if they had been my oldest friends. When I told them that I had been to Windsor to see the Kellys, and that they were not the persons I wanted, Mr. Rafferty remarked, with a comical expression of face,—

"Shure, thin, I thought it was mighty queer that you should be in such a hurry to find thim crathers. It worn't for the like of me to ax questions, but if ye'd tould me the girl and her mother you were looking for were pritty and handsome, I'd have sed in half a minute, 'Then shure enough it isn't the Kellys you want,' for there's nothin pritty at all about 'em, as my wife says of her Cochin-China chuckies."

"The Kellys are a dishonest lot," said Mrs. Rafferty with warmth. "I can show you, sir, how shamefully they have cheated me and my husband—the wicked rogues!"

"Well, well, never mind, Sally. It's a good job they can't say we are rogues. We are not ruined entirely, but I don't think it would take long to do it if we stopped in this place; for though we work like sailors, dear knows it isn't half a soger's pay we get for it all."

"Judging from the comfortable appearance of the homesteads that I passed on the way here, I thought that farmers were a well-to-do class," I remarked; "and I have seen a good many of them driving in smart buggies."

"Any of the farmers about here as is well off have better luck than I have myself, that's all I got to say about it," replied Mr. Rafferty with a sigh. "The very last keg of butter that I sint to market only fetched me ninepence a pound, and it was as lovely a bit of churning as anybody ever tasted this side of ould Ireland. And seven prime porkers, as we sent to Sydney three days afore Christmas, only brought six pound ten the lot, forbye one that was whacked to death by the sailors in the steamer."

"Beaten to death by the sailors! Do you mean that, Mr. Rafferty?" I asked, with surprise and indignation.

"Indeed I do mane it, sir. They whacked it wid ropes' ends bekase the poor baste didn't want to be the first pig to go up the landing-stage on to the wharf in Sydney, on a dark night, and a crowd of fellows on shore yellin' and shoutin' like cannibals, to coax the scared animals out of the steamer."

"It was wanton cruelty of the sailors to beat your pig to death."

"No mistake about that same. But they do whack and hammer things about in thim steamers sometimes, whin they are in a hurry to get the decks clear to make a double trip; an' it's a pity somebody can't stop it. T'other day our neighbour fornint there, sint a fat calf up to market; and when all the live stock was being rushed ashore in Sydney, wid a howlin' and hallaballoc-ing enough to frighten all the fat off the animals, a gintleman on board seed one of the sailors take hold of the calf's tail and screw it round to drive the baste ahead like a steam-launch, and he fancied he heard the bones of the tail crunch all to dominoes. When our neighbour's children knew of it, they almost cried their eyes out, poor little things, for the calf had been a home pet wid 'em all."

I said, "I think the Society for the Prevention of Cruelty to Animals should let one of their agents look on board those coasting steamers now and then, and prosecute any one whom they saw committing such acts of cruelty. I will speak about it the first opportunity I get."

"Troth, thin, all the farmers about here would be for ever obliged to the Cruel Society if they wud do that same, sir. And by the same token, if they wud stop the sailors from piling up our kegs of butter near to the red-hot funnel, it wud be a mighty savin' agin loss of weight; besides, some delicate folks in Sydney don't like to ate fresh butter whin it looks just like castor oil and soft soap."

"The Cruelty Society won't interfere about that, Tim, because kegs of butter are not live stock, you know," said Mrs. Rafferty; and she added in a desponding tone, "When I persuaded my good man to buy this place, sir, I had in my mind's eye the comfort my cousins have on their farms in Yorkshire; but rich as this district is, in general, I am very sure we shall never live and pay our way on our farm, because all the goodness has been worked out of the land, and weeds have been left to grow to seed, by the slovenly folks that owned it last."

"We'll try what we can do on it, Sally, till young Misther Cockle comes out agin, and thin maybe he'll help us to clear out of the unlucky concern altogether; and afore we go, we'll make a grand bonfire wid all the ould combustibles in the dairy, that ye're allers fretting about. Cheer up, honey! I believe there's better times coming for us; but if so be that worse times come, we can't help it, and grumbling won't mend 'em a bit, I'm thinking."

After breakfast, Mr. Rafferty kindly offered to drive me in his cart to Belambi, where I hoped to find Mrs. Cameron. As we rode along, he explained to me that the mountains to the left of us were choke-full of coal, and he added,[1] "Troth, the Sydney folks needn't be afraid for the next hundred years or two of running short of coal or butter, nor of bacon nayther, if the land in this fine district is sensibly worked, both inside and outside, and if proper attention is paid to the rearing of pigs of a raysonable breed, instead of thim long-jowled crathers, same as you saw on my farrm, what wud ate for everlastin' and niver git any flesh on 'em. Yes, sir, it's a lovely district, as you say, and if I could git a decent living here, I wouldn't wish to go anywhere else;

---

[1] See note at end of book.

but every man to his trade, as the cabin-cook said, whin they axed him to go aloft in a gale of wind to send down the fore-royal-yard."

At Belambi I learnt that a man named Joe Winkle had lived there for a short time; but that he left one day in a collier vessel, and no one could tell me where he had gone. It was supposed that he decamped in order to get away from a woman, whom I concluded was Clara Cameron. I further learned that the said woman had gone to live with her uncle at Maneroo. I could not hear anything about Ella, and I supposed that she had not been living with her mother of late. That supposition afforded me some comfort in my disappointment at not finding her.

We stayed an hour or two at Belambi, and Mr. Rafferty, in his sailor-like style, expressed strong admiration for the cleverness and pluck of the gentleman (Mr. Hale) who had planned and built a long, strong, wooden jetty on an ocean beach, and exposed to breaking waves, heavy enough in easterly gales to smash up a whole navy. At the time of our visit, there were two vessels alongside the jetty, loading coal. We were told that a second ocean jetty was being erected in a bay a little to the northward of Belambi, by another enterprising colonist (Mr. Somerville). It is now owned by one of the most flourishing mining companies in the land; but the original owner is not a sharer in the profits. Without assuming that Mr. Somerville has any claim at all on the Bulli Coal Company, I will venture to say, that if some of the rich shareholders knew as much as I know of that good old gentleman and his worthy wife, they would offer them a small annuity. I am not sure, however, that the trustful old pair would accept of it.

Mr. Rafferty admitted to me, soon after we started from his house, that he was not expert at driving a horse in a cart, though he could steer a ship with any able seaman in the navy. I soon discovered that he really was not a clever driver; still, I was not at all nervous, for we were merely going at an ambling pace, which was the quickest motion we could get out of the horse without a constant application of the whip, to which Mr. Rafferty seemed averse. But when the animal's head was turned homeward, his paces improved in an exciting degree; for he began with a spirited jog-trot, and gradually quickened into a brisk canter, as if he wished to show me what he could do when he was in a humour to go. Mr. Rafferty was just assuring me that there was no vice in the crather, and that he had no notion of running away, but was only making natural haste homeward to get his feed of corn, when the off-wheel suddenly plunged into a mud-hole, of which there were many in the road, and in a moment the cart turned over.

Rafferty managed to spring clear of the cart, but I was not so fortunate, for it fell upon my right leg. I distinctly heard my knee-bone crunch, and then I fainted from the extreme pain. I was carried on a rude sort of litter to Rafferty's house, and a surgeon was sent for who set my fractured bones cleverly, and warned me to lie perfectly still if I wished ever to walk again on a sound leg.

I dare say that some experienced writers—men of uncommon moral fortitude—if they were laid up for several months with a compound fractured joint, might be able to teach some excellent moral lessons therefrom; but it does not seem in my power to make my painful experience in any way pleasant reading, and I think that a detail of my sufferings and symptoms would be less useful than the diary of a cattle doctor. The least I can say about it is, that it was a troublesome time for me. Mr. and Mrs. Rafferty nursed me with as much tender care as if I were their own son. The remembrance of their kindness gushes up like a hot spring whenever I hear whining folks lament the absence of disinterested friendship in the world. I could write some pleasant chapters about honest Tim Rafferty and his practical philosophy, and it would be amusing to me, but Saul positively objects to it. He says there is already ten times more philosophy in print than anybody in the world can understand.

As soon as I could walk without crutches, which was fully six months after my accident, I returned to Sydney. Good old Mrs. Dyke was overflowing with sympathy when I told her of my misfortune. In return for her patient attention to my sad story, I felt bound to listen to some particulars of her family affairs. It was rather flattering to me, a comparative stranger, to be taken so far into her confidence; still, I did not care much for it. Foremost amongst the items of domestic news, she told me that her Selina was going to be married on the fourth of next month to Mr. Burney. I was sorry to hear it, for the girl's sake; and I thought it was a pity that she should bestow her young heart's affection on a man whom I could but despise for his foppish effeminacy and for his apparent lack of virtuous principles.

It would have been sheer presumption for me, a young single man, to offer advice or words of caution to the mother of two grown-up daughters, on the delicate subject of the choice of a son-in-law. Indeed, I have since observed that the suggestions or monitions of *old* married men, or even of old women, are not always heeded in such cases. I simply said, "I hope Selina will be happy, Mrs. Dyke;" at the same time I thought I would suffer almost unlimited trouble or penance to save any girl related to me from becoming the wife of Mr. Brutus Burney.

While Mrs. Dyke and I were having our confidential chat in the little back parlour downstairs, I heard a strange noise in the drawing-room upstairs, which for a moment startled me, for I thought some of the ceiling cornice had fallen, or that the large life-size portrait of the late Captain Dyke had come down, from the wall on to the cabinet of curiosities beneath. My late illness had made me nervous, no doubt. Mrs. Dyke saw me start at the noise, and she smirkingly remarked, "Don't be alarmed, Mr. Larksway: it's only Annie and Mr. Gorff, our new lodger, having a romp together. He is such a funny gentleman—so full of life and spirit! You never did hear such games as they have up there sometimes."

I tried to imagime what my dear old father and mother would have said or done if Mr. Gorff, or any other funny gentleman, had romped in that uncivilized way with my sister Emmy when she was approaching her sixteenth year; but I only said, "Your new lodger is very noisy at his fun," and then I asked how Master Bob was getting on?

"Oh, I think he is getting on pretty well, thank you. He is now junior clerk to Mr. Docket, the broker, and gets ten shillings a week. Mr. Mackintosh, the ironmonger, kindly offered to take him as apprentice without a premium, for his poor father's sake; but Bob didn't like to go. It is not a very clean business, you know, sir. Bob is a clever boy, though I say it."

I thought it was a pity that Bob should slight a chance of learning a useful business with a good master; but I did not tell my opinion to Mrs. Dyke, for I knew it would not influence her in any way, except perhaps to make her vexed with me for insinuating that she did not know the best way to train up her son. The wisest of mothers are apt sometimes to differ with any one who expresses a doubt of the goodness or cleverness of their darling boys or girls.

No doubt a berth in a smart office, with light work and short hours, is enticing to a boy who has just left school; and perhaps eight out of a dozen boys, if left to their own choice, would prefer it to the drudgery of learning a mechanical trade or a business.

My Cousin Saul, for example, chose to take a clerkship in a gas company's office when he left college, rather than go into his father's engineering factory, and now he sorrowfully owns that he missed his way. I by no means wish to underrate clerks. They are as necessary in a trading community as sailors are on board a ship; but they are becoming too numerous for the requirements of trade, and their pay is cut down to a modicum, in many cases too small to support their families in a style becoming their respectable position in society. Every year clerks increase faster than the increase of commerce. The keen competition of the times also militates against their interests; for employers in general strive to get the work of their offices done by as few hands as possible, to save expense; and preparing for the out-going English mail is often a plea with some Australian employers for working their clerks all night as well as all day. They have no alternative but to submit; for it would not be safe for clerks to strike while there are so many in their line out of employment, and willing to accept work on almost any terms, and to submit to any extent of drudgery, for the sake of the dear ones depending on them.

These significant facts are worthy the consideration of parents, who are perhaps puzzled how to place their sons, about to leave school, in positions for earning an honest livelihood. My remarks have special reference to the Australian colonies that I have visited; but I can well remember the many exciting discussions in my own early home, before I was launched on to life's busy stream. The anxiety of my dear mother that I should have some light, indoor occupation, where I could always keep my hands and feet warm ; and the concern of my sister, lest my chosen calling should not be of a genteel kind, and lest I should be snubbed by some of my old schoolfellows for wearing an apron. I now regret that my father's proposition to apprentice me to a cabinet-maker or a farmer was not unanimously agreed to ; for if it had been, I am almost sure I should find myself in a better position to-day.

CHAPTER XII.

> "Passing through the forest,
> Chewing the cud of sweet and bitter fancy."
> —*Shakespeare*.

To find an ordinary individual in the extensive pastoral district of Maneroo would seem about as unpromising an undertaking as it would be to find another ordinary person in the woody dells of Derbyshire, or on the Druidical plains of Wiltshire. Mr. Jeremiah Badkin, innkeeper, Maneroo, was the only address I had of that personage; and it ought to be held as indicative of my perseverance and pluck, that I resolved to find him, or perish among the snowy plains and rocky gullies of that wide region. Being over 4,000 feet above the sea level, it is cold there in the winter season.

I might tell a thrilling story of my adventures on the road from Sydney to Cooma, for it was in mid-winter, and at a time when a notorious gang of bushrangers were in the height of their marauding glory; but, as Saul truly remarks, there would be no fun in such a story; besides, I have not room to spare for it. Few mail-coach passengers escaped a ransacking in those days of error, and some of them received a bullet as a memento of the event. I was "stuck up," as it is called, and was awfully scared by having a loaded revolver held before my eyes by a great, rough fellow, who seemed almost as willing as he was able to kill me in half a minute, if I made any resistance. I am thankful to say that I was not maimed in any way, and my pecuniary loss was not serious, for I had taken the reasonable precaution of leaving all my valuable effects at home, except a little loose cash for my expenses on the road, and a change of linen, which I need hardly say changed owners. While the rifling was going on, I noticed that one of the passengers seemed as cool and composed as if the coach was merely stopped to grease the wheels. He afterwards remarked that he was sure the bushrangers would not molest him, for he had known each man in the gang ever since he was a baby; and he called them by their Christian name, of Tommy, Ben, and Charley, as familiarly as if they were his own grandsons. He was evidently proud of the acquaintanceship. It certainly was an advantage to him then, for they did not rob him, nor even feel in his pockets.

By another of the happy occurrences which have so often favoured me, I learnt from the first person I inquired of at Cooma, that Mr. Jerry Badkin kept the Flying Fox Inn, a few miles on the road to Kiandra. I was so anxious to get to his house, that I resolved to set off at once, although it was nearly sundown. A man, who had been having a solitary tipple at the bar of the inn where the coach stopped, said he was going in his cart within a mile or two of Badkin's, and he wouldn't mind driving me there for five shillings. I agreed to

L

his terms, and we almost immediately set off on our journey. A storekeeper, in Cooma, obligingly cashed me a cheque on my bank in Sydney for a small amount for present expenses.

It was a cold evening. Snow lay on the ground several inches in depth, and the wind howled through the wild bush like the ghosts of warmer times. My driver said his horse knew every inch of the road, which was somewhat consoling to me, for I had misgivings as to the man's knowledge of anything useful for the occasion. If the road track had not been covered with snow, he was too tipsy to see it, even if he had kept his eyes open. All my faculties were painfully awake (a common virtue with nervous people, who "suffer a thousand deaths fearing but one"), and I suffered a score of fractures—in imagination! I believe that no spring cart ever had a more violent trial of its endurance on any road in the world, and it is scarcely possible that any ordinary steel springs could stand a more severe testing. It was a succession of ups and downs of the most rasping kind that I ever experienced. Over rocks and roots and stumps, and through holes and ruts and quags innumerable, we slowly wheeled our way: and only the ardent desire of seeing Ella Cameron before I slept, and of comforting her with the message from her departed father, kept me from leaping out of the cart at half a dozen fearful crises and walking back to Cooma.

Night came upon us—a starless night,—and still we plodded onward through the dreary bush. The dead limbs of the ring-barked gum trees looked like gigantic skeletons sparring at us. But my companion was insensible to all the poetical features of our situation and surroundings. He was in a state of tipsical drowsiness, and he never uttered a word except to curse the eyes or limbs of the horse whenever he stumbled at a snag in the road. Becursed as that horse was, I envied him, for he was sweating while I was half-skinned with cold. That benumbing ride has several times since come shivering up to my memory, when I have glanced over some gushing young rhymer's eulogiums on this glorious Austral land—that knows no winter, where the winds are warm and soft and balmy, and where the busy bees have nothing to hinder them from "gathering honey from opening flowers" all the year round. I think if the poets and the bees were to flit to Kiandra in the month of July, they would cease their humming, and their rhyming would not be of a merry turn.

At length, from the eccentric movements of the horse, I feared that we were lost in the bush; and I was about to propose the forlorn expedient of stopping and making a fire with the cart, when my gloomy driver suddenly gave utterance to four of the most cheering words that I ever heard from a tipsy man: "That's Jerry Badkin's house."

"Wh-wh-where is it, mister?" I asked, with an eagerness which was startling, for my words sounded like the giggles of a frost-bitten goblin, as they shivered through my purple lips.

"Yonder it is, in the bush. Can't you see the light?"

I did see a light, and though it was dim and distant

it seemed for a moment to warm my whole inner man like a flash of love. After a few more mighty tugs from the horse, and some death-like struggles of the cart, we were clear of a lot of fallen trees, and I alighted at the front door of the Flying Fox inn; safe, but not sound, for my skin in some parts had been sorely rubbed. Nevertheless I was glad, anomalous as it may seem.

There are various degrees of gladness or joy in this our world, to sweeten "life's cup of misery," which some ascetic beings often sigh about. Mine just then was the gladness of a man who had had his crushed thigh cleverly taken out of its socket,—or perhaps it will be a prettier figure to say, mine was the joy of a woman, who is taking the first quiet look at herself in her new set of teeth, after a long and trying ordeal with a dentist. The recollection of the obstinate stumps she had had gouged or punched out, would scarcely cause her more peculiar shrinkings than my recollection of the skinning jerks and jolts over the rocks and stumps in that spring cart caused me. I was glad that my exciting journey was over for the night, and that I had a roof over my head, although it was merely a stringy-bark roof.

In scanning the adventures of Dundrearyite tourists which are often printed, it is sometimes too much for my patience to notice the squeamish fastidiousness they show about their personal comfort. The soup at a certain hotel they patronized had a dry-bony flavour; or the game was too fresh, or there was no ice to be had, so they could not enjoy their claret! I think it would do foppish epicures good to set them down on a frosty night at such an unpromising-looking hostelry as the Flying Fox; at any rate, they would not lament that they could not get their drink cold enough, or their meat either.

The bar or tap into which I entered was as unpromising a groggery as ever was licensed by a bench of magistrates. A jolly-faced man was behind the counter, looking at two customers who were playing at puff and dart at the farthest end of the room. I supposed him to be the landlord, so I asked, in the humble tone of a poor beggar, if he would accommodate me with board and lodging for the night. He replied, in a rather doubtful way, "You must ask the missis about that; she will be here in a minute or two. I never meddle with her part of the house."

He then addressed my late driver in a more lively strain: "Hallo, Mick! What brings you up this way to-night? Has the old woman been fighting with you again?"

"No fear! I drove this gentleman from Cooma. Give us a gill o' rum, Jerry. I'm frost-bitten all over."

The rum was drawn, and Mick was about to swallow it whole, when the landlord cried, "Hold on, mate! What has old Jerry done? Isn't he to go halves with you?"

"Draw yourself a nip if you like, Jerry. A gill isn't too much for me at a gulp this cold night. Ugh! I can hardly get my jaws open wide enough to swallow it."

The rum had the effect of thawing Mick's tongue, and

of stimulating his fancy, and he grew talkative to a degree that was astonishing when contrasted with his moody taciturnity on our journey. He was well up in the latest bushranging news, and the gamesters left their puff and dart to listen to his comical account of the last "sticking-up" case. He evidently was not aware that I was one of the victims on that occasion, or he would not have ventured to add so much from his imagination to the facts of the case. The sympathies of Mick and his listeners were strong on the wrong side, and it grew less a source of wonder to me that bushrangers should have such lengthy careers of lawless plundering, and that the police should have so much difficulty in tracking the rogues, while there were so many applauding Micks and Jerrys throughout the country, who no doubt would sooner help the bushrangers to escape than help the police to capture them. But sympathy with lawlessness is not confined to the residents of the backwoods of Australia, I am sorry to say.

Presently a stout old woman huddled into the bar, and I repeated to her my request for board and lodging for the night. She replied, "Come into the parlour." There was a surliness in her look which seemed to say, "We don't want such customers as you in our house, and for two pins I'd turn you out." I felt uneasy, but I strove to master my feelings, and followed her into a room which was nearly as dirty as the bar. It was indeed a comfortless apartment—I thought it was a shame to call it a parlour. It had a table in the middle of the bare floor, and a dozen gaunt straight-backed cedar-chairs stood against the wall. That was all the furniture. A grimy glass lamp was on the table, and as I tried to warm the tips of my fingers over its blaze, I asked the hostess if she would oblige me with a fire. She mumbled out something as she left the room. I did not hear whether it was yea or nay; but in a few minutes I was somewhat revived by seeing a slip-shod woman enter, with a shovelful of live cinders and a few sticks.

"Thank you!" I said, with real gratitude in my tone. "I will try to make the fire burn up; and if you will be good enough to get me a cup of tea soon, I shall be much obliged to you."

The woman said, "Yes, sir;" and as she shuffled out of the room in her loosely-fitting slippers, I felt convinced that she was Clara Cameron; for though the grace of her figure was lost in fat, there were to be traced symptoms of early beauty in her face above her double chin, and there was still some sparkle in her large blue eyes. She appeared to be verging upon forty years of age, and she had a profusion of fair hair, though it sadly wanted combing and brushing.

When the fire crackled up, I felt more lively. As I squatted on the hearthstone to warm my back, I took a survey of the room, and I daresay a hundred spiders or more were at the same time taking a survey of me from their webs in the bark roof. My mind always will be occupied; and I wondered how many times those straight-backed chairs had each held a tipsy man; and then I wondered if all the tipsy men who had ever sat in those chairs were in the land of the living! And if not in the land of the living, where were they? And if they could possibly come back to this earth, would they ever again waste their precious time in getting drunk? These speculations were making me dismal again, when suddenly the door was kicked open, and in shuffled the woman with a tea-tray; so I jumped up from my indecorous position on the hearthstone, for I was always taught to behave with politeness, even to the humblest servant. While she was arranging the supper on the table, I took a fair look at her, and felt confirmed in my belief that it was Clara herself; for there were still some of the dimples in her cheeks which poor Cameron had so tenderly alluded to when dilating on her maidenly beauty.

Cold pickled pork and dry bread, and tea without milk, are not enticing viands to set before a jaded traveller on a frosty night. Still, I did not murmur; indeed, I should have been afraid to complain if the pickled pork had been raw, lest I should be ejected from the house—turned out to perish in the snow. I ate my supper, and tried to feel thankful for it; for poor as it was, it was better than no supper at all. My extreme meekness on that occasion will perhaps be called pusillanimity by some bold spirits who have never lodged at the Flying Fox, or any similar bush-groggery. Of course I cannot help what anybody thinks of me; but I am quite sure that if I had possessed the pluck of an arctic explorer or an elephant tamer, I should not have shown it in any way. To "knuckle down" was my policy for the time being; and that is the policy which hundreds of millions of our race have to study all their lifetime. It is only a privileged few that can afford to show all the pluck they have in their nature.

I ate my cold supper as a duty—not for pleasure—and it was soon over. There was a rusty old bell on the table; but I was afraid to ring it, lest it should summon Mr. or Mrs. Badkin into the room, and I did not want to see them again. When I had finished my meal, I sat by the fire and considered how I could best open a conversation with Mrs. Cameron. After awhile, she came into the room to remove the tea-tray, and I said to her very persuasively, " Pray may I ask, is your name Clara Cameron ? "

"Yes, sir, it is," she replied, and she blushed slightly. For a moment I thought she looked pretty. I also thought of her handsome daughter, whom I hoped to see presently; so I said, with the pleased expression which such thoughts would naturally throw into my features, "I would like to have a little private conversation with you, if you do not object."

In an instant there was a changed expression in her eyes which I did not like, and she whispered jauntily, " I'll be with you as soon as the old woman is gone to bed." She then gave me another peculiar glance of her eyes, and left the room with a sort of mincing or half-skipping gait, which might have looked playfully graceful in a merry girl of fifteen years old, but it was not at all becoming to a woman of her mature age and portly figure.

As I sat toasting myself at the blazing fire, the charming picture of Ella came before my mind's eye for the thousandth time; and much as I longed to see her—for her poor deceased father's sake—I ardently hoped she was not in that comfortless house, exposed to the everyday scenes of drunken debauchery, and to the dangerous influence of a wanton mother. The soothing effect of the fire gradually lulled me into a fanciful mood, and all the straight-backed chairs suddenly became animated and began talking in random style of politics, and dummy-selection, and bushranging, and that old bone of contention, "the educational question," just as naturally as a common gathering of wrangling colonists; and of course there were the usual signs of fighting when the subject of religious instruction to children was touched. After awhile, they seemed to have settled everything harmoniously, for they all began to sing Robert Burns' well-known bacchanalian song,

"We are nae fou, we're nae that fou,
But just a wee drap in our ee!"

the song which has made so many scores of whisky-loving Scotchmen to drop under the table—from enthusiasm. My laughter at the comical scene aroused me, and I found that I had been taking a short dream. But there was a peculiar hubbub in the tap-room, and I might have concluded that some mounted bushrangers had just come in to see us; but I soon found that the row was merely a convivial one. Mr. Jerry Badkin was singing in lofty strains, "Rise upon gad!"; and his tipsy customers, including my late driver, were giving the usual sort of clog-dance accompaniment to that funny old Irish song. Discordant as the performance was, I was really glad to hear it, for it helped to divert my mind from the exciting contemplation of those vacant chairs; indeed, I think I would even have tolerated a few barrel-organs under my window, though I never did enjoy that sort of music.

CHAPTER XIII.

"Sic a wife as Willie had,
I wadna gie a button for her."—*Burns.*

THE clock in the tap-room struck eleven, and I still sat musing by the fire. Presently the door opened, and in came Clara, with extreme softness considering her solid weight. She closed the door again noiselessly, then carried a chair to the fireplace and sat down, rather closer to me than I approved of.

"O mercy! it's stinging cold to-night. Just feel my paw." She put one of her fat hands in mine, and it felt like a dead frog. I shrank from her and pushed back my chair.

"Ha, ha! I make you shiver; but I shall soon warm up, never fear! I couldn't come in before, because the old woman wouldn't go to bed till we carried her upstairs. She is awfully troublesome when she has had a drop too much."

"Does she really get tipsy?"

"When trade is dull, she takes a little drop extra to keep her spirits up. But she is fast asleep and snoring now; and there is no fear of Jerry showing in the parlour to-night, so we are snug enough. If there was anybody here who would shout for drink or gamble a bit, you would have seen the governor in long ago. Ugh! my toes are like wedges of ice; I'm glad you asked aunt to let you have a fire." Clara then shuffled off her slippers and put her feet on the hearth, in a very free-and-easy style.

"I wish to have a little quiet conversation with you, Mrs. Cameron," I said, and I fixed my gaze on the chimney, for I knew that she was looking at me, and I dreaded the leer of her eyes. "I have something to tell you of your husband."

"My husband!" she exclaimed sharply. "If that's what you want me for, I am sorry I came in. I don't want to hear anything about him. I hope he isn't in this part of the country, that's all."

"He is dead, poor man!"

"Dead, is he? When did he die?"

I told her some of the particulars of his death, and that with his latest breath he prayed for her and for their daughter; and how that he had implored me to search for them both, and to tell them that he fondly loved them; and especially I was to tell her that he forgave her for all the sorrow and loss she had caused him.

"Forgave me, indeed! Did he tell you to ask me to forgive him? He has left me to fight for myself the last seventeen years, and has never sent so much as a pound note either for me or the girl. I daresay he was ashamed of himself at last; and so he had need to be, after the cruel way he treated me. Did he leave any money behind him?"

"He left enough to pay his liabilities and his personal expenses, and——"

"I wonder he left as much as would do that," she said, stopping me short in my report of his finances. "He was always a fool with his money, and anybody could get it out of him—except me." She then, in a whimpering tone, told me of her sorrows and trials since the unlucky day she married Cameron. It was an old-fashioned story, perhaps founded on fact, but, like many other sad reports of family disagreements, it was built up with prejudice and misrepresentation. If I had not heard her dying husband's version of the whole affair, I should perhaps have sympathized with Clara as an ill-used wife; and that proves to me the necessity for hearing both sides of such conjugal disputes, if you really *must* hear them, before you can possibly form a correct judgment on their merits. She grew pathetic towards the end of her story, her sharp tone softened down, and I thought she was going to weep. A woman's tears always make me feel a sort of ready-to-die-for-her disposition, and the sympathy which was swelling in my breast was just about to vent itself in some soft way, which I should perhaps regret to this day, when her facial expression suddenly changed, from the pensive to the pert, as she held up her finger and said, "Hist! I hear Jerry shutting up. I am glad of that, for I am getting as dry as a fire-stick." She certainly did look dry just then! as unlike a sorrowing widow as any woman I ever beheld.

"Your uncle keeps his bar open rather late," I remarked, for I thought I must say something; and I was glad I had not wasted kind words of condolence on the heartless woman.

"Oh, we don't call this late. He wouldn't shut up now if there was any trade going on; but it is a slack time with us, on account of the Kiandra diggings getting poorer than they used to be."

"Has your uncle been in this business long?"

"He hasn't been in this house a great while, but he was in the public line in other places in this colony, and in New Zealand."

"I suppose he has made some money?"

"Yes; no doubt about that, for he has been insolvent twice since I have lived with him."

"But surely that is not the way to make money!" I remarked, with natural surprise in my tone.

"I don't know much about it myself, but I often hear fellows talking about it in the bar. I heard uncle himself say, one night when he was tipsy, that he did well out of his first smash up; but the second time, what with law charges and other drawbacks, there wasn't much profit for him, and it isn't worth his while to try it on again. He makes a poor mouth to me whenever I ask him for money; but for all that, I know he must be pretty well in, for we do a rare trade here sometimes, when fellows come down from the diggings with their pouches full of gold dust, but especially after sheep-shearing time, when the shearers drop in with their big cheques. They are the boys to shout."

"I suppose the diggers are very profitable customers?"

"Only middling in these times; for gold is not so easily got as it used to be, and the diggers are more wide awake to its value. They know to a threepenny-bit how much their gold is worth an ounce; and there are often rows with them and Jerry over the price, and over the weighing of the dust. But when the shearers come in for their regular spree, they hand their cheques over to the governor like men; and they don't often bother their heads about the way the money goes, till Jerry tells them that their cheques are all knocked down. Then after a day or two of coaxing, they stagger off to their huts in the bush, with a bottle or two of rum in their pockets, to keep them lively enough to get home. My word! we do see roaring life here once a year with the shearers!"

"And I suppose you have awful deaths here, sometimes?"

"There have not been any deaths in the house since I came here; but we have had some fellows crazy with drunkenness, and I don't like those characters at all, because they are dangerous. I'll say this for uncle, he is fair and square with his customers; and though he puts plenty of 'snowy river' into his rum kegs, he doesn't put anything worse in, and good water will never hocuss a man, or make him savage. Hark! the governor is going upstairs now, so I'll slip into the bar, and smuggle a bottle of Old Tom. Sit still— I won't be half a minute away."

Heedless of my protest, she tripped to the door with the lamp in her hand, and left me in darkness.

I felt very uneasy lest the landlord should overhear her, in which case he would certainly have accused me of conspiring with her to rob him, and he would have turned me out of the house with disgrace. Clara soon returned from her raid on the bar; and as she placed a bottle and two tumblers on the table, she said, with an ill-meaning leer, "Now we'll have a nice quiet boose all to ourselves. Nobody will disturb us. Jerry has taken his nightcap, and is fast asleep by this time; and I warrant he wouldn't wake up if a wool-dray were to back up against the bar door. Will you take your grog hot or cold?"

I said, "I don't like spirits, Mrs. Cameron; and if I did, I should have a decided objection to drink any of the stuff that you have stolen."

"Ha, ha! I know what you mean, but you needn't be afraid of it. It's good cordial gin, just as we get it from the merchant. Look at the label and the cork. There's no fear of me making a mistake." She then poured some of the liquor into a tumbler, and swallowed it without coughing, which showed me what habit will help a woman to do. "I wish you would take a little drop, just to be sociable, Mr.—er—er. I forgot to ask your name before."

I told her my name, and I again protested against her act of petty larceny; then I asked her where her daughter was.

The spirit seemed to blaze out of her eyes, as she replied: "I don't know where she is, nor I don't care. It is more than three years since I saw her last."

M

"Then she is not in this house?"

"No fear! Jerry wouldn't let her come here if she was inclined to it. You had better ask him for her character if you would like to hear it in plain English. She is every bit as bad as her father."

"I am sorry you cannot tell me where she is, for I received a message for her from her father just before he died."

"A rare lot of good it would do her, I daresay. But whether or not, I don't know where she is, so I cannot tell you. She left me one day when I was living at Illawarra Lake, and I have not seen her since. There was a meddling parson in Wollongong who was always talking religion to her, and I believe he persuaded her to run away from me. She went off to Sydney, and I never ran after her, you may be sure. I did hear that she was in a ladies' school, but I haven't troubled to ask many questions about her. She never behaved properly to me after she grew up, and I don't care if I never see her proud, stuck-up figure again as long as I live. Why don't you drink some gin, Mr. Luckspot? I tell you there is no hocussing stuff in it."

"I never drink spirits, Mrs. Cameron. I will go to bed if you will please to tell me the way to my bedroom."

"You are in a precious hurry to go to bed, and I am only just beginning to get lively. Sit still a bit, and let us talk about something pleasant."

I thought that if I sat there for three hours longer, I should not get any more information from her respecting her daughter that would be of service to me, It was also clear to me that she was in a fair way to get drunk very soon; so I said, "I feel tired after my long journey, and I pray you to excuse me sitting up later, Mrs. Cameron."

"My word! you are a sleepy-headed fellow. I wouldn't have run the risk of stealing this bottle of gin, if I had known that you wouldn't help me to drink it. Come, sit still and make your mind happy!" She tried to take hold of my arm, but I eluded her grasp, and said firmly,—

"I will not stay up any longer, madam."

"Oh! call me madam, do you? Well, if you must go to bed, there is your state apartment, my lord," she said, pointing to a door at one end of the room. I bade her good-night, and went into my room and fastened the door. She then stirred up the fire, and began to sing "Shades of evening." Whether she was singing for her own amusement or for mine, I cannot say; but if she hoped to charm me in that way, it was a complete failure, for to my ears her half tipsy voice was not more musical than the grinding of a coffee mill. Presently I heard the guggle-guggle of the gin, as she poured some more from the bottle, then a few heavy strides across the room, and the door slammed. She was gone, and I was as thankful as a sailor who had just escaped from the jaws of a shark or the paws of a crimp, which are equally cruel.

There was no ceiling to my room, and neither plaster nor paper on the walls, and the icy draught through the chinks in the slabs seemed to pierce my very marrow. For the first time in my life, that I can remember, I turned into bed without saying my prayers; but I had no sooner turned in than I turned out again, for the musty smell of the bed reminded me of my dear mother's kindly warnings, "Roger, my dear boy! beware of damp sheets! Remember that un-aired linen caused the death of your poor Aunt Hannah." I snatched off the sheets and made counterpanes of them; then I got into the single pair of blue blankets and rolled myself up as round as possible. I tried to say my prayers with my nose between my knees, but my tongue seemed afraid of my chattering teeth, and would not act for the sternest appeals of conscience. In dread of being frost-bitten, I was half tempted to go into the parlour and finish the bottle of Old Tom, if Clara had left any; but I thought again, that to get a temporary thaw for my stomach at the cost of an aching head next day, would be almost as silly an act as that of the man who burnt down his haystack to roast a snake. So I lay still, and when my brain got warm enough to think, I thought of poor Cameron.

I fancied what he might have been at the present time, if he had not had the ill-luck to fall in with Clara Bond on his voyage to Australia. If he had kept disengaged until he got safely past the susceptible period of adolescence, and then married a woman his equal in rank and of a kindred mind to his own, I pictured him as a wealthy and an influential man, living in that luxurious homeliness which is the charm of a squatter's life in the bush. I pictured his wife a lady of refinement and cultivated taste, an ornament to his home, the idol of his heart, and the honoured mother of his children. I pictured half a dozen bright boys and girls gathered around the social hearth, a healthy, intelligent, loving group, their father's pride and mother's delight; children whose minds were expanding under the genial influence of the moral precepts and examples of their parents, and who showed cheering promise of maturing into men and women who would become lights in the land.

It was not stretching fancy too much to suppose that Cameron would have married a lady of refined breeding if he had waited until his calm judgment guided him to such a choice; for he was a man of education, and of a good family, and he was possessed of a moderate fortune. At that time, too, he was of gentlemanly habits, and withal a fine, manly looking fellow, whose addresses perhaps no sensible lady would have slighted, if she had not a tender reason for so doing. But poor fellow! he was bewitched by Clara's pretty young face, and he thought, boy-like, that his life would be a dreary blank without her. He had no judicious friend at hand to advise him to take a fortnight to consider, before he made an engagement with her; but urged on by youthful passion, he wooed the willing maid; he made her his wife, and she made him miserable for life, a natural result in accordance with the fixed laws of cause and effect.

As I lay shivering on that cold, mouldy bed, under the same roof with poor Cameron's tipsy widow, I resolved that his unhappy marital experience should be a solemn warning to me. If I ever tumbled in love with a pretty face, I would keep a philosophical check-rein upon passion, and make the best use of my judgment in finding out the qualities and disposition of my charmer, before I ventured to say a word to her on the subject of my attachment.

After making that sensible resolution, I repeated some of the Proverbs of Solomon, many of which I have stored in my memory, and I found them a pleasant sedative for my excited mind. My good father was a dear lover of the Bible; and to please him, I have often learnt a chapter by heart and repeated it to him. He used to say, "The Book of Proverbs is a safe chart to give a boy or girl for the voyage of life." On several occasions since I left my home, I have seen the practical wisdom of King Solomon's inspirations, and especially of his warnings against the ways of "the strange woman."

The next morning, after an early breakfast, I left the Flying Fox, and was glad to get away. I thought perhaps Clara would ask me a few tender questions about her late husband before I left; but not another word did she say about him; and when I looked at her and said "Good morning" at parting, there were no more traces of sorrow on her face than I might have expected to see if she had heard of the death of old Wallabadaba, the blackfellow in the bush. I walked back to Cooma, and from thence I went to Sydney by mail coach. I luckily escaped the bushrangers on my return journey; and, though the roads were in a very bad condition, the coach only upset once.

CHAPTER XVI.

"Oh would I were dead now, or up in my bed now,
To cover my head now, and have a good cry."
—*Hood.*

WHEN I reached my lodgings in Sydney, I found the whole house in disorder from bottom to top, and Mrs. Dyke and her daughters in a state of excitement, which set me wondering what was the matter with them all. I soon learned that on the previous night a large building close by had been burnt down; and although Mrs. Dyke's house was unscathed by fire, it had suffered damage from water which was poured upon it to keep it cool; and moreover, she had lost many valuable chattels which thieves carried off under the specious pretext of removing them beyond the reach of the flames. Most of the household effects had been turned into the street topsy-turvy; and when I arrived, she had just finished the work of getting them inside again, with the aid of her son and daughters and Mr. Burney, who all looked fagged with the exercise. The furniture, too, looked nearly worn out with the rough handling it had received from the active salvors and smashers.

Mrs. Dyke was glad to see me home again. She sat in an easy chair to rest herself, and was just beginning to give me a full account of the terrific disaster which had aroused her from her midnight slumbers. But I was naturally anxious about my own personal baggage, so I ventured to interrupt her story, and asked, as composedly as possible, if my trunks were safe?

"Oh yes, sir; I am glad to say they are safe enough. I took special care of them, and stopped Bob from throwing them out of the window. If he had done so, there is no saying where they would be by this time. But I fear they are wet, for the fire engines were playing upon your room, full pump, for half an hour before we could get inside to carry anything out. Your trunks are where you left them, beside your bed; but you will find the room terribly upset, for we have not had time to put it to rights or wash it out. Fire engines do make a sad mess in a house, sure-ly; and firemen don't care whose property they pump upon."

I hastened upstairs, and on overlooking my trunks, a disheartening spectacle of damaged effects met my gaze. If the volunteer brigade had squirted on my trunks all night long, they could not have more thoroughly saturated everything inside them. It would have made my mother and sister weep to see the condition of my new linen shirts and my white waistcoats; and my album and other valuable items, mostly *souvenirs* from dearly beloved friends, were in a still more pitiable state. I lifted out the saturated articles one by one, and laid them on the floor. Presently I came to the parcel which poor Cameron had sealed up and addressed to his daughter. It was sodden with water, having been placed at the bottom of the trunk for greater security. In lifting it out, though I was as tender as possible with it, the paper wrapper gave way under my touch, and out rolled a lot of jewellery. I was about to gather it up again, when my eyes caught sight of the gold locket with the portrait of Mrs. Cameron and her daughter in it, and I became almost overwhelmed with a rush of feelings, powerful as gas and electricity combined. In an instant I perceived that the portrait of Ella represented the face and figure of the girl whom I had specially noticed at the restaurant in Melbourne.

Thus the mystery which had kept me awake for so many anxious hours was solved in a twinkling. That I had seen the girl's face in Greenwich, I had all along felt as certain as that I had seen my own face every morning since I first learned to shave; but who she was, I could not for the life of me recollect. *Now*, it was as clear to me as sunlight that it was Ella Cameron, and I had seen, not the girl herself, but the picture of her sweet face, whilst sitting beside her father on a bench in Greenwich Park. Yes, that very picture in my hand was Ella, and Ella was Bella, the finest of all the waitresses at the popular restaurant, where I left my silk umbrella.

I kissed Ella's side of the picture, and enjoyed it (though of course it was mere fancy, like a child sucking a glass sugar-plum) and then I put it into the heart-pocket of my waistcoat. I would have taken her mother's picture out of the locket first, but I did not like to deface the thing. Without stopping to replace anything in my trunks, I ran downstairs and said, "Mrs. Dyke, can you tell me when a steamer will go to Melbourne."

I daresay my excited look startled her, for she turned pale as she replied, "No, sir; I cannot tell you. I have not the least idea."

"Then I must find out," I said, and I seized my hat from a peg in the hall, and left the house. I ran all the way to the steamers' wharf, though I cannot give a sensible reason for my extreme haste. There I was told that a boat would leave for Melbourne the next day at noon. I have no doubt that Mrs. Dyke peeped into my room during my absence, and saw all my effects strewn about the floor, including the collection of jewellery, and perhaps she thought I was going crazy; anyway, her conclusions were unfavourable to me, for when I returned to the house, hot and still highly excited, she seemed afraid that I was going to attack her. Mr. Burney stood by, looking as if he were ready to fight in defence of the family, while Selina and Annie clung to his side, like interesting emblems of timidity and trustfulness crouching under a poplar tree in a hailstorm.

I had some difficulty in assuring my good landlady that I was not leaving her house so suddenly on account of the dirty state of my bedroom, a condition which was clearly unavoidable. I would scorn to desert friends at a time of disaster. I told her that very important business demanded my return to Melbourne as soon as possible; but I did not tell her the nature of my business there, although I could see that she was very wishful to know it, and her daughters were trembling with curiosity.

On the following day I went on board the Melbourne steamer, and it had no sooner started from the wharf than I wished myself on shore again. Never did a steamer go to sea in a more hazardous trim than the *Petrel* did on that occasion. It was fortunate for me that the weather was clear and calm. Had it been stormy, it is deadly certain that all that remained of me at the present time would be some scattered bones at the bottom of the sea off Gabo Island, or somewhere else along the rugged coast.

Blessings on the head of Mr. Samuel Plimsoll! His chivalrous crusade against unseaworthy ships is talked of all the world over, and many sailors' wives and children remember him in their prayers. He has undertaken a Herculean task; and who can wonder that he sometimes rather loses his patience over the apathy and opposition that he meets with? I have often wished I could give him an encouraging smile, and say, "Go on, my brave brother!" But if Mr. Plimsoll thinks that he is the only man who can tell a thrilling story of seamen's risks and wrongs, and shipowners' cupidity, I could convince him to the contrary by a hundred ghastly facts. Rotten or badly built ships and wicked owners are not all on his side of the world, and London is not the only port where they load steamers down to within a few inches of death's door-sill.

The foredeck of the *Petrel* was filled nearly to the top of the bulwarks with boxes of oranges, bags of onions and oysters, and other delicacies that the Victorians are fond of. Under the bridge were sundry horses and other live stock, and actually *upon* the bridge were several carts or drays. The poop deck was lumbered with passengers' luggage, and the quarter boats were full of vegetables. There was a rush of passengers up to the moment of the steamer leaving the wharf, and I estimated that there were twice the number on board that the vessel was legally allowed to carry, and three or four times more than the boats were really able to carry, if there were a necessity for using them.

I will venture to say that I am not the first landsman who has looked with calculating eyes at the physical development of the captain, to whose nautical skill and courage he had entrusted his life. I scanned our captain as we were steaming out of Sydney harbour, perhaps more carefully than his sweetheart scanned him before she said "Yea" to his wooing. His stout figure and his bronzed face gave me a passing thrill of comfort at my first glance, for they were sailor-like traits. Though the confusion and bustle on deck kept me for awhile in a state of nervous fidget, the captain seemed as composed as if he were sitting in a Turkish bath. He stuck to his post on the paddle-box platform, and did not appear to trouble himself about the hubbub on the deck beneath him. It was plain to me that there was no fear about him, and by degrees I reasoned down my dread of being swamped. I daresay the nice bright weather and the smooth sea helped my philosophy; for I find from experience that I can always reason best upon a calm day, on the wisdom of making one's mind easy when at sea—or in other words, I am seldom afraid when I am quite sure there is no immediate danger. No doubt there are warriors in the world who are brave on like conditions.

Never perhaps had a captain more need for nerve and patience than our captain had on that short voyage, for it seemed to me that everybody on board was more or less drunk, except himself and his officers; and rows and wrangles were the general pastime. It was lucky for me, in one important particular, that there were so many tipsy passengers, or I might have been hungry all the voyage. By information I got from the steward, it appeared that there was not enough provisions or the large number of steerage passengers that had been induced to rush on board by the telegram on the previous day announcing the finding of a monstrous nugget of gold at one of the new diggings in Victoria ; and the ingenuity and tact of the steward were severely tested, to make his scanty larder hold out from port to port.

"What will you do, steward," I asked, "if, as you say, you have not sufficient victuals for the passengers on board?"

"Oh, we have lots of grog, sir; and if we keep them well supplied with that, they won't want much to eat. One fellow roused up just now from his roost abaft the funnel, and said to me, 'Steward, I say, when are you going to give me any dinner?'—'Dinner! my wig! are you hungry again?' said I. 'Didn't you eat half a leg of mutton not two hours ago?'—'Did I?' said he, rubbing his tipsy eyes open. 'I forget all about it. Well, give me another bottle of porter.' He is taking a fresh nap now, but I shall have to talk to him again when he wakes up; and I have other fellows on the same lay. Ha, ha! That's the way I manœuvre, sir, when we run short of provisions in these golden times."

We arrived at Sandridge pier without any mishap, and I soon took a cab and set off for Melbourne. On the road I remembered that I had left the steamer without saying good-bye to the captain, or thanking him for his polite attention to me on the passage. The truth is, I was apprehensive that my luggage might be mistaken by some of the other passengers, in the general hurry there was to get ashore. I felt sorry for my remissness, but I forthwith sent the captain a small box of cigars, and I daresay he received them as a satisfactory apology, for he was a smoker.

On reflection, I felt rather ashamed to admit, even to myself, that my veneration for the watchful captain had decreased as my sense of personal risk dulled down; that my trustful regard for him was far less when we were safely moored at the pier, than it was when, during the dark nights on our voyage, I used to anxiously observe him at his post of duty, keeping a sharp lookout for squalls, and for coasting vessels without sidelights; or when he was guiding us through the hazardous rip at Port Phillip Heads, and skilfully keeping clear of a fleet of outward bound ships and tug-steamers. Other casuists might define my blunted feelings in a more delicate way than my cousin Saul does, but perhaps they would not be much nearer to the truth after all. He says it is the way of the world all over to respect a man or a beast in proportion as he is presently serviceable; and he furthermore says, by way of analogy, that he has known a scrubby traveller, after riding his horse a forty miles' journey, to drag the saddle off the jaded beast, and then hit him across the tail with the bridle, to stimulate him to jump over the middle slip-rail into a cold paddock, there to nibble a scanty feed of grass while his owner ate his own hot supper ready prepared for him. And Saul also says that he has known fussy passengers to almost worship a captain during a storm at sea, but they showed him a cold shoulder when they afterwards met him on shore, if he did not happen to be a stylish-looking man.

I took up my temporary lodgings at an hotel in Flinders Street. Soon after tea, I made myself look as smart as possible, and off I went to the restaurant, hoping that I should have the happiness of seeing Ella, and disburdening my mind of her late father's message before I slept. I walked past the house twice before I had courage to go in, for I felt an unconquerable dread of those quizzing girls in the saloon. Presently I walked into the shop. I could see only one girl behind the counter, in the pie department, and I asked her if she would be kind enough to tell me if Ella Cameron was within?

"Ella Cameron! I don't know her, sir."

"She lived here about ten months ago. I saw her serving in the dining saloon behind there. I think she was called Bella when I was here ; yes, I now distinctly remember, she *was* called Bella."

"It is the 'Countess' the gentleman wants," whispered another young lady, whom I had not seen on my first entrance.

"Oh, yes ; I forgot her ladyship. Bella is not living here now, sir. She left months ago, to go to some other place."

"Pray can you tell me where I may find her? I have a message for her from her relatives in England."

"I cannot tell you where she is, sir. I was not intimate with her, so I do not know any of her connections. Perhaps some of the young ladies attached to the saloon may be able to tell me. I will ask them, and if you call to-morrow about one o'clock, I will let you know."

I left the shop, and returned to my lodgings in a very dissatisfied mood. The next day I began to carry out a plan of operations, which I had designed during the sleepless hours of the previous night : namely, to visit every respectable restaurant in Melbourne, in the hope of meeting with Ella. Troublesome as the scheme promised to be, I much preferred it to the alternative of calling at one o'clock at the pie shop, to meet those laughing girls in the dining saloon.

Let me hasten over the record of the trying week that ensued, each day of which I breakfasted, dined, or supped at a separate house of refreshment, without meeting with Ella, or with any girl who I thought was at all to be compared with her. Goaded on by a feeling like desperation, I again went to the pie shop one evening, and saw behind the counter the young lady whom I had seen on my previous visit. She politely informed me that not any of the girls in the saloon could tell me where Bella was at present, though one of them said she saw her serving in a confectioner's shop about six or seven months ago. I furthermore learned that Ella had been a waitress at the pie shop for only a few weeks.

I next resolved to visit all the confectioners' shops in the city. That was a far more critical task than my former one, and it took me another week to accomplish. I did not find Ella; but I found that gooseberry tarts and raspberry rolls, and such-like rich dainties, some of which I was obliged to eat at each shop, did not agree with me as a daily diet; and if I had not had timely recourse to a few of my good uncle's famous vegetable pills, I should doubtless have been laid up with bilious fever or cholera morbus.

CHAPTER XV.

> "In the centre of a world whose soil
> Is rank with all unkindness, compassed round
> With such memorials, I have sometimes felt
> That 'twas no momentary happiness
> To have *one* enclosure, where the voice that speaks
> In envy or detraction is not heard."
> —*Wordsworth.*

TWO days after I first landed in Victoria, I had, for the first time in my life, the pleasure of seeing my name in full print, Mr. Roger Larksway, in the *Argus* newspaper's report of the wreck of the *Stormberg*. I sent the paper home for my friends to see me thus honoured! Some persons may perhaps say it is silly to notice such trifling matters; but I believe that if we were to take more notice than we do of the small joys or comforts that come to us every day, we should not so often be disposed to grumble or to complain of our condition. Mine is an uncommon name, and it is often accidentally misspelt by my correspondents. I was anxious to see if the *Argus* had again spelt my name correctly in the list of passengers when I left by the *Columbus;* so I went to the office, and a gentleman there politely allowed me to look at all the old files.

It happened that while I was searching for my name

in the *Argus* of the right date, I saw an advertisment which made my heart flutter for a minute or two. I could hardly believe my eyes, so I tried my ears, and read softly as follows : "Will the gentleman who so courageously rescued the little girl from drowning at Sandridge beach yesterday, kindly call on or send his address to Mr. Moss, Rose Villa, Prahran." I bought the paper with the advertisement which had so much interested me, and I walked straightway to the Carlton Gardens, where I sat down to calmly consider what to do next.

As far as my memory can stretch back into my childhood's history, I have been subject to seasons of depression, when my heart has been as heavy as a leaden coffin. I suppose it is a constitutional infirmity, for I cannot help it. While the depression lasts, I can never see anything cheering in my life's lot, either by looking back or by looking forward, and I feel as dreary as if I were going to be locked up in our family vault, never to see daylight again. These gloomy visitations usually go away as mysteriously as they come on; but I find that an hour's chat with a cheerful friend, or a frolic with some nice lively children, are wonderful alleviatives, far more effective than physic.

A book has been written by a learned author, entitled, " Is Life worth Living ?" and no doubt the question is ably argued to the best conclusion. The other day I saw a small handbill, issued by a very practical chemist in London, and he too asks, " Is life worth living ? " He laconically decides the question by adding, "It depends upon the *liver*"; and then of course he recommends his dandelion pills,—for it is merely a business affair with him. Now I know that my liver is not so good as it ought to be—at least, our family doctor used to tell my mother so. I have often wished when I was a boy that I had no liver, but I did not then know that I could no more get along without it than a watch could go without a mainspring. The harassing speculation has sometimes engaged my thoughts, whether it is owing to weakness of brain that my liver tyrannizes over me so often, and I have wondered again and again if great statesmen and lawyers and prelates, and other men high up on the intellectual level, are ever slavishly forced to allow any inferior organ to master their minds; or if by sheer power of brain and logic they can compel their livers to act properly? I wish I knew enough of the right sort of science to solve all these perplexing moral and social questions.

As I sat on the bench in Carlton Gardens, that mystical subject again occupied my thoughts; but as I could not see any clearer into it than I had ever seen before, I gave it up as a profitless study, and resolved that if I could possibly help it, I would never again waste the bright healthful hours that are allotted to me by brooding over sad days gone by, or in dreading gloomy seasons that may or may not come; or, in other words, I would take no anxious thought for the morrow, but accept the consoling words of Truth itself, that "Sufficient unto the day is the evil thereof." I soon became more composed, and I left the gardens humming over a song that I had often heard my dear father sing in his merry way,—

"All's for the best, be sanguine and cheerful!
Trouble and sorrow are friends in disguise."

I took a car and rode straightway to Rose Villa, Prahran, which I had no difficulty in finding. As I walked through a well-kept little garden towards the house, I saw an old gentleman sitting in Turkish fashion under a rose-bush smoking his pipe. He stood up as I advanced, and said, pointing to some dead insects on the ground: "You see, tobacco smoke does not agree with aphides, though worms like it."

"Indeed, sir! I can hardly believe that it agrees with worms."

"I did not say that it agrees with them, but that they like it. I mean worms of the earth, as poets call the like of us. Do you smoke?"

"No, I never smoked a pipe or a cigar in my life."

"Glad to hear it! Ah, you may smile, but I mean what I say, though I have only just put my pipe out. I have smoked on an average three pipes a day for the last forty years, and I have consumed, I daresay, quite three hundredweight of tobacco. Just think of that! If all the smoke that I have puffed out of my mouth could be collected into one cloud, it would be enough to poison all the aphides in Prahran, and would make a smother something like the burning of the great bonded warehouse in Melbourne last week. Don't learn to smoke, my lad, or you will wish you hadn't long before you have burnt half a tierce of tobacco."

I told him that I did not mean to learn to smoke, and that before I was in my teens, my father cautioned me against acquiring the slavish habit. I then asked the chatty old gentleman if his name was Moss?

"Yes, my name is Moss; but I daresay it is my son that you want. He is at his office: won't be home till past six o'clock."

"Has he an office in Melbourne?"

"Yes, to be sure. Don't you know my son?"

"No, sir, I do not know him. I have called here in answer to an advertisement in the *Argus*—which I did not see until this morning—for the person who helped a little girl out of the sea at Sandridge, not quite a year ago."

"What! are you the man that saved our Nelly? Why didn't you say that before? Come inside. Hoy! Maria, call your mistress downstairs directly!" He then half pushed me into the drawing-room, and soon a lady entered, to whom I was bluntly introduced as the man who had saved all their hearts from being crushed with sorrow, and then I received such an overwhelming amount of thanks, that I was half sorry I had answered the advertisement. I tried to explain that my main object in calling was to disclaim some of the praise that had been lavished on me in print; but I was answered by a fresh outpouring of grateful expressions from both mother and grandfather. It was almost too much for my nerves, though of course it was gratifying.

I remember when I was returning to Sydney from

one of my short sea trips, a few months before, that as the steamer was going up Sydney harbour, one of the seamen accidentally fell overboard. The vessel was stopped, and a boat was lowered to pick the man up. But he seemed wisely disposed to help himself; for he no sooner rose to the surface of the water after his dive, than he struck out for the shore, about a hundred yards off. In the meantime, I observed a kind-looking young lady flitting about the quarter-deck in a very excited manner, and I wondered what was the matter with her. But it was not long a mystery, for she applied to me, as well as to most of the other passengers, for help towards making up a sum to present to the sailor as soon as he came on board. Presently the boat returned alongside with the swimmer, who was quite unhurt; nor did he seem at all disconcerted, until the romantic young lady stepped up to him as he mounted the gangway, and put a little purse of money in his hand. I shall never forget the puzzled looks of the man as he walked forward in his dripping clothes, nor the comical looks of some of his messmates as they followed him, each man, perhaps, wishing he had been lucky enough to fall overboard and earn a purse of shillings. Doubtless they all thought it was a queer thing for a man to get paid for merely trying to save his own life—a thing that even a monkey would have done. And I thought it was a strange way for generosity to shape itself; but I have since then seen money testimonials given with even less show of reason than rewarding the sailor

for his cool bravery in trying to swim ashore out of
the way of sharks. The gratitude I got for my small
service to little Nelly Moss was almost as striking a
case of unearned guerdon. By the way, it is not often
that common sailors get a testimonial of any sort
(though it is common enough for the captain of clipper
ships and steamers to receive deserved marks of regard
from grateful passengers); indeed, I do not remember
ever hearing of passengers giving a testimonial to either
sailors or stokers, though perhaps those poor fellows
have the hardest work to do in the ship.

After awhile, Mr. Moss, senior, trotted out of the room,
and soon returned leading in Nelly and three or four
other bright, curly-headed little girls and boys, whom
he presented to me in his merry style. They were
lovable children, with very little shyness in their nature,
for they were soon clinging about me as familiarly
as if I were their uncle; so much so indeed, that their
grandfather feared they were becoming tiresome. So
he "hooshed" them all out of the room, as though
they were a lot of intruding chickens; and the rompish
little rogues ran out, laughing and capering with the
happy old gentleman, in a way which showed that
there was no dignified stiffness to stop their familiarity
with him as a playmate. A minute or two afterwards
I looked out of a window, and saw him lying at full
length on the lawn; the children had succeeded in
putting him down, and would not let him get up again.
The sight almost brought tears into my eyes, for it
reminded me of my dear grandfather, who was just

such another merry old man; and though he had been for many years captain of a Greenland whaling ship, he was like a capersome boy when he was amongst his grandchildren, and was always ready to have an innocent romp with us, no matter who was looking at him.

I have sometimes wondered how parents could possibly fondle children that were, to my cold bachelor eyes, unbearable little nuisances; I mean the sort of children that are usually called "mischievous monkeys!" But I suppose it is quite natural for parents to love their own children, whoever else may slight them. I could not wonder at old Mr. Moss being so fond of his little pets, for they were honest-eyed young romps. I would have spent a whole day looking at them sooner than go to see a coronation or a Lord Mayor's show.

I sat for a while chatting pleasantly with Mrs. Moss, who was an amiable lady. She had such an easy, sisterly way of talking to me and of listening to me, that I soon found myself giving her an outline of my colonial history, in which she seemed much interested. She said her husband would be very pleased to see me, and she made me a promise to take tea with them one evening in the ensuing week. I was writing my address on a card at the table, previous to taking my leave, when a sort of wild "corroborree" * outside startled me. Mrs. Moss observed my concern, and said calmly, "It's only the children."

---

* A "corroborree" is a peculiar dance of the Australian aborigines, accompanied with shouting.

I said, "I hope none of them are hurt, ma'am?"

"Oh, no! They are having some fun with grandfather. They are very noisy sometimes; but I am so used to their riot that it seldom disturbs me. I know it is only innocent mirth."

As I walked to my lodgings, I felt thankful for the little accident which had been the means of introducing me to a family who seemed to be the sort of people whose society I should enjoy. Since then I have happily proved that my first impressions of them were correct; and I have had many pleasant opportunities of observing the moral and physical development of their dear little children. I shall have to touch on that subject again presently.

Very lately I saw, in an old copy of the *Christian Treasury*, some verses (by an anonymous author) headed "Only the Children," and they tenderly reminded me of Mrs. Moss's remark, when her merry little group were playing on the lawn years ago. I will take the liberty of copying the verses into my book, and I daresay some loving mother will read them with interest. They always seem to thrill my heart with recollections of dear ones, "whom I have loved long since, and lost awhile."

"ONLY THE CHILDREN."

Beneath a wide-spread tree,
 Which cast a pleasant shade,
Five children, full of mirth and glee,
 One sunny morning played.

Loud were the sounds of merriment
Which o'er that daisied field they sent,
　For theirs were hearts untouched by care,
And eyes that seldom owned a tear.
" What are those sounds," asked one, " I hear?"
" Only the children playing there."

Only the children ! Years have flown
　Since that bright summer's day ;
And they have men and women grown
　Who then were at their play.
The eldest of that little band,
Who threw the ball with skilful hand,
　Who rolled the hoop by far the best,
His country now attempts to guide,
And fashions laws, which, when applied,
　Shall aid and rescue the distressed.

The next, a gay and dashing girl,
　With blue and sparkling eye ;
Whose hair was always out of curl,
　Whose frock was oft awry :
Is now a lady full of grace,
In whom we vainly seek to trace
　The carelessness which marked her youth ;
And to whose gifted pen we owe
Those sweet and simple tales which show
　How lovely is the way of truth.

That rosy boy, so full of fun,
　The first in every game,
Whose ill-learnt task and sums not done,
　Exposed him oft to blame ;
Why, he is quite renowned for knowledge,
Was senior wrangler when at college ;
　And has a world-wide fame attained.
His brother, robed in rustling gown,
Is rector of a country town,
　Which from his labour much has gained.

The youngest, gentle as a dove,
  As sweet as she was fair ;
Who gave her doll such words of love,
  And nursed it with such care ;
Far from the scenes of early life,
Is now a missionary's wife,
  And oft her weary husband cheers.
Together patiently they toil,
And hope to reap, on India's soil,
  The fruit which they have sown in tears.

"Only the children !" Yes, they seem
  But ciphers unto some ;
But I, who often sit and dream
  Of things that are to come,
In children, full of mirth and glee,
Our future generation see;
  Mighty for good or else for ill.
God bless and guide them ! so that they
May scatter blessings on life's way,
  And all His wise behests fufil.

CHAPTER XVI.

> "Oh, many a shaft at random sent,
> Finds mark the archer little meant!
> And many a word at random spoken,
> May soothe or wound a heart that's broken."
>
> —*Scott.*

I HAVE before explained, that soon after my arrival in Australia, I advertised for Mrs. Cameron and her daughter, without receiving an answer. Having tried all other feasible means I could think of, without success, it occurred to me, as a sort of forlorn hope, to advertise again for Ella alone. Accordingly, I sent the following advertisment to each of the daily newspapers: "Ella Cameron will oblige by sending her address to A. X., Post Office, Melbourne." A few days afterwards, to my great comfort, I received a note informing me that Ella Cameron was living at Ivy House, La Trobe Street.

I went to Ivy House at once. I gave my card to a servant, and was shown into a drawing-room. In a few minutes a clerical-looking gentleman entered, and I briefly explained to him that I was the person who had advertised for Miss Cameron's address, and that I particularly wished to see her. He politely bade me take a seat, and said he would see if Miss Cameron was disengaged. He left the room, but soon returned, with Ella herself close behind him. I felt my heart begin to flutter again as I arose and bowed to her. She gave a timid glance at me, and evidently recognised me as the young man who had summoned her downstairs at the restaurant; I could see as much by her significant look at the gentleman, which seemed to say to him, " Pray do not leave me for an instant." The idea struck me that she thought I had some wicked design on her person, or that I was not right in my head, and I felt sorely disconcerted.

She drew herself up with captivating haughtiness, and gave me such a searching look that I had scarcely vigour enough left in me to reply to her question, " Pray, what is your business with me, sir?"

Presently I said, "I wish to have a few minutes' private conversation with you, madam."

She cast an appealing glance at the gentleman, which he understood, for he said promptly, "Miss Cameron very properly declines to have a private interview with a stranger. Will you please to state your errand at once."

The righteousness of my intentions seemed to nerve me again, and I replied proudly, "I have a message from Miss Cameron's late father, but I do not think I am warranted in delivering it in the hearing of a third person."

"Then I must decline to hear it, sir," said Ella. She bowed slightly and left the room.

I felt extremely hurt. After all the trouble I had

taken, and the risk of life and limb that I had encountered in finding poor Cameron's beloved daughter, to be treated with such disrespect and ingratitude by her, was almost too much for me. The gentleman noticed my perturbation, and no doubt he saw that it was honest feeling, for as I was walking towards the door, he put his hand gently on my shoulder and said, "Wait awhile, sir, if you please. Sit down and let me plead for Miss Cameron. I am sure she does not mean to be rude to you ; but—but—there are circumstances connected with her family history, as I daresay you are aware if you knew her father, which cannot fail to cause pain and embarrassment to her sensitive mind. In plain terms, she knows that her father was a bad man."

"Pardon me, sir ; but if Miss Cameron had patiently listened to all I have to tell her of her late father, she would not feel such repugnance at the mention of his name."

"Alas, poor girl! she has heard too much of his profligacy and of his cruelty to her unfortunate mother, for her to feel anything but horror when she hears him spoken of."

"Sir, may I take the liberty of asking your name, and whether you are related to Miss Cameron?"

"My name is Benson. I am a clergyman, as I presume you are aware. I am not related to Miss Cameron ; but she is a member of my church, and she is living in my family as a nursery governess. She has made my wife and myself acquainted with her whole history, and we both sympathize with her very deeply. She is a young lady of superior mind, and she has nobly struggled against a more than ordinary share of difficulties. I esteem her highly for her consistent, Christian principles, and I shall continue to give her my support and protection as long as she needs such help."

I said, "I promised Mr. Cameron when he was dying, that I would, if possible, deliver a certain message from him, with a parcel, to his daughter, personally. I will, therefore, not tell my message to any one except Miss Cameron; but you may say to her, sir, if you please that I can prove to her, by certain evidences, that her father was not a low-minded, profligate man; in fact, I know that he was a gentleman."

Mr. Benson gave his head a dubious shake, and sighed; so I continued, with a little warmth in my tone, "I have no wish to impugn Miss Cameron's mother—far from it—but I ask you, sir, as a man of experience in the world, is it not very easy for a mother who has had the care of her child from the first dawn of its comprehension, to influence the mind of that child in any way she wishes? Miss Cameron has heard her father's character only from her mother's point of view, so it is no wonder to me that she loathes the memory of a man who she has been taught to believe was destitute of all honest feeling."

"You surely will not try to justify Mr. Cameron's cruel conduct in forsaking his wife and young child, and leaving them to struggle on without any help from him whatever?"

"I would not attempt to justify the misdoings of any man, sir. But I need not remind you that it is not safe or just to judge a man's conduct from *ex parte* statements or charges. I have papers that I found in Mr. Cameron's desk, which would give Miss Cameron a more correct idea of her late father than she has obtained through the teaching of her mother. I will leave you my address, sir; and if, on a calmer reflection, Miss Cameron should think it proper to grant me an interview, I shall be glad to wait upon her at her convenience; but if not, I will, with your permission, call here in a day or two and deliver to her, in your presence, a packet of jewellery and some legal documents which her father enjoined me to hand to her personally. I will add, sir, what will surely be comforting to Miss Cameron to know, as she is a religious girl, that I saw her poor father die, trusting on the merits of Christ for salvation."

Mr. Benson said he was delighted to hear that good news; he further said that he and his wife would talk to Ella, and advise her to consent to see me. I then left the house.

I had a nervous headache that night, which kept me awake for several hours. As I lay fidgeting about on my bed, my mind was occupied with disturbing thoughts of my undeserved rebuff that afternoon. If my dear father and mother had turned me out of my old home, and my loving sister had thrown a brick at my head from the attic window, I don't think I could have been more inclined to be broken-hearted than I was at the haughty ingratitude of Ella Cameron; indeed, I was half amazed to feel myself so much hurt at it. My fancy was active, and it took me back through all the perils and discomforts that I had experienced since the night when I first saw John Cameron; and the silly wish that I had never set eyes on him came into my head again and again. I fancied what a vast amount of inconvenience I might have saved myself—including a fractured knee—if I had stopped contentedly in my uncle's shop at Greenwich, instead of wandering over the world, incurring all sorts of risks and wrongs, merely to oblige a dead man—a perfect stranger to me—to find a girl, and give her some jewellery which she would never wear! Then I tried to imagine what I should have said or done if any kind stranger had taken even half as much trouble to find me out and give me a packet of jewels. I felt convinced that I should have shown joy and gratitude, instead of treating that stranger with dignified contempt. In my moody humour it never struck me that, taking the pie-shop incident into consideration, Ella's cool demeanour towards me was not unlike the cautious, maidenly conduct I should have wished my sister to observe towards a stranger under such circumstances. But a man seldom reasons soundly when he is love-sick.

The next morning I was sitting in a back parlour, with a wet compress on my aching head, when a waiter brought me the Rev. John Benson's card, and in another minute that gentleman entered the room.

"I am sorry to see you are looking poorly this morning, Mr. Larksway," said Mr. Benson, after shaking hands with me more cordially than he did the previous day. "I have called to see you in behalf of Miss Cameron; and in the first place let me say, that she wishes me to express her regret for the seeming rudeness to you yesterday. She explained the mistake to me. She has seen you before," continued Mr. Benson, smiling. "I daresay you remember the occasion; and she thought you had called on her yesterday merely for a silly frolic—you understand me? That is all about it in a few words. I hope you will accept this explanation—or apology."

I replied, "Oh, certainly, sir; I accept it gladly—it is very satisfactory." My heart was relieved of a load, and my head felt better immediately. That prompt effect shows me more convincingly than any doctor's book could do it, how tenderly the heart and the head sympathize with each other. It was marvellous!

"And now let me say that Miss Cameron is very anxious to see you, Mr. Larksway. Can you come and take a quiet cup of tea at the parsonage this evening?"

I told him that I should be very happy to do so; and then, after a pleasant chat for a few minutes longer, Mr. Benson took his leave, with the air of a man who had work to do, and a definite way of doing it.

That evening I dressed myself with extra care, and taking poor Cameron's packet under my arm, I set off

for Ivy House. I was very kindly received by Mr. and
Mrs. Benson, and by Ella also, who shook hands with
me almost as warmly as a cousin. I felt there was
gratitude in her gentle pressure. After tea, Mr. Benson
explained that he could not stay any longer with me, for
he had to speak that evening at a public meeting in behalf of a school for the Aborigines. I was pleased to
know that the Victorian public were considerate for the
poor black sons of the soil. Soon after Mr. Benson had
left the house on his errand of justice and mercy, his
wife begged me to excuse her, as she had something to
do in the nursery; so I was left in the parlour with Ella.

I should like the reader to have a fair idea of the
charms of Ella Cameron; but I am not a poet, so I do
not know how to describe perfect beauty. And if I were
to try even to outline her singular graces with my prosy
pen, I should as certainly fail as if I had tried to paint
a flock of king parrots flying half a mile above my
head. I will merely say then, in plain words, that she
was beautiful in face, and her figure—as far as I could
properly judge—was as symmetrical as the finest marble
statue in our Melbourne Gallery of Art. Here let me
briefly remark that that admirable public resort, and the
extensive Free Library adjoining, are institutions of
which the colonists of Victoria may be justly proud.
The benefits they confer are incalculable.

Ella's affable manner encouraged me to talk unrestrain-
edly about the curious coincidence of our meeting at the
restaurant, and how I was struck with the belief that
I had really seen her living face before, when I had only

seen her portrait on ivory. She expressed regret that she had misunderstood my attention to her on that occasion, and especially as it had caused me so much trouble and suffering in my search for her. Although she manifested an interest in my epitome of my travels, I could see that she was desirous of hearing what I had to tell her of her father; so I told the story from my first meeting with him to the moment of his decease, and I gave her his biographical statement to me almost in his own words, only omitting to mention the name of his family, in accordance with his wish. In the course of my recital, I closely observed the varying expression of her features. She had doubtless prepared herself to hear much that was distressing; and when I began, her face showed mental calmness and fortitude. As I proceeded, wonder and pity were severally indicated; but when I described her father's peaceful death, and told her of his devoted love for her and for her misguided mother, her firmness quite gave way, and she wept. I felt such a very strong sympathy for her that I could hardly keep my seat.

We were sitting on opposite sides of the fireplace, silent and sad, when Mrs. Benson returned to the parlour. Her coming in so abruptly just at ten o'clock was prearranged no doubt; and perhaps it was well that she did come in, for my heart at that moment was almost irresistibly prompting me to soothe poor Ella. It is uncertain to me, as I reflect on it now, what course I should have adopted for that kind purpose, and it is possible that I might have been too softly demonstrative in my condolence. Young men cannot always depend on the coolness of their judgment in such circumstances. I was glad that the good pastor's wife did not catch me in any act of brotherly sympathy which might have been misconstrued into something of a less platonic nature. After speaking a few kind words to Ella, Mrs. Benson drew me aside, and suggested that I had better not say any more to the poor girl just then, and she invited me to come again to tea on the morrow.

I dare say millions of young masculine heads have ached over the effort of conjuring up new poetical figures to express the tenderness of their first heart-yearnings for the darling girls of their choice; but I shall take the easier way of explaining to the reader my soft feelings for Ella, by simply saying I was in love with her. Anybody will understand what that means.

CHAPTER XVII.

"So sweetly she bade me adieu,
I thought that she bade me return."
—*Shenstone.*

I SUPPOSE that if every man's courting experience could be fairly written out, it would be seen that there is a distinctive feature in each case, and perhaps as strange a variety of love's manifestations as there is of eyes or noses on the faces of the great human family.

It has been insinuated (I need not say by whom) that I was quite as soft as John Cameron in my love development. But I would appeal from that unfair judgment to all my young manly readers; and let me summarize the leading facts of the case for their impartial re-consideration. First of all then, be it remembered that I was shown the portrait of Ella in a perfectly innocent way, and was told that it was taken when she was about eleven years of age. It was a very pretty picture; and I ask, was it not as natural as winking for a youth of a warm quick fancy to add seven to eleven, and form his ideal of her as a charming, courtable damsel of eighteen summers? Then my interesting commission from her dying father to search through the world till I found her, and my solemn promise to do so, tended to keep her perfect image fresh before my fancy's eye; and how vividly it was impressed there is evident by my quick notice of Ella at the restaurant, instinctively, as it were, picking her out from the ten thousand fine maidens of Melbourne. Furthermore, my long and hazardous search for her, the favourable season for quiet rumination of love thoughts and fancies when I was laid up with a broken leg, together with the proverbial influence of deferred hope. Then the sudden joy of at length finding her, the stimulating effects of her scornful rebuff at first, and our next friendly meeting, the touch of her gentle hand, the gushing of tears from her lovely eyes, her exquisitely tender emotions at my story of her poor father's end, and her look of genuine gratitude at me! Consider all that, my susceptible young male reader, and tell me if you think I was blamably soft in falling in love with Ella! Could anything in life be more reasonable than my doing so?

On the following evening I went to tea at the parsonage. I found Ella sorrowful but composed. After tea I was left in her company, and I gave her a copy of her late father's will, and other documents, from the executor to the will. Then, in the most delicate way I knew of, I told her that I had not expended much more than half of the money which her father left me to pay my expenses, and that what I had left was at her service. She warmly expressed her thanks, but said she did not need money just then, and would not take any from me. She asked me not to divulge the fact of her father having left her any property except his jewellery and added, after a few minutes' pensive cogitation, "I have a special reason for making this strange request, Mr. Larksway. I cannot explain it to you at present but you shall know all about it soon."

 I felt an almost overpowering inclination to take hold of her hands, and implore her to give me a legal liberty to soothe and share every care and sorrow in her heart. I fancied I would willingly be half choked with sorrow for her sake. A war seemed to be stirring up in my breast between prudence and passion, such a conflict as I had never before felt within me, and prudence was getting the worst of it, when Mr. Benson re-entered the room without knocking. I was thankful he did not catch me in the act of making love, which he certainly would have done had he been a minute later. I could see that it had been pre-arranged to shorten my interview with Ella, and I confess I thought they were rather strict with their young governess.

 Mr. Benson chatted with me very cordially, and I gradually calmed down into myself again. I had purposely taken all my testimonials in my pocket, so I showed them to him, and he was much pleased with them, especially those from my dear old pastor and from the organist of our church at Greenwich. He said he should be glad if I would join his church, as he was in want of able singers in his choir. I said I should be delighted to do so if I succeeded in getting employment in Melbourne. Before taking my leave, both Mr. and Mrs. Benson said they should be happy to see me at the parsonage occasionally.

Having now fulfilled the mission which I had specially in view in coming to Australia, or having done as much of it as I could, for the time being, I began to think seriously about getting a situation ; for pleasant as it may seem to have one's liberty to roam about without restraint, it leaves a reacting influence on the mind of any young man who has an ambition to rise in the world. So long as my object in finding Ella was unattained, I felt that I was rightly employing my time in searching for her ; but having found her, I could no longer spend a sort of listless life without uneasiness of body and mind. " Pleasure is the reflux of unimpeded energy." So says Sir W. Hamilton. I never heard of any good authority saying that there was either pleasure or profit in a life of indolence.

I did not wait for a situation that was exactly to my liking, but took the first one that offered, which was as clerk to a corn merchant in Flinders Lane. The work was new to me, but I was always willing to learn. Mr. Hazelton was a good man—perhaps rather too good to make money in those times, when competition in his line was ruinously active, and when the banks gave such liberal encouragement to bold speculators and kite-flying schemers. He was conscientious to a fault—at least, some of his neighbours said so ; but for my part, I never could see any fault in a man being scrupulously upright in all his dealings. I dare say Mr. Hazelton lost a chance customer now and then while he was conducting religious services in the upper floor of his store with all his employés, and he perhaps suffered loss occasionally through petty thieves, who robbed his lower store while he was praying upstairs; but for all that, he continued his practice of having prayers every morning before beginning the business of the day. Some of his trading neighbours, who were too busy to pray at any time, looked upon it as a mere whim or crochet of his, indicating weakness of character; but Mr. Hazelton said he was sure it was right to ask for Divine aid in anything that it was right to do, and if he were seemingly a loser by the practice just now, he knew he should be a gainer in the long run. He certainly had a long run of mercantile losses and crosses; still, he stuck to his old system of shaping his course by the Bible chart all the time he was in business in Melbourne.

I should have mentioned before that I accepted an invitation to tea from Mr. and Mrs. Moss, and enjoyed a pleasant evening in their little family circle. I found that though Grandfather Moss could be as frolicsome as a kitten when he was playing with his lively grandchildren, he was merry and wise, for he could be sedate enough when it was a time to be thoughtful. I got many sensible hints from him, which were calculated to be helpful to me as a young colonist; and if I had since then paid more practical heed to his counsel, I should perhaps be an independent man to-day. Mr. Moss, junior, was a thriving merchant in Melbourne, and an active worker in public affairs of a benevolent character. He was exceedingly kind and hospitable to me. He alluded more frequently than I wished to the service I had rendered him in saving the life of his beloved child;

indeed, I have seldom seen so much real gratitude as that whole family displayed for what was after all a simple act of duty on my part. Mr. Moss applauded me for taking the first situation I could get, rather than be idle; but he advised me, as I had learnt a business, to keep to it; and he added, "You may have a shop of your own by-and-by, Mr. Larksway. I do not see why not, for you seem to possess the essential qualities of a successful man."

I thanked him and felt encouraged, for he was a man whose good judgment was pretty generally confided in. He promised to use his influence to get me a situation in my own line; nor did he forget his promise, as some friends are apt to do, for about three weeks afterwards, through his recommendation, I was engaged by Mr. Cudbear, the well-known chemist and druggist, as his assistant, at a salary of £150 a year, with board and lodging.

That was three times as much salary as I received when in my uncle's service, so I reasonably considered that I was making progress in the world, and that thus far this new land was better to me than the old one. Most spirited youths have had secret longings for a married life. It is quite natural, so I need not be ashamed to own that even as early as my twentieth year I used now and then to think how pleasant it would be to have a wife, and a nice little home with a flower garden in front, and some cabbages, etc., and a fowl-house at the back. I was not really extravagant in my ideas of housekeeping, and I used to think that

£150 a year would keep me and a tidy, careful wife very comfortably. It was merely a boyish speculation, for I had then no prospect of receiving such an income, nor had I seen a girl I really cared for, except perhaps Laura Cleff; but she was too musical for me—that is to say, she studied music to the neglect of domestic duties. I should certainly like my wife to be fond of music, but I should like her to be capable of directing her servants in the house work, or of doing the housework herself if circumstances should change with us so that we could not afford to keep a servant. I don't think I could enjoy music in an untidy house. Now that I had a salary of £150 a year, and more than £200 in the bank, and I knew and loved a girl who I believed was in every way calculated to make me a good wife, and withal, that I had arrived at a fair marriageable age, it was rational for me to decide to get married as soon as I could. I was sorry I could not consult my parents before taking such an important step; but as that was impracticable, I took another week to deliberate over it, and then having made up my mind that I thoroughly loved Ella Cameron, I wrote her a letter to tell her so.

For three days afterwards I watched for the postman almost as anxiously as any shipwrecked sailor ever watched for a sail from his lonely perch on a bare rock in the ocean. I trust I made up my prescriptions all right, but in some of my gloomy seasons I have had distressing doubts if it really were ice-creams and cucumber that took poor old Mrs. Dunn off so suddenly. On the fourth morning, to my great relief, I received a letter from Ella. It was short and polite, but not loving. However, it gave me an invitation to tea at Mr. Benson's that evening, so I argued down my fears, and gave my hope all the encouragement I could think of. That seemed a very long day to me—all the longer because there was not much business doing. My master gave me liberty for the evening, and punctually at the time appointed I was at the parsonage, attired with befitting neatness, and carrying a basket of cherries and some sugar-plums as presents to the little Bensons. I thought it was wise policy to get in favour with them, for they were Ella's pupils, and they would perhaps talk kindly of me in her hearing.

When Ella entered the drawing-room, I thought she looked pale; at which I was rather cheered, for it seemed to explain the reason why she had kept me waiting so long for an answer to my letter. She had evidently been unwell since I last saw her. She received me kindly, but with embarrassment, which I further interpreted to my comfort; for I mentally argued that girls of the right sort are usually embarrassed at such critical times. Presently Mr. and Mrs. Benson came into the room, and soon afterwards the tea bell rang, so we all went into the parlour. Ella was silent at the tea table, but Mr. Benson was unusually chatty, so she had not a chance to say much if she had been disposed to talk. He said he was glad to know that I had a permanent situation, but he wished that I had found one in a wholesale drug house, for then I might have been able to spend my Sundays profitably.

"Sunday work is the most objectionable part of my occupation, sir," I replied. "My working hours every day are slavishly long. Ours is the double eight hours system. Then the night-bell is a cruel disturber of my short slumbers; besides, it is often rung by practical jokers, who seem to think it is fun to summons a weary fellow from his bed down to the shop door to be made a fool of. However, those are miseries which long experience has taught me to put up with composedly; but my Sunday work in Melbourne really makes me irritable. My good uncle always kept one of his assistants at home on Sundays to make up prescriptions, or to sell any medicines that were urgently needed; but on no account would he allow perfumery or hair oil, or any similar article of trumpery trade, to be sold for love or money."

"Your uncle was quite right," said Mr. Benson; "I commend him for his generous consideration for his employés and his respect for the Lord's day."

"Yes, sir; and I honour him for it. I wish my present master, and every other retail chemist in this city, would adopt my uncle's plan in that respect; they might easily do it if they had the will, and it would be a great relief to their assistants. I assure you that Sunday morning is quite a busy time in our shop, selling soda-water and drunkard's draughts, called 'pick-me-up,' besides many little fancy trifles from the glass cases on the counter; trifles which reasonable customers would have bought on Saturday night, or that they might well wait for till Monday morning. I never object to make up prescriptions on a Sunday—that I call a work of necessity or mercy—but the other sort of traffic I do thoroughly abhor. If I ever have a shop of my own, I will adopt my good uncle's plan, and I am sure I shall not lose by it in the end."

"I like to hear you talk so sensibly on that subject, Mr. Larksway. I am grieved more than I can express to see so much unnecessary trafficking in this great city on Sundays; and my mind is often disturbed as I am going into my pulpit, by the sound of carriage and cab wheels, bringing members of my congregation to church, some of whom are as well able to walk there as I am myself."

Soon after the tea was over, Ella asked me if I would be kind enough to step with her into the drawing-room. Of course I said I would do so with much pleasure. I felt that I was blushing all over, but neither Mr. nor Mrs. Benson seemed to notice it. I could tell that it had been prearranged by them for Ella to give me a private interview, and I felt grateful for their confidence and their delicate consideration.

We entered the drawing-room, and I shut the door. Ella then sat down in an arm chair and wept like a child. My inexperience misled me for awhile, and I thought her tears sprung from joyous, maidenly emotions. I had often heard of a girl weeping even on her wedding morning! I stepped up to her and gently strove to remove her hands from before her face, and I uttered a few tender words; I forget what I said— but 'tis no matter. I felt intensely disposed to kiss her sweet quivering lips; but before I could make bold to do so, she partially recovered herself, and said pensively, as she pointed to a chair on the opposite side of the fireplace,—

"Mr. Larksway, please to take a seat; I am going to speak to you confidentially. I received your kind note four days ago. I should have replied to it immediately, but at the advice of my dear friends, Mr. and Mrs. Benson, I waited till I was sufficiently calm to see you personally, and fully explain my unhappy position. You have been a kind friend to me. I cannot express the comfort you have afforded my heart in——"

"Dearest girl!" I interposed, as I arose in a rapture of soft feeling; "your words overpower me with happiness!"

"Pray sit down and listen to me, Mr. Larksway," she said mournfully. "I have a painful story to tell you. I was about to say that the good news you brought me respecting the peaceful end of my poor father has given me much comfort. I shall ever be deeply grateful to you for the trouble you have taken on my behalf. I feel that I can safely tell you of all my trials, and I will make an effort to do so."

"Tell me everything, my sweet Ella! Tell me all, and let me share your sorrows and your joys for life,—in short, let me call you my wife!" I said that with real feeling, and again I started up and was stepping towards her with a delicately loving motive, when she said,—

'Stop! Do pray stop, Mr. Larksway! Sit down again, sir, and hear what I have to tell you. I am married!"

By a desperate effort I stifled a groan that struggled for vent; and I sat down again a blighted man. All my fondly cherished pictures of domestic bliss faded away like dissolving views, and my life's prospects seemed to be blocked up by a dismal high wall of bluestone, which my hope could not even peep over. Never shall I forget the smarting influence of those three words, "I am married!" Three buckshots in my legs could not have hurt me so much, or—in a metaphorical sense—so effectually have knocked me down. How long we sat in mournful silence I cannot remember. Ella was the first to speak, and she said, in tones which showed the depth of her sympathy,—

"I am sorry indeed, for your sake, Mr. Larksway, that I did not explain my unhappy position to you at our first interview; but I had no idea that you were becoming so fondly attached to me. I have suffered much on your account since I received your expressive letter. You have taken a deal of trouble to fulfil my dear father's dying request, and I feel grieved that I should unwittingly cause you so much distress. But do not reproach me, Mr. Larksway!"

"My dear madam," I replied with emotion, "far be it from me to reproach you. Believe me, that though your disclosure is an unexpected blow to my happiness, I am still your true friend, and I shall ever remain such. Pray tell me all you wish me to know of your affairs, and if I can in any way help you, I will do it with brotherly goodwill."

"Thank you! thank you! my generous friend! I am truly grateful. But I feel unable to tell you my sorrowful story to-night, for the trouble I see you are suffering unnerves me. If you can conveniently come here on some other evening, I shall esteem it an additional obligation."

I promised to come the next evening; and after asking Ella to excuse me to Mr. and Mrs. Benson for leaving their house without seeing them again, I shook hands with her, and walked homeward at a funereal pace.

Our shop was not shut up, so I went behind the counter. There, on the shelves around me, were drugs of various kinds, which I knew would procure me a temporary oblivion from my overwhelming love-sickness; and for the first time in my life I was possessed with an almost irresistible desire for some powerful stimulant or opiate, which would deaden my sense of present misery. I had had some experience, in the trade in Melbourne, of compounding stimulating or steadying draughts for a few regular morning customers; besides, I had often seen my late tippling shopmate, Mackay, mix up a strong dose for himself, when it was not practicable for him to run out to the public house for his more favourite dram of whisky. My hand was on a bottle labelled "Laudanum," when a warning voice from the dead seemed to whisper in my ears, and by a strong effort of will I restrained my craving for the stupefying draught. It was a hard struggle, but I conquered.

My late beloved father had often cautioned me against encouraging the first morbid desire for any kind of intoxicant, which might grow by use into a confirmed habit, and would soon tyrannize over all my powers of body and mind. His timely counsel has hitherto saved me from acquiring habits by which I see so many men around me, old and young, hopelessly enslaved. I went to bed that night depressed beyond all former experience, but I did not seek to get temporary relief at the cost of a debilitating reaction the next day.

Sleep quite forsook my eyelids that night. There I lay, puffing the teasing mosquitoes off my nose, and brooding over my hopeless attachment until my brain seemed to be shrivelling up, like passion-fruit blasted by hot winds. Soon after the post-office clock struck three, I heard loud shouts of "Fire!" and our night bell was pulled by an impatient hand. I sprang out of bed, and at once saw that a grocery store adjoining our shop was blazing furiously. I soon slipped into my clothes; but before I could get downstairs, an excited mob had forced our shop door open, and were carrying out the goods with more haste than care. Flurried as I was, I could see that our stock, which the salvors were flinging pell-mell into the road, would be almost useless to us, if it was not all stolen, and that it would be wiser to let the bottles and jars remain on the shelves and take their chance, as our shop was not actually on fire. So I managed to barricade our doorway up; and, armed with a revolver (which was not loaded), I stood sentry outside, and scared the crowd off with my warlike antics, until the brigade inspector arrived. In an hour or two the fire was put out, without injuring our premises beyond blistering the paint on the shutters and cracking our show lamp.

That was a timely blaze for me, whoever lost by it, for it afforded me something to think of distinct from my own personal troubles; and I have since fancied that it saved my brain from getting "crazed with care" on that memorable night. I do not mean to say that to afford excitement enough to chase away one's sombre reflections, or blighted love throes, a neighbour's shop should catch fire,—that would be an atrocious sentiment, akin to incendiarism; but I do experimentally affirm, that active occupation of some kind is one of the best things in the world for diverting one's mind from distressing subjects, which, in harmony with the general laws of cause and effect, gather strength from being fostered.

I was very unpopular with the noisy rabble outside for an hour or two; but it did not trouble me much, for I know that it is natural for rogues to hate any one who tries to keep them from picking and stealing. They hooted and howled at me like cannibals all the while I was getting our stock back into the shop; and a ferocious-looking sailor proposed that they should catch me, and make me swallow a bottle of horse-physic.

CHAPTER XVIII.

"We bear it calmly through a ponderous woe,
And still adore the hand that gives the blow."
—*Pomfret.*

ONE of the Melbourne newspapers, in its report of the fire, commented very nicely on my sagacity and courage in protecting my master's property from the ravages of unauthorized salvors. I was pleased, as most men are when their efforts to do good are rightly estimated; but my gladness was soon afterwards extinguished when I read the report of another daily paper, which harshly condemned my conduct in firing off the six barrels of my revolver over the heads of the mob, and endangering the lives of some young ladies at an attic window of the house over the way. I was grieved at such flagrant misrepresentation. The mute evidence of my pistol convinced the inspector of police that I was innocent of the charge of firing it off, for its rusty condition proved that it had not been loaded for several months. Still, the false report had gone far and wide, in perhaps twenty thousand broadsheets, one of which might possibly reach my parents' eyes, and make them fear that I was savagely altered since I left home. A pushing young lawyer wanted me to begin an action for libel; but when I got over my vexation, I declined to go to law, and took the softer course of writing a polite explanatory letter to the erring editor, which he inserted in the next day's issue of his paper, and I was pacified.

My master lived at Boroondarra. When he came to business the next day, he found his shop in disorder, and myself and all the other employés busily putting it to rights. As I was the only assistant who slept on the premises, I had to give Mr. Cudbear all the particulars of the disaster. But he did not even look thankful to me for my exertions in saving his premises from being destroyed. From the peculiar tone in which he remarked to the senior assistant that he would have altered his shop-front if he had been burnt out, I judged that he was well insured.

That evening I went again to the parsonage, according to promise; but I would rather have stayed at home. On my way there I found myself encouraging, for a minute or two, a burning jealousy for Ella's husband, though I had no idea who he was or where he lived. I feel shame in making this confession, but I wish to be candid. If Morton had ran away with all my personal effects, and with my sister Emmy as well, I could hardly have felt a stronger grudge against the young man; I think I would have turned the handle of a machine to half skin him. Of course I soon scouted such wicked thoughts.

After tea, Ella again asked me to walk into the drawing room with her. She seemed more composed than she was on the previous night. She sat down in an easy chair, and I modestly took the chair opposite to her, and tried to look calm, though my heart was sadly ruffled. It took her some minutes to conquer a rising emotion; at length she said, in a low but sweetly clear voice,—

"I will be as brief as possible with my disclosures, Mr. Larksway; but I fear I shall overtax your forbearance. My earliest history you are already acquainted with. I have but a faint remembrance of my life in New Zealand. I think I was about six years of age when my mother returned with me to Sydney. Soon afterwards she went to live at Illawarra. The farm we lived on was then two miles from any school; and I should probably have been as untaught as many neglected children on this great continent are, but for the disinterested kindness of a good woman who lived on a farm adjoining ours. She had two little girls of her own; and as the public school was too far off to send them to it, she taught them at home, and she offered to teach me at the same time. My mother did not object to it, so I went to Mrs. Bell's house every day. Though not a well-educated woman, she had a happy way of imparting what she did know to young minds, and I learned from her the elements of a plain education, also to comprehend and prize the Bible, and to shape my life by its holy precepts. I shudder when I reflect what my moral character might have been to-day, if dear Mrs. Bell had not pitied my forlorn condition, and taken me under her training. I always picture myself when

I see a poor, neglected little girl in the street. My heart yearns to take her into my charge, and teach her the right way of life from the wrong one, and perhaps save her from drifting into the way that leads to ruin. If I could devote my life's energies to work of that kind, Mr. Larksway, I think I should be happy.

"Mrs. Bell used to take her own children and me in a cart to a Sunday-school; and there a good minister took notice of me, and became a real friend to me. When I grew old enough to know the immorality of my unfortunate mother's way of life, I became very unhappy about it. Many times I implored her to leave the man with whom she was living. But my entreaties were all disregarded, and I was cruelly treated for presuming to offer advice. When I was a little over fifteen years of age, my mother wished me to encourage the visits of a young man of a low, profligate character, who wanted to marry me. I repelled him in disgust, for which I was subjected to a persecution too painful for me to relate. When nearly driven to despair, I sought the protection of the kind minister, whom I before mentioned. At his advice, and through his pecuniary help, I went to Sydney, and was hospitably received into the family of a respectable mechanic, who had formerly lived near Wollongong. I soon got a situation as assistant in a confectioner's shop; but the young man I have alluded to found me out, and renewed his hateful overtures. I refused to speak to him, and he threatened my life. I dreaded violence from him, so I wrote to my good friend the minister for his advice and aid. He immediately came to Sydney to see me ; and in order that I might live more privately, he got me a situation as pupil teacher in a ladies' school. For more than two years I lived there in quietude. My mistress was very considerate to me, and I acquired a sound English education, and some little knowledge of what are called the accomplishments. I studied hard, in the hope of qualifying myself for taking a situation as governess in the far bush. But that project was frustrated and my peace was again disturbed by the young man—my loathsome admirer. I somehow learned that he had been in jail for two years ; but soon after his release, he renewed his persecution to me, both by letter and by calling personally at the school where I was engaged. To avoid him, I determined to go to Melbourne. It seemed a desperate course, for I knew no person th're ; but I hoped that by being far away from the scenes and connections of my early life, I should have a better chance of living quietly, and earning a respectable livelihood. The secret of my purpose I entrusted to the mechanic and his wife, whose house I first went to in Sydney. They had a brother in Melbourne, whom they wrote to in my behalf. He was a cabinet-maker in Lonsdale Street—a reputable tradesman and a member of Mr. Benson's Church. He met me at the steamer on my arrival at Melbourne, and took me to his house. Both he and his good wife treated me as affectionately as if I were their own daughter. I was anxious to be employed, for I did not like to be burdensome to them ; so I took the first situation that offered, which was at the restaurant where you first saw me. I was in that place only a few weeks, for the duties of a waitress did not suit me, or I was not expert enough for them. Though perhaps the majority of the daily customers in the dining saloon were gentlemen, and knew how to behave with dignified civility to a servant, the manners of some of the men who came there were not at all times decorous, and I could not endure their jocular familiarity. After the dinner hour, I usually had to retire to my room suffering from severe headache, caused by nervous excitement. Most of the young ladies there misunderstood me: they thought my reserved manner was pride, and that my extreme nervousness was affectation. Many cutting remarks were made, which were meant for me to overhear. I thought if those girls only knew the sadness of my heart, every one of them would have pitied me; but I had not courage to make a confidante of either of them. At length I left the place, and went to serve in a confectioner's shop in Collins Street.

"You see, Mr. Larksway, I have hurried over my history—have given you but the bare outlines of several eventful years," said Ella, with a sigh. "But now comes the most painful part of my story. I fear I shall weary you with my troubles; and it is perhaps wrong for me to intrude so much upon your time."

Poor Ella's forced composure here quite failed her, and an uncontrollable fit of grief checked her utterance for awhile. I said, feelingly, "My dear madam, let me persuade you to defer any further disclosure until some other time; I see that it is causing you much distress, and on that account it pains me to listen to you. You are looking ill; shall I call in Mrs. Benson?"

"No, pray do not call her, sir; she is with her sick infant. I have already given Mrs. and Mr. Benson much trouble with my affairs. I will finish my sad story to-night, if you will kindly listen. When I have told you all, my mind will be more composed."

She sat for a few minutes as if trying to collect her thoughts, and then she said, "Amongst the daily customers at the dining-saloon, when I lived there, was a young man who usually came in by himself, later than the first rush of guests. He never seemed in hot haste, and he always took his hat off before he sat at the table. Those little marks of refined manners did not escape my notice, and I concluded that he was a gentleman. I soon observed that he invariably gave his orders to me, and I liked to wait on him, for he was polite, and he never rudely joked with me, as some of the other guests did. I often thought to myself, that young man has sisters. He was genteel in appearance, but I need not further describe his exterior: I will show you his portrait presently. One day, as he was leaving the table, he took a beautiful white camellia from his coat and put it into my hand. That act was noticed by some of the girls in the saloon, and I was much teased about it. From that time I avoided waiting on him. Soon afterwards I left the restaurant and went to serve in a confectioner's shop in Collins Street. About three days after I had been in that place, the same young gentleman came in at lunch-time, and asked me for a cup of chocolate and some pastry. He bowed politely when he saw me. For several weeks he came every day to lunch. He did not speak much to me, and he never offered me another flower; but I could tell, from various signs which I cannot explain in words, that he was rather partial to me. It was but natural for me to feel a growing respect for a person who behaved towards me with such uniform gentlemanlike civility; but I never, either by word or look, wittingly encouraged him to show me attention. I was naturally distrustful of the advances of strangers. One evening he accosted me in the street, as I was going to my home in Lonsdale Street; but I went on my way without speaking, and he did not follow me. That is the course I usually adopt if I am spoken to in the street by a stranger, and I think it is the safest way for an unprotected girl to act.

"The next day the same gentleman put a letter in my hand as he was paying me for his luncheon, and he immediately left the shop. I did not venture to open it until I went home, and then I found that it was a declaration of love and an offer of marriage. I showed the letter to my friends, Mr. and Mrs. Flitch. After some consideration, they advised me to write Mr. Morton (that is his name) and invite him to their house, and they would afterwards give me their opinion of him. I took another day to deliberate over it, and then I followed their advice.

"The ensuing evening, when I returned home, Mr. Morton was there conversing with Mr. Flitch. He stayed till a late hour. Before he went, I promised to give him an answer to his letter in a day or two. I need not go into particulars; it is enough to say that my own inclination and the opinions of my friends coincided. Mr. Morton told us that he was a clerk in the —— Bank, in Melbourne; that his salary was £250 a year, with a prospect of a rise, and that he had some valuable mining shares. Moreover, he told us that he left a bank in London three years before. From documents he produced, it appeared that his family connections in England were respectable; he said he had no relations in the colony. He invited Mr. Flitch to call at —— Bank and make any inquiries he chose as to his character. The next day Mr. Flitch called at the bank, and the manager's report was satisfactory. My friends both congratulated me on the good match I had a chance of making. Can it be wondered at that I felt elated at the prospect, poor and helpless as I was? I thought it would be nice to have a comfortable home of my own, and some one to protect me. I disliked serving in a shop, and I could see no chance of getting a situation as governess, for I was not thoroughly qualified. I confess that I did not feel the warmth of attachment that I had always thought I ought to feel for the man I married; but I expected that my love would grow on a better acquaintance with him. Briefly let me tell it: I accepted him, and after five weeks' courtship, we were married by the Rev. Mr. Benson, at the house of Mr. and Mrs. Flitch. We spent a week at Geelong, and then went to live at Emerald Hill, in a rather stylish cottage, which had been furnished for us by an upholsterer in Melbourne, far more extravagantly than I could have allowed if I had been consulted in time.

"For several weeks we lived very harmoniously. The only disquietude I felt was on account of my husband's reluctance to accompany me to church, and his entire disregard to the sanctity of the Sabbath. Sunday, indeed, was a day of feasting in our house. I did not at first object to a little extra cooking, because it was the only day that he could dine at home; but after a time it became my regular task to provide dinner for four or five of his bachelor friends. I then ventured to tell him the difficulty I had in persuading our servant-girl to do so much work on Sundays, and I hinted that those dinner-parties very much increased our housekeeping expenses; for our guests drank an immoderate quantity of wine. My husband replied kindly, that he really did not wish to keep so much company, but he was afraid to appear shabby to his old friends now that he had a house of his own. He meant, however, 'to turn over a new leaf' very soon. As to our house expenses, he said, I need not be uneasy about them, for he expected his mining shares would very shortly turn him in dividends, which would treble his income. I felt relieved, and then I took courage to say, in the most gentle way I could, that it would so much add to my peace and happiness if he would go to church with me on Sundays. At that he looked sorrowful, and then he confessed to me, that previous to his coming to this colony, he was a member of a Church and a Sabbath-school teacher, and that his father and mother and sisters were all religious. He also said that after his arrival in Melbourne he had been tempted to neglect his religious duties, and at length, he added with a sigh, 'I have become a complete infidel. Oh, dear! it is terribly true that "Evil communications corrupt good manners," but I mean to reform, Ella, and I want you to help me to do it. I shall gradually cut off all my gambling acquaintances; that is the first step for me. I made a grand effort to do so four months ago, and for a while I was very steady; but my tempters have made a dead set at me lately, and they have proved too many for me. Cheer up, dear Ella! I will make another solemn resolution very soon, and you shall see that I have some manly firmness left.'

"I cannot tell you how comforted I felt, Mr. Larksway; but I grieve now that I did not say more to him just then, that I did not press him to begin to reform at once, and tell him that the only way he could keep right was by beseeching Christ to help him. Poor fellow! I believe he meant to do all he said, but he put it off till it was too late.

"We had been married about ten weeks, when I remarked that at times he looked exceedingly depressed, and I was sure that something was preying on his mind. My nervous fancy suggested that he was disappointed in me, and I became unhappy. At length I ventured to tell him what I feared, and then he said that the cause of his depression was temporary embarrassment in money matters; that in anticipation of realizing largely from his mining shares, he had incurred liabilities, some of which were pressing. Then for the first time I knew that our household furniture was all bought on credit. I am sure you are pitying me, Mr. Larksway, but you have not yet heard the saddest part of my disclosure.

"For a fortnight or more after that, my husband was absent from home every evening; sometimes it was past midnight before he came. He told me that it was a busy season with the bank, and that he had to work overtime. I was pacified; still, I used to feel very lonely. One night—I never shall forget it—he did not return; but just before daybreak next morning he came home, looking so haggard and excited that I became alarmed, and was going to rush away for a doctor. He begged me to be still and listen to him. He was compelled, he said, by urgent business in behalf of the bank, to go away for a week. He could not stop to explain more, but would write me particulars as soon as possible. He did not stay quite ten minutes. After hastily thrusting a few articles of clothing into a valise, he kissed me fondly, and fled away by our back garden gateway. I will not try to describe my agonising distress, nor my horror half an hour afterwards, when two detective officers entered our house, with a warrant to apprehend my husband on a charge of embezzlement and forgery."

Poor Mrs. Morton here became so much overpowered with emotion that I went into the parlour and fetched Mr. Benson. He quite concurred with me that it would be unwise to allow Ella to say any more about her sad affairs just then; and we prevailed upon her to retire to her bedroom. Soon afterwards I took my leave, after accepting Mr. Benson's invitation to tea on the ensuing Monday evening.

CHAPTER XIX.

"This is the truth the poet sings,
That a sorrow's crown of sorrow, is remembering happier things."
—*Tennyson.*

THE next Sunday morning it was my turn out, so I went to Mr. Benson's church. Ella was there, with Mrs. Benson and the children. I could see them, but they could not see me; for I sat on the opposite side of the floor, behind one of those heavy gothic pillars which are so convenient for shy sinners and flirting couples. Though I tried to tone my mind down to a devotional frame, my eyes were constantly wandering from my book to the minister's pew, where sat poor Ella, looking pale and careworn, but sweetly composed and devotional.

Mr. Benson preached with great energy; but I might as well have been at home for any profit I derived from the sermon. I was thinking all the while how happy I might have been on that bright Sabbath morning, with dear Ella sitting beside me as my wife, if I had only had common sense enough when I first saw her at the restaurant, to ask her name in a civil, manly way, instead of assuming a jocose simper, and asking her if she came from Greenwich, making her fancy that I was some impudent booby beginning to flirt with her; for poor girl! she had never been to Greenwich, and perhaps did not know that there was such a place under the sun. Thus, through assuming a fast man's affected style for once, I had lost my chance of getting an amiable wife, I had spent more than £200 unnecessarily, and I had fractured my knee! moreover, I had wasted more than a year of my life in a sort of wild-goose chase, and, worse than all, I felt that I had overburdened my heart with hopeless love. Then I thought of Ella's noble struggle against vicious and degrading influences, which had beset her from her childhood, and I thought of her persevering efforts to secure mental and moral culture; of her struggles for an honest livelihood, and of her Christian-like stand against the temptations and dangers to which her personal beauty and her unprotected condition constantly exposed her in the gay city of Melbourne. I thought also of her more recent trials, most of which I might have saved her from if I had only used my wits for a single minute.

Although my conscience sternly reminded me that to encourage such mundane reflections in church was a waste of time and opportunity, I still kept turning them over in my mind, until I became as wretched as if I were going to be tried that afternoon for poisoning a customer. A more miserable sinner than I was on that fine Sunday morning never sat in a church pew. When I went home, I could not eat my dinner, and I lay on my bed all the afternoon, nursing my woe as if it deserved tender consideration.

On Monday evening I again went to the parsonage. After tea I retired to the drawing-room with Ella; and without much preliminary talk she resumed her sad story, as follows:—

"I told you that the detective officers came to our house, Mr. Larksway. They did not stay many minutes. I honestly answered all the questions they put to me, but I could not give them much information. I did not know where my husband had fled; if I had known, I should perhaps have gone after him, and that would have been a rash step. Soon after the detectives had gone, a gentleman called on me, who said he was a friend of my husband and a lawyer, and that he wished to help me. I cannot remember all he said, for my brain was almost distracted. I thought I should have gone mad. He advised me to keep possession of the house, and not to allow any one to enter it to seize my furniture; but I did not follow his advice, for I knew the furniture was not honestly mine. That same afternoon I gave up possession to some official, who I think was sent from the bank. I took with me only two trunks containing my own wearing apparel, and I went in a cab to my friends, Mr. and Mrs. Flitch, who received me as affectionately as ever. I was dangerously ill for a fortnight; but thanks to their kind nursing, I recovered. Sometimes I have wished that I had died then, but that was a sinful wish. I have since learned the only true way to find resignation and comfort in every time of need. When I got well, the Rev. Mr. Benson offered to take me into his family as a nursery governess. I gladly accepted the situation, and I have lived here ever since."

"Have you had any tidings of your unfortunate husband since he left you?" I asked, feelingly.

"Yes, sir, I have. A fortnight ago I received this letter. It was written on board ship. I cannot read it to you now; but you may take it with you if you please, and read it at your leisure. You will find a photograph of my husband in the envelope. It was taken before our marriage."

Ella handed me the letter, which I put into my pocket. I then said, "I hope Mr. Morton was well when he wrote to you, ma'am?"

"Yes, he was pretty well in health, Mr. Larksway; but poor fellow! he seemed to be in great distress of mind, as you will judge by his letter. He was on his way to Fiji when he wrote to me; and I suppose he is there now. But what he will do there I cannot tell, for he has taken very little money with him—if he has taken any. When you first told me that my late dear father had left me a section of land in this colony, I thought of selling it and paying off my husband's debts, so that he might return to Melbourne safely. But Mr. Benson tells me that the bank directors cannot lawfully receive repayment of the money which my husband got from them by forgery and embezzlement, and let him go free from the legal penalties of his dishonesty. I am now thinking of selling my land, and going to Fiji to search for my husband. If I find him, we may be able to go together to California; and there—where his misdoings will not be known—he may retrieve his position; for he has good ability, and I verily believe that when away from the influence of the unprincipled associates he had in Melbourne, he will be steady and honest."

"May I ask you, Mrs. Morton, if Mr. Benson approves of your design in going to Fiji to look for your husband?"

"I have not yet told Mr. Benson all my plans. I do not like to trouble him, for he has overmuch work to do."

"It seems to me a very hazardous undertaking for you, my dear madam."

"I know it is, Mr. Larksway. It is hazardous and very uncertain; for I have no idea what part of Fiji my husband is in, and many parts of it, I am told, are quite uncivilized. Still, I am willing to incur any risk if I can help him, poor fellow! The Melbourne newspapers have printed many harsh things about him since he absconded, which have pained me excessively. I know that he is deserving of censure and of punishment, but I also know that he is not thoroughly debased. He has some good principle left. He may be saved from utter ruin, and I will try to save him. Though he is forsaken and despised by persons who once seemed proud to call him their friend, I will never forsake him. Sadly as he has misconducted himself, he is my husband, and I will act a true wife's part."

Poor Ella again began to weep. I did not know what to say to comfort her, so I sat still and said nothing. I was glad when Mrs. Benson came into the room. Soon afterwards I left the house, in a very sorrowful mood.

When I went to my bedroom, I sat down to peruse Morton's letter; but first of all I looked at his photograph, and as I did so a wild, fiery feeling seemed to stir up again in my breast. I had the picture of a fine-looking young man before me, but my prejudiced eyes could not see any feature to admire. I flung the photograph on the table and read his letter, as follows :—

"MY DARLING ELLA,—
"Words cannot convey to you a conception of the misery I have endured since the morning when I tore myself from you so abruptly. I could not stop to explain anything to you, and it is a bitter reflection that my last words to you were falsehoods. You have doubtless since heard much to my dishonour. The only gleam of comfort I feel springs from the hope that you will not judge me too harshly. I own that I have heinously transgressed, —have brought disgrace upon myself and you. I am a criminal and an outcast, fleeing I scarcely know whither, from the hands of justice. Would that I could escape from the stings of an upbraiding conscience!

"Let me tell you, my much-injured wife, a little more than you know about my unhappy history. Every word that I now write is strictly true. I have before told you, that in my parental home I was taught all that was virtuous and good, both by precept and example. The testimonials which you have seen in my desk will prove that my character was highly esteemed by the minister of my church, and by the manager of the bank in London where I was employed for several years.

"I voyaged to Melbourne in a large steamer. There were nearly five hundred passengers; many of them young men, and some of them very unsteady. There I first acquired a taste for gambling, and for conversation which was worse than frivolous. Immediately after my arrival at Melbourne, I went to the —— bank. I had a kind of letter of introduction to Rev. Mr. H——, but I regret to say I did not deliver it. You may find it in my desk. My irregularities on shipboard had deadened my religious feelings, and the influence of some of my profligate companions inclined me to scepticism. I lodged in the same house with four young men, who were perhaps more vicious than myself; and I became a confirmed Sabbath-breaker and a midnight reveller. I do not know whether the managers or any of the directors of my bank knew of my unsteady habits, but if they did, they never spoke to me on the subject. Perhaps they thought they had no right to interfere with my doings out of the office, as I did my work satisfactorily. A few kindly words of advice might have saved me; but no person spoke a word to me in that way.

"During my first year in Melbourne, I won nearly £300 by betting on horses, and gambling in other ways. I was greatly elated at my success; and I then speculated in gold mining shares, and I made money rapidly. At one time I had shares which were supposed to be worth £5,000, and I thought my fortune was made. About twelve months ago I was unable to attend to my official duties from illness, and I got leave of absence for two months. It was supposed that I was suffering from low fever, but my illness was the result of dissipation. I went to Dalesford for change of air and rest. I lodged with a good old couple, whose kind attention and Christian counsel I shall never forget. While living there, I made a solemn vow that I would give up gambling and drinking, and every other vice to which I had been addicted. To aid me in keeping my vow, I took fresh lodgings when I returned to Melbourne, and as far as I could I cut all my wild associates. I forsook the expensive *café*, where I formerly used to lunch, and I went every day to the *restaurant* where I first saw and admired your sweet face, my beloved Ella!

"Soon after we were married, I was tempted to break my vow of total abstinence, which I had rigidly kept for nearly seven months; I then began again to gamble more intensely than before. My aim was to win enough money to clear off some debts which were harassing me. Thus I was again led into the society of some wild, reckless young men. When I saw that you were unhappy on account of my inviting so much company to our house on Sundays, I fully resolved that the next New Year's Day I would renew my broken vow,—that I would forsake all my dissipated companions, and thenceforward live soberly and righteously.

"I cannot linger on this painful topic; my brain is almost bursting as I now write. My luck at cards and billiards turned against me, and instead of winning money, I lost heavily. To enable me to pursue my luck and retrieve my losses, I *borrowed* some money. I know that the law calls the act embezzlement; but I solemnly declare to you, my dear Ella, that I meant to return every penny of it, and I had a fair prospect of doing so, for it was supposed that my shares in the Nabob Gold Mining Company would soon become immensely valuable. I *borrowed* some more money from my bank, and gambled with desperate earnestness, hoping to retrieve all; but still I lost money. To prevent my defalcation being discovered at our half-yearly balancing, I had recourse to forgery—simply as a temporary expedient, and not with a fraudulent intention. You know the rest.

"I left Melbourne in this schooner, the *Dora*, which is bound for the South Sea Islands, on a trading voyage. I had but a faint hope of getting clear away when I left you. Why I was not searched for in the vessel is perhaps best known to others. I do not wish to implicate any one, so I will mention no names; but it will be seen in the day when all secrets shall be revealed, that I was not alone to blame, though I dare say I am now made a scapegoat.

"We are nearing Haabai, and I am writing in the hope of sending this letter by some vessel that may be going from thence to Sydney or Melbourne. We shall go on to Fiji, and it is probable that I may remain there for awhile; but my future plans are all dim and undefined. I think if I could by some means get to California, I might have a chance of earning an honest livelihood, and perhaps of sending money for you to come to me; that is, if you will ever again link your lot with a wretched felon. The bare conception of what you are suffering, my beloved Ella! and of the agony of my dear father and mother and sister, when they hear of my disgrace, almost drives me to despair.

"May God have mercy on a miserable sinner,
"HENRY MORTON."

CHAPTER XX.

> " Oh, it is excellent
> To have a giant's strength ; but it is tyrannous
> To use it like a giant."
> —*Shakspeare.*

My brief experience in Mr. Cudbear's service gave me more convincing proofs of the unsatisfying nature of money than all the sermons I had heard Parson Blanche preach, or all the homilies I had ever read on the subject. Mr. Cudbear was moderately rich, though a few years before he was as poor as his present stable-boy, Ben. He had a fine house of his own at Boroondarra, with highly cultivated gardens around it, and perhaps all kinds of luxuries inside it. He rode to Melbourne every morning in a smart buggy, drawn by a fast-trotting horse, and he had no turnpike to pay. All day long he could hear ready money tinkling into his till ; for ours was a busy shop, and he knew full well that two-thirds of the takings were net profit. Moreover, he had an income from rents more than enough to support five city missionaries, and yet the man seldom looked even half satisfied ; and I never saw him look joyful for three minutes on a stretch. The sound of his buggy wheels in the morning was a warning for all the porters and apprentices to look sharp, and the senior assistant used to put on a subdued look, like a man going to gaol for stealing a loaf. He was too valuable a help to be scolded by a master; and he might have shown respectful dignity of manner, without fear of being summarily discharged for it; besides, he had no wife or children to make him feel extra humble, but as he had expectations of succeeding to the business, he thought it was his duty —or his policy—to be servile, until he could afford to be otherwise.

I had been so long used to the pleasant freedom of my uncle's establishment, that from the first day I went to Cudbear's shop, I felt it difficult to do my work well while my employer's stony, suspicious eyes were always watching me. I usually got on better when he left in the afternoon; and then the senior assistant always grew chatty, sometimes extremely jocose. But I rather despised the man for his lack of independent spirit, so I could not make a friend of him or enjoy any of his jokes. For my part, I never would admit the right of any employer in the world to bully his servants, no matter how humble their capacity; and I quite concur in a celebrated author's opinion, "That a man has no more right to say an unkind word to me, than he has to knock me down."

I had heard Mr. Cudbear "blow up" every one in his employ, except the senior assistant and myself, and his blowings up were like hot hurricane blasts and hailstones. I wondered whether my turn would ever come, and if it did come, how I should bear it, for I had never had a strong scolding in my life. But I was not long left in suspense. On the very morning after I had sat up half the night thinking over Morton's letter, Mr. Cudbear came to the shop looking dreadfully upset. Some thief had got into his garden overnight and stolen all his early cucumbers. He was uncommonly cross, and there was a general discomfort in the establishment all the morning. An easier feeling prevailed while master had gone to lunch, but that was only one hour's respite. On his return I happened to be the only person in the shop. Had there been merely a dog there besides me, it would have been kicked out, and I should perhaps have escaped for awhile; but there was nobody save me for Mr. Cudbear to abuse—so I caught it, as the saying is. I was making up a prescription, and the tincture bottle that I held in my hand was almost empty; that was a sufficient plea for his beginning to grumble at me. I calmly told him that I was going to make some more tincture that afternoon; but instead of receiving my explanation, as a reasonable man would have done, he blazed up and called me "a miserable crawler."

His words seemed to lacerate my breast like a scratch from an old kangaroo's hind claw. Miserable I was, sure enough,—but crawler! ugh! snakes! I was disgusted at the epithet. I politely asked my master to retract his words.

Retract, indeed! Mr. Cudbear was not a man to show such weakness to an assistant whom he could do without. He was further annoyed at my appeal, and said anything that came into his head—as angry men often do—without reference to truth or reason or common sense. I tried to keep calm, but I was very nervous. As a mild wind-up to his abuse, he said I was a wooden-headed fellow, and might take myself off as soon as I chose.

"Then I choose to go immediately, sir," I said; and I went forthwith upstairs, packed up all my effects, and an hour afterwards I was riding in a car to a friend's house at South Yarra, where I knew I could be accommodated with board and lodging. As I rode along, I wondered what sort of a disposition Mr. Cudbear had when he was a chemist's assistant, a few years ago; and I thought it likely enough that he was just such another cringing, common-souled fellow as his present head shopman. Mr. Cudbear owes me a small balance of wages; and it is probable that he will always owe it, for he is too mean to pay money without being dunned for it, and I will never go near him again.

It was not till I had lived for a week in the quiet rusticity of my new lodgings, that a full view or sense of my unhappy circumstances and prospects seemed to burst upon my mind. The explanation is, that I had had nothing to do but to sit and ponder over my troubles, and they naturally grew heavier, until they seemed to press me down like a whole cargo of coal, or a mountain of snow on the top of me. Never did I feel such a dead weight of depression since I was born. Mr. Cudbear's savage words were always grating on my memory; and at length I got to believe that I really was "a miserable crawler, and a wooden-headed fellow." I could see that the reason why I had always disliked my calling was because I had not capacity enough for it. I had served my apprenticeship to a trade which would not now yield me an honest living—because I was a dolt. Oh, I was miserable! I blamed my worthy uncle for not candidly telling me of my defects, years ago; and I blamed my sainted father for not making me a potter or a brickmaker, or some such calling, where mud is more needed than brains. How I could earn a bare living—after my little stock of cash was gone—next occupied my anxious thoughts; and I could not decide what I was fit for, except for grinding at the pestle and mortar; but that way seemed to be shut up when I remembered that drug-grinding is now done by steam power. I was forced to conclude that I was useless—a mere drone in the great human hive. Sleep forsook me, my appetite failed, and I got weak and very nervous. I longed for seclusion from the busy world; and at length I resolved to go and live a week or two at Queenscliff, that being the quietest place I had ever seen. Accordingly to Queenscliff I went.

I took lodgings, and whiled away my time strolling about the grassy streets, or along the shores of the bay, watching the fishermen, and wishing I had learned the fishing business instead of chemistry. I seldom spoke to any person, and I dare say the villagers thought I was a very unsociable fellow. The poor little children used to shy off from me, as if they were afraid I was going to pinch them, and I fancied that even the street dogs used to lower their tails when they saw me coming.

One fine day I walked to Cape Otway. From the top of a cliff I could see the identical rock on which I sat shivering with cold and hunger on the morning of my shipwreck. I remembered how uncomfortable those limpet shells were to sit on or to walk on without shoes or stockings; and I also remembered the jumping joy I felt when I was rescued from my hazardous perch. But now, though I was dry and well clad, and was neither cold nor hungry, I had not a sparkle of joy in my breast—was indeed more miserable than when I was tossing about in the surf, with my mouth half full of sand and seaweed. It was to me a mysterious anomaly, and that was all I could say about it. Of course I know now that I ought to have got medical advice, for my liver was sadly affected as well as my heart.

I wandered along the cliffs till I found a sort of cave under a rock, and there I sat, like a native troglodyte, encouraging all sorts of gloomy forebodings, until (with a shudder I confess it) the terrible idea of suicide rushed into my mind. Some influence suggested how easily I could dive from my cave into the seething waves beneath, and end all my woes with a few struggles. I thank God that I was not overcome by that satanic temptation. Like John Bunyan's old pilgrim, resisting the attack of Apollyon, in the Valley of Humiliation, I resolutely wielded the same weapon that Christian did, and the tempter fled from me. To divert my mind from such fiendish imaginings, I again took Morton's letter from my pocket and read it. Then I lay down in the cave, covered my handkerchief over my face, and began to reflect on poor Morton's condition as compared with my own; and I thought, that downcast as I was, I had the consciousness of possessing an unblemished character, while he was an escaped felon—a wandering outcast. Then all at once it occurred to me that I could be of some use in the world, however low old Cudbear had rated me; I might go in search of poor Ella's unhappy husband, and in that way I could serve the dear, sorrowing girl, for whom I felt that I could gladly sacrifice my life, if need be. It was a happy thought, and the more I revolved it, the more clearly the way seemed to open, and the more strongly I felt impelled to undertake the work of mercy. I had still more than £200 of Cameron's money left; and I thought, as it honestly belonged to Ella—though she would not take it from me—that I could not expend it more properly than by trying to find, and perhaps helping to reclaim, her misguided husband. She was planning to undertake that duty herself, but I knew it was utterly impracticable. As I pictured poor Morton's disconsolate condition, and thought of the anxiety of his wife, and also of his relatives in England, on his account, all selfish, jealous feelings left my heart, and I pitied them intensely. "What though it should occupy me another year?" I reasoned; "the time and money will be well spent if I can give ease and comfort to so many sad hearts!" I thereupon resolved that I would go in search of the fugitive, and if I found him, I would try my utmost to help him to retrieve his position in life. Strange to say, after I had come to that decision, I gradually grew more lively, and I longed to begin my errand at once. But I would recall the first word in the preceding sentence. It was *not* strange that I should be lively; for I was feeling the glow of comfort which naturally springs from the purpose to do good. Any honest heart may understand it.

I returned to South Yarra without delay. Throughout that night I slept soundly, and did not dream of Cudbear. It was the first good sleep I had enjoyed since the memorable night of Ella's painful disclosure. The next morning, though suffering from weakness, my spirits were buoyant, and I felt my appetite returning. I thought I had better make all my arrangements for the voyage before acquainting Ella with my design, so I set about it with an alacrity which almost surprised me. I soon found that there was a schooner loading at the Queen's wharf for the South Sea Islands, on a trading voyage. When I first applied for a passage in her, I was told that she had no room for passengers; but through the influence of a friend of mine, the captain was persuaded to make up a sleeping berth for me in the hold. It was by no means a comfortable-looking berth; still, I was so fully bent upon my mission, that I think I would have gone if I had been obliged to sling a hammock on deck all the voyage. I bought a necessary outfit, and when I had seen it safely on board, I called on the Rev. Mr. Benson and told him what I had resolved to do.

At first he seemed incredulous, and I thought he looked suspicious; but that was only my fancy; he could not doubt the disinterestedness of my motive, for what selfish end could I possibly have in view? He soon saw that I was in earnest, and that my purpose was a kind one; so he took my hand again and shook it heartily, and said some eulogistic things, which were encouraging to me. It would hardly seem modest of me to print all his compliments, but there can be no harm in my telling that he said he wished I had been trained for a missionary instead of a chemist. I have often indulged a similar wish, since I have seen how much useful work there is for missionaries to do.

He further said, "Ella has told me of her design of going in search of her husband, and no arguments that I could use seemed to shake her determination. My wife is quite shocked at the idea of a young woman going alone to an uncivilized land on such an uncertain errand; but I am sure Ella would have attempted it if you had not made this self-sacrificing offer. I thank you, Mr. Larksway, with all my heart on her account, for sparing the poor girl so much hardship and risk. I hope you may find her unhappy husband, and help him on to his feet again."

At my request Mr. Benson said he would tell Ella

all about it, and I promised to call the next morning to receive any instructions she wished to give me, and to take letters and messages for her husband.

When I called the next day, Ella's heart was too full to say much to me, but I could see that she was very thankful. Her beautiful eyes were swimming in tears of gratitude. She gave me a letter for her husband, and a small sealed packet which I presumed contained money. I said a few comforting words to her, assuring her that I would use every effort to find her husband, and I would help him in the way that I deemed most expedient. She again tried to express her thanks, but her tongue faltered and she could not utter a word. I did not stay more than ten minutes, for I could not see any sensible object in prolonging the interview. I shook hands with her and left the house, with my heart full of a precious feeling which I cannot clearly describe, but it can be realized by persons who are conscious of having done, or being about to do, an act of genuine kindness for some one in distress.

I took tea that evening with my esteemed friends, Mr. and Mrs. Moss, and spent a few hours very agreeably in their hospitable home. Little Nellie ran up and kissed me as soon as I entered the doorway. She is a sweetly interesting child, but I do wish she would not so often remind me that I saved her from being drowned; indeed, the whole family seem to be perpetually thinking of that little service I rendered them. Gratitude is nice, no doubt, like many other scarce things, but too much of it is embarrassing to me.

When I told Mr. Moss that I had left Mr. Cudbear's employ, he smiled and said, "I did not expect you would stay there long, Mr. Larksway. I refrained from saying anything to prejudice you against the place, but I have been on the look-out for something better for you. When you return from your tour to the islands, don't forget to call on me before you make any other engagement. I may perhaps have something ready for you."

On the following Sunday morning, at daybreak, the schooner *Ariel* got under weigh, and proceeded down Hobson's Bay with a fair wind. I was the only passenger on board.

CHAPTER XXI.

"I see the right, and I approve it too ;
Condemn the wrong, and yet the wrong pursue."—*Ovid.*

As I before hinted, my accommodation on board the *Ariel* was not in keeping with the high sum I paid for it. It would have been dear at almost any price. The only ventilation I got for my berth in the hold was through a sliding door in the cuddy bulkhead, and I got a glimmering of light through the same aperture. The captain warned me to be careful of fire, as there was half a ton of gunpowder stowed just below my berth; so I could not carry even a bull's-eye lantern with any degree of comfort. For the first two or three nights I used to fidget about the awful position I might suddenly find myself in if the captain were to let a spark from his pipe fall through the lazarette hatch, or if the clumsy cabin-boy should upset the kerosene lamp. I daresay that thousands of persons on ship-board have incurred even greater risks of sudden death, without knowing anything about it, and I wished that I had been kept in peaceful ignorance of the dangerous explosives under my bed; for I am sure that no unsuspicious person who was ever blown up by half a ton of gunpowder suffered a fiftieth part of the mental worry that I endured, in the mere anticipation of a catastrophe which did not happen. I sometimes think that a dull, stupid-headed fellow would have more enjoyment, of a negative sort, than I get when travelling; and I wish I were not so quick to discern danger or to realize remote contingencies.

Few travellers ever had a better opportunity for studying the characteristics of rats in a dark place than I had in the hold of the *Ariel;* and it is perhaps a loss to the cause of science that my fancy for animals does not extend to such vermin. There were hundreds of rats on board; and we found when we got into port that they had nibbled away one of the ship's timbers, in the hope of getting something to drink. They could hear the sea-water splashing about the rudder casing, but of course they did not know it was salt. Man usually forces the brute creation to serve him in some way, or to stand clear of his vengeance; but one would almost judge that rats have not had terms of service fairly propounded to them, that they continue, as a race, to be revolters from human authority or rule. I leave the subject for the consideration of anybody who does not mind spending time over a whimsical study; but this much I may say about it, that no man, whether on shipboard or elsewhere, could wish inferior animals to show a greater disposition to fraternize with him than the rats in that ship did to me, for they frolicked about my berth like pet kittens, and I was sometimes awakened by the peculiar tickle of a rat's tail and paws as he trotted across my face in the dark. Their tameness was really startling.

I had letters of introduction from the Rev. Mr. Benson to several missionaries in the Fijian and Tongan groups of islands; and on the arrival of the *Ariel* at Tonga, I met with a cordial reception at the house of a missionary. I might give some interesting particulars of mission work in those islands, but I wish to hasten on with the report of my own particular work; i.e., the search for poor, wandering Morton. I will say, however, that in no part of the world that I have seen are the happy fruits of Christianity so apparent as in the peaceful little kingdom of Tonga. I thought some of the natives made losing bargains when they bartered their cocoa-nut oil for bad spirits with the captain of the *Ariel;* but it would have been hazardous for me to express my opinion on the subject, for such traders are apt to get cross if interfered with.

After staying a few weeks in the Tongan group, we sailed for Fiji. At Ovalau I got a clue to Morton's whereabouts; so I left the *Ariel*, and went in a small coasting vessel to Bau. There I got further information, upon which I went to Rewa in a native canoe. At the northern entrance to the Rewa river the canoe was upset by a breaking wave, and I had a narrow escape from drowning. After being three hours in the water, clinging to the canoe, I was rescued, and taken to the mission-house at Matai-Suava, where I was hospitably cared for.

Saul wants me to let him sparkle up the story, just now, with a racy chapter about those friendly rats in the *Ariel*. He says that seven-tenths of the folks in Christendom do not care a farthing for missionaries, or their useful labours, and would sooner read a comical sketch about vermin than read a mission sermon. I admit that my cousin is not far wrong this time; at any rate, there are millions of well-to-do persons who never give a farthing to the support of missionaries, or show any interest in them in other ways, but I think it is because they do not understand the important nature of mission work. I could tell them a good deal about it, from personal observation; and I hope to print something about it soon, but I cannot do it in this book, for Saul would certainly object to topics of so serious a character.

For several days I suffered a little from the effects of my immersion and exposure to the scorching sun. My kind host insisted on my remaining quietly within doors; and I am perhaps indebted to his friendly restraint from my escape from an attack of fever or dysentery, diseases which are fearfully prevalent in Fiji.

Perhaps I had better remind my readers that at the time of my visit Fiji was not a British colony. Except the missionaries and their families, the white population consisted of a few traders, and a sprinkling of runaway sailors and refugees from the Australian colonies, who preferred taking their chance among cannibal natives, to facing their creditors or the officers of justice. I had not much difficulty in tracking

Morton from Ovalau to Bau; and I had reason to believe that I was still on his track, for I learnt from Mr. Goodson, the missionary, that a young man had lately gone to live with a small cotton-planter, a few miles up the river. Mr. Goodson saw that I was very anxious about the young man; so in order to relieve me a little, he agreed to send one of his native teachers, "a sagacious fellow, to make a few quiet inquiries;" and try to find out if the stranger's name was Morton.

If there had been a newspaper in Rewa, with a circulation equal to any of the Melbourne or Sydney papers, and I had advertised in it for Mr. Morton, I could hardly have given my business greater publicity than I did by employing the sagacious teacher to make quiet inquiries. A few hours afterwards there was scarcely a native in the district who did not know that there was a white man in the mission-house at Matai-Suava who wanted to find another white man up the river, named Mortoni. The teacher returned in the evening, to inform me that he had found a young white man up the river, but he said his name was not Mortoni, but Browni. I suspected that he was the man I wanted. Brown is a modest old name that is often stolen by rogues and shams.

As soon as it was deemed safe for me to leave the house, Mr. Goodson lent me his boat and two men to pull it, and I went up the Rewa river to the house of the planter. I landed at a rough wooden jetty, and walked to a shanty a few roods from the river bank. I was met in the doorway by a man whose external appearance was very unprepossessing, but I knew as soon as he spoke that he was not an uneducated man. I could hardly, however, mistake him for a gentleman, for he kept me standing in the hot sunshine, and I thought he seemed to be fiercely determined that I should not enter his house. To all my questions he replied with the wariness of a sharp police-office lawyer. He would not admit that a young man named Morton or even Brown had been under his roof; in short, he would admit nothing; but he looked savagely disposed to knock me into the river. I began to fear that I had missed my track. He evidently noticed my concern, for he presently said in a milder tone,—

"You have asked me a good many questions; now, sir, may I ask you if you are a Melbourne detective? Tell me candidly."

"Detective! No—certainly not!" I replied. "I have come in search for Mr. Morton with the purest desire of assisting him, and thus relieving the minds of his distressed relatives. You may be convinced of that fact if you will only read this letter."

"Why did you not tell me all this before?" said the man, excitedly. "Come inside the house. That poor wretch may be dying while we are palavering here."

I followed him into the house. He went to the back door and shouted to some black men who were working in the plantation. When they came up, he said a few words to them in a language which was unintelligible to me, and the men scampered off in various directions.

The planter then said to me, "Morton has been lodging with me; but a few days ago he heard that some fellow from Melbourne was tracking him. Of course he thought you were a detective, so he set off out of this directly, though he was scarcely able to crawl. Where he is now I don't know exactly; but I am sure he could not have gone far away, for he was bad with dysentery. I have sent four of my kanakas to look for him, so you had better wait here till some of them return."

My host then opened a corner cupboard, and took out part of a cold yam, some boiled pork, and a bottle of spirits. He said his fare was not tempting, but such as it was I was welcome to it. I declined to take any refreshment, whereupon he helped himself to some spirits, and said as I was not going to eat he would light his pipe. After he had puffed away for a few minutes, I asked him if he liked Fiji?

"No, indeed, I don't like it; but it suits my convenience to stay here for awhile." Presently he added, with a sigh, "I have a wife and three children in Melbourne. I wish you had brought me tidings from them, poor things!"

I hardly knew what to say to him, fearing that he might suppose I wished to pry into his affairs; but after he had taken a second glass of spirits, he grew very communicative. He told me that three years before he had had a thriving business in Melbourne. That he was tempted to go out of his ordinary line to speculate largely in oats and gram, and to do so he had imprudently used some trust money. The horse fodder market became glutted, and prices fell. He was hopelessly involved; and to save himself from a criminal prosecution for breach of trust, he absconded from the colony. "Here I am pretty safe from the law," he added, with another sigh; "but it is a wretched life for a fellow who has been accustomed to a stylish home and a jolly circle of friends. The truth is I am weary of it, and I should not care if the detectives were to ferret me out and carry me back to Melbourne. If I were in Pentridge stockade, I should be forced to work, so I should have less time to brood over my folly, than I have in this swampy solitude; besides, I should see my wife and children occasionally."

I could not but pity the man's forlorn condition. I asked him if it were practicable for his wife and children to come to Fiji to him?

"No, I would not bring them here if they could come. I think this locality is the most unhealthy part of Fiji; it is very low as you see, and the river sometimes overflows part of my land. Besides, the natives of Bau and Rewa are often at war, and it is not very safe to be between two fires as it were. Oh, dear; mine is a hard, lonely life!" he added, as he helped himself to another glass of spirits from the bottle. "But if it were not for this cursed stuff, I should not be in my present plight. Grog is to blame for all my mishaps. It has been the bane of my life."

"Then why do you drink it?" I asked, and I shuddered to see him pour the raw spirit down his throat in such immoderate quantities.

"Ha, ha! why do I drink it, indeed! That simple question proves to me that you don't know much about the clawing power of drinking habits. Happy for you if you never do know it. Grog is my master now. I would gladly give up drinking it if I could; but I cannot do it. I have tampered with the cursed thing too long, and I believe it has weakened my brain."

"Were you in the habit of drinking to excess in Melbourne?"

"It is hard to determine what excess really is. I did not consider myself a hard drinker, in comparison with some of my neighbours; still, there is no doubt I kept the steam up pretty well. I knew scores, or I may say hundreds, of commercial men in Australia, who were constantly doing the same thing: they fancied they could not do business if they were quite sober. There is no mistake about it, young fellow, the tippling system is cankering the very heart out of our mercantile life. Ah, you may stare; but it is true enough what I say, though I am half drunk."

He looked at me as if he expected me to say something in reply to his startling proposition, so I ventured to say I thought he was mistaken.

"You are right; I am mistaken, though not in that particular. I have mistaken my way in life's high road, and have got into a bog, literally and figuratively. I was once as steady as you seem to be; but I was lured by the prevailing fashion around me to begin a fast style of living, and I wanted to make money fast in order to keep up my expensive establishment. I gradually left my old honest sober track, and took the devil for my guide or driver on the broad-gauge line to ruin. You see where he has shunted me, for awhile. But dreary as my lot is now, it is perhaps luxurious and happy compared with what I may expect after I reach the terminus of death, if it be all true that the missionary over the river tells me, and he seems an honest sort of man."

" Then the missionary comes to see you sometimes ? "

" Oh, yes, he comes often enough ; but it is no use of his talking to me—he would have a better chance of converting a cannibal native. Perhaps I might have been influenced by Christian counsel a few years ago, when I was just switching on to the main line to destruction ; but it is too late now. Here I am like a blasted tree in the wilderness, or more like an old storm-battered wreck on a quicksand. There is no hope either in life or death for poor Tom Ryan."

He sat for some minutes apparently absorbed in gloomy reflections. I had just summoned courage enough to take out my pocket Bible, to read some words of direction and comfort to him, when he again clutched the bottle, and exclaimed mournfully, " Ah me! God only knows how my poor wife and children are situated. They won't get overmuch sympathy from the world around them, poor things ! Anxiety about their condition makes me half mad, and then I fly to this hot stuff for relief. Bah ! 'tis like pumping coal tar or turpentine on to a burning house. I don't know what your name is, mister ; but no matter. You are one of the great human family, so you are my brother, and I warn you to beware of the grog bottle. I am not a teetotal lecturer exactly—but never mind that; I know what I am talking about, if I am almost drunk, and I say again, Beware of strong drink, young man, or it will perhaps blast every glint of joy out of your life, and fill your soul with the horrors of despair; that is what it is doing for me."

As I gazed on the poor hopeless man, I again felt thankful that I had hitherto been saved from contracting habits which yield such a terrible harvest of woe.

CHAPTER XXII.

"What shadows we are, what shadows we pursue!"—*Burke*.

PRESENTLY two of the black messengers returned, with news of the whereabouts of Morton; so the planter volunteered to go with me to see him.

After crossing the river, he led me by a zigzag course through several swampy taro plantations, abounding with mosquitoes, until we stopped at a small native hut. I had to crawl through the low doorway on my hands and knees; and when I got inside, it was some minutes before I could see anything for the smoke which filled the place. There was a smouldering fire in the centre of the floor, and beside it lay a man apparently unconscious, for he took no notice of my entrance. His clothing was ragged and soiled; he had evidently taken a straight course through the swamps, in his eagerness to get to his hiding-place. His hair was long and unkempt, and altogether his appearance was abject in the extreme. As I looked at his emaciated face in the dusky light, I could not trace any resemblance to the handsome picture I had seen of Morton, and I fancied that I had mistaken my man. Soon, however, he opened his eyes, and I shall never forget his ghastly look of error when he saw me.

"I told you you had better let me crawl in here first, mister!" said the planter, who was close behind me. "See how you have scared the poor wretch. Hallo, Harry! Don't be frightened, old fellow! This gentleman has brought you a letter from your wife. He is not a detective."

The expression of Morton's face changed in an instant. He gasped, "Where is the gentleman? Tell him to come to me directly. O Ryan! I have been awfully bad since I left your house."

"Here, take a drop of this stuff, Harry. It will perhaps brighten you up a little." Ryan then poured some spirit into a cocoa-nut shell which lay on the floor and handed it to Morton. It seemed to give him temporary strength, for he sat upright and extended his hand to me as I approached him.

"I am sorry to find you in this sad condition, Mr. Morton," I said feelingly. "I have brought you some good news from your dear wife, and I have a letter for you from her."

"Please to give it to me, sir," he said eagerly.

"I think you had better first let me help you out of this close place."

"No, no; give me the letter now. I shall never go out of this hut alive. It is all up with me."

"Don't trifle with a dying man! Give him his letter!" shouted Ryan peremptorily. I thought I had better obey, for Ryan was too tipsy to be reasoned with. So I gave Morton the letter; and then I told him that I would go and get some dry clothing for him, and would come back again as soon as possible. I was glad to get out of the hut, for the stench inside was almost overpowering. I returned to the boat, and made signs for the men to pull as fast as they could. In about an hour I was back at the mission-house at Matai-Suava.

When I told Mr. Goodson the state I found Morton in, he shook his head and said, "I fear this will be a fatal case, Mr. Larksway. But we will do all we can for the poor fellow, and we must do it promptly." He then put a mattress and two blankets into the boat, and taking a small medicine case and a valise, also a suit of my warmest clothes, we set off together in the boat, with four natives as oarsmen.

I scarcely had an opportunity of asking Mr. Goodson what he meant to do with Morton, until we were seated in the boat, for he had been so busy with his preparations. "I mean to carry him down to the mission-house at once," he replied. "He will certainly die if we leave him where he is; indeed, I wonder that he is alive now, if he has been lying in his wet clothes on the floor of that hut, as you say, for two days. Dysentery is the scourge of this land."

When we got to the hut we found Morton in great agony. He was moaning piteously. His wife's letter was clasped to his breast. Ryan was lying on the floor asleep, with an empty rum bottle beside him. While Mr. Goodson was preparing a dose of medicine for the patient, I whisperingly asked what he thought of the case? He replied,—

"While there is life we will hope. Put a cheerful face

on when he is looking at you, Mr. Larksway. Many a patient has been frightened to death by the desponding looks of his nurse. We must handle him tenderly, poor fellow! But he must be taken out of this place at all risks. He will inevitably die in a few hours if he remains in this fetid air, and we could not stop with him long without fatal results to ourselves."

When Morton saw us making preparations to remove him, he begged us to let him stay where he was. He said he knew he must die, and it was not merciful of us to prolong his sufferings. I was afraid Ryan would awaken, and then it is probable that he would have insisted on the sick man being allowed to remain, and there would have been an unpleasant scene; but fortunately he slept on. With the aid of our boatmen we carried Morton on a mattress to the boat, and rigged an awning over him.

"It will be inhuman of us to go away and leave a helpless drunken man lying in that foul hut," said Mr. Goodson. "Let us drag him out into the fresh air before we start."

Accordingly we returned to the hut, and taking hold of Ryan's heels we dragged him as gently as we could through the doorway, and were about to place him under the shade of a clump of bananas, when he awoke; and being too stupid to comprehend our kind motive, he flew into a rage, and would probably have stabbed us with his knife if we had not made haste to our boat. We pushed off, leaving him on the bank of the river, cursing us more fiercely than Shimei cursed King David.

"What a living picture of the degradation and misery of intemperance that poor man's history presents," I remarked, with a shudder at his frantic denunciations. "I wonder if his sad state would have a reforming influence on the fast men of Melbourne and elsewhere, if they could see him just now?"

"Not much permanent influence, I fear," replied Mr. Goodson. "Surely they have enough miserable examples of this kind in civilized life, without coming to poor Fiji for them. I have tried my utmost to influence that unhappy man for good, but apparently to no purpose. I will not give him up while he has life and a glimmer of intellect left; but oh! it is heart-sickening to see a man who knows the right way so well, persistently going headlong to ruin."

We made all the haste we could down the river, but before we got to Matai-Suava, Morton exhibited the worse symptoms of dysentery, and his pains were extreme. We carried him to a room in the mission-house, and administered such alleviatives as we could prevail on him to swallow; but we saw that his end was near. Mr. Goodson and I sat beside his bed, and during the temporary cessations of his agony Mr. Goodson spoke to him, tenderly but plainly, of the awful change that was at hand. Poor Morton covered his face with his hands and wept bitterly. All that we could distinctly hear him articulate was, that he was a wretched sinner, without a hope of mercy. Mr. Goodson then prayed earnestly for him, and read many passages of Scripture which were appropriate to his case, still he seemed to take no comfort from them, for every now and then he would mutter, " Dark! dark! mercy, good Lord! mercy! mercy!"

".Do you believe the kind words of affection in your wife's letter, Mr. Morton?" asked Mr. Goodson, softly. "Do you believe that she still loves you, and that she forgives you for all the sorrow you have caused her?"

The dying man pressed the letter, which he held in his hand, to his breast, and feebly gasped, "Yes—yes, Ella loves me, wicked wretch that I am. Yes, Ella forgives me. I believe that."

"And God loves you, and is willing, for Jesus Christ's sake, to forgive all your sins. Can you not believe that, after all the encouraging invitations and comforting promises I have read you from God's own book?"

Morton's lips moved as if in prayer, but we could not distinguish a word he said. Soon afterwards he became delirious, and in his ravings he loudly cursed his luck in betting on a losing horse. Then he seemed to be having an angry dispute with one of his old companions named Charlie, whom he accused of cheating him at cards. Presently the scene in his troubled vision changed, and he was imploring the manager of his bank to wait till he received the dividend from his gold shares, and he would pay back every penny he had embezzled. Then he would fancy that he was again taking a hurried leave of his wife. During these various phases of his mental aberrance, the contortions of his features were shocking to look at.

The mission-house was enclosed by a fence of

bamboos, about six feet high, lashed side by side, like long rows of organ pipes. Some of the canes were split by the sun; and as the wind rushed between them it produced the most mournful music conceivable. I shall not soon forget my melancholy thoughts and feelings as I sat watching beside Morton's bed, through the weary hours of that night, listening to his dying groans and to the weird moaning of the sea-breeze through the bamboo fence, like sounds from the spirit world. I tried to picture him as he was four years before, setting out from his parental home with the wide world before him, looking very promising, no doubt; and perhaps he was cherishing a hope in his heart that he would, a few years thence, return to his home with honestly earned wealth, to be the comfort and stay of his aged parents. Alas! he had dashed all his life's hopes to ruin, like a child ruthlessly destroying its toys. Then I thought of the terrible grief his parents and sister would suffer when they heard of his untimely end on the far-off shores of savage Fiji, with only strangers to close his eyes. Then involuntary thoughts of poor Ella, and of my own strange connection with her sad history, filled my mind and aroused feelings of a painfully conflicting kind, which I have not courage to describe. It was indeed a dreary night; and I longed for the morning light to cheer the sombre chamber of death.

When I have since tried to picture any state or position that is most calculated to drive a man melancholy, my mind has at once flown back to that lonely night-watch in the mission-house on the sandy shore of Matai-Suava, perhaps one of the dreariest spots in all the islands of Fiji. And whenever I hear persons captiously ignoring the useful services of missionaries, I call to mind the self-denying zeal and patient endurance of the Rev. Mr. Goodson and his exemplary wife. I feel morally certain that nothing but pure Christian love for their great Master's work could influence a lady and gentleman of refined tastes to live in that dismal locality, and labour on from year to year in oft-disheartening efforts to evangelize the poor black natives, and to wean them from uncivilized habits.

Just as day was breaking, Morton opened his eyes. I could see that consciousness had returned, and I took his proffered hand in mine. He softly whispered, "Yes, sir; I do believe it. Tell my Ella that I am going to heaven! God be merciful to me, a poor, wicked wretch, for Christ's sake!" His voice failed and his eyes closed again. I ran out of the room to arouse Mr. Goodson from his bed; I had promised to call him if I saw any change in the patient. In less than two minutes we were back by Morton's bedside; but he was again unconscious, and he remained so until he died.

The mortal remains of that once promising young man lie beside the neat little native church at Matai-Suava. The ocean surges on the beach close by, and the winds, moaning through the bamboo fence in front, are mournfully chanting a perpetual requiem over him.

Three days afterwards a ship called at Rewa, on its way to Sydney; so I sent by that opportunity full particulars of Morton's death to the Rev. Mr. Benson; and I requested him to break the sad news to Mrs. Morton.

CHAPTER XXIII.

*" Messmates, hear a brother sailor
Sing the dangers of the sea!"—Dibdin.*

IN the preceding chapter I used the phrase "Savage Fiji"; and lest it should be thought unfair to that fine young British colony, I would state that my experience of it dated several years ago. Then there certainly were many savages to be seen, both black and white; and I am not sure which were the most depraved or treacherous. Fiji is now under British rule; so it is far more civilized, and most of the savages have been taught better manners. But though the comforts of social life may be more readily obtained now than they formerly were, the climate is much the same as ever, and it is a trying one for European constitutions, especially in the low, swampy parts. The prospect of a free and easy life, which new colonies usually present, is no doubt alluring to some of the restless spirits of Melbourne and elsewhere; but it will be well for such adventurous ones to consider the risk they run in going to Fiji. Persons who have been used to what is called a "fast life," had better resolve before they go there to be "temperate in all things," or it is sadly probable that they may soon fall victims to the prevailing diseases, fever and dysentery.

But notwithstanding these drawbacks, Fiji will doubtless become an important colony; and its rich soil and but partially developed mineral and other natural resources offer tempting scope to British enterprise and capital.

My object in going to Fiji was accomplished sooner than I expected. I will not say much about my feelings at the untimely end of Mr. Morton; but I certainly was glad to report that it was the firm hope of Mr. Goodson, as well as myself, that he died truly penitent. Had I acted wisely I should have returned to Australia, and began to work for an honest livelihood. But I somehow found that steady work, in my old line, had grown more distasteful to me than ever. There was such a delightful difference between skimming about as free as a bird or a fish amongst those lovely fragrant islands, and being confined fourteen hours a day behind a druggist's counter, with an employer to please and physic to smell continually, that I could not help liking the change, and I half wished I were a black-man, "for the glorious privilege of being independent" of tailors. I found it quite easy to persuade myself that I might reasonably take a month for enjoyment, after my exciting work; and as I had no friends near to object to my doings, my liberty was as perfect as I could desire. All I seemed to lack was an agreeable travelling companion.

The latter part of my stay in Fiji was real holiday pastime. I should feel a delight in writing a few chapters from my notes, of what I saw in that interesting group of islands; but instead of overtaxing my descriptive powers in that way, and digressing again from my story,

I would refer my readers to the report of a much more experienced visitor than myself. A book has lately been written by Miss C. F. Gordon-Cumming, entitled "At Home in Fiji," which I have read with great interest. I am glad to know that the book has been widely circulated, for it cannot fail to be useful. I have seen some of the reefs or fields of coral which that enterprising young lady describes so pleasingly, and I have rusticated on some of the beautiful little green isles which her clever pencil has so graphically portrayed. I have sailed over the blue waves, with the swiftness of a mail steamer, in large double canoes, cleverly managed by Fijians, and I have seen a little of the domestic life of the natives. To the scientist as well as to the friends of Christian missions, Miss Cumming's book will be very interesting, and I cordially recommend it. It had a peculiar fascination for me, and I could hardly lay it down until I had almost read it through. I can, from personal observation, endorse much that the gifted authoress has stated about the evangelizing efforts of the Wesleyan missionaries in Fiji and elsewhere; and I know many of the ladies and gentlemen, and some of the native converts, whom she has named in her book.

On the night before I left Fiji I was a guest in the hospitable home of a missionary at Rewa; and at bedtime my host showed me to my chamber, which was a room detached from the mission-house, and built on a sort of conical mound, for the sake, I supposed, of being above the reach of flood waters. I remarked to my host, as he was about to say good-night and shut me in, that I hoped it was not a gigantic ant-hill or a hornet's nest, that my bed-room was built upon; when he smilingly said, "No; but it is the tomb of one of Fiji's most terrible cannibal chiefs." I forget the native name of the late chief, whose bones were buried beneath me, but the English of it was "The ground shark." Ugh! I did not forget that awful name all the time I lay awake that night, and I wonder I did not dream that the late notorious old cannibal was exercising his idle jaws on some of my limbs. I rather wished that my worthy host had waited till next morning to tell me who my dead neighbour was. When I had spent as much time as I could afford in Fiji, I started for Samoa, in a small trading brig called the *Bouncer*, and a hard time I had of it.

I may here remark, that it is not uncommon for passengers, now-a-days, to write grumbling letters to the newspapers about the ships they have travelled in, if everything on board was not up to their mark of perfection. Formerly we heard comparatively little about the discomforts of ship life, not that there was nothing to complain off, but because fussy travellers were then not so numerous as they are now. I have not the least respect for ships that are unseaworthy, nor for dishonest owners; but I do love fair play, and I think there is some danger of our over-estimating maritime abuses in our zeal to cure them all with pen and ink, and a risk of blaming honest owners for unavoidable casualties. Break up rotten ships, I say to any one who wants a useful job, and punish all the roguish owners, too, if you can catch them; but do not condemn good ships, nor scold honest owners for mishaps which may be fairly put down as ordinary perils and dangers of the sea.

Though I have had a more disastrous experience at sea than most persons would care to have, I do not call myself a professional sailor; and I would not presume to say much about ships or their tackling in the dogmatic way that I have heard some simple young fellows talk, after their first voyage, perhaps, to the annoyance of seamen who may overhear their gabble. It would have been mere presumption if I had gone quizzing about the *Bouncer*, to judge if she were sound or rotten, before I took my passage in her; and I went on board in confidence that I was protected by British navigation laws, as the majority of my countrymen do when they go to sea. But I had not been twelve hours from port, before I felt in danger of being drowned, and I wished myself on dry land again. I repeat it, I am not a seaman, but mere instinct would tell any man, when he heard the water sousing about over the ballast in the hold that the ship was not tight, that there was a hole in her somewhere. Unquestionably the *Bouncer* was a leaky vessel. The crew pumped in a deliberate way, which showed that they were used to it, and the water came out of the pump-spout clear and sparkling; still, I was not comforted so much as I should have been if the water had been pumped up thick and stenchy. The mate coolly told me that the ship was only leaking in her topsides. But even that official statement did not relieve my anxiety, for I thought it would be much the same to me whether the ship filled from the top or from the bottom; for in either case she would sink, and I could not swim. I grew very uneasy. At length I politely asked the captain to put back to the nearest harbour in Fiji, and land me, and he might keep my passage money. I shall not print his answer to my request. I simply say it was a very ungentlemanly negative. I felt chagrined, and I went below to the cabin, which was by no means a convenient one. I knew beforehand that the accommodation was rough, but I reasoned to myself, "the distance is merely five hundred miles or so." I had forgotten, however, that Samoa lay dead to windward, and that we should probably have to beat all the way there against the trade winds. The cabin boy told me it would take us a month of sundays to thrash there. What he meant by that ambiguous reckoning I could easily guess.

That night the captain got drunk and seemed disposed to quarrel with me, so I left him alone in the cabin and went on deck. The mate was sober, but he was a very dreary man, and would only speak when I spoke to him. He told me, in answer to one of my anxious questions, that the reason why he was carrying on so much sail was that there was a coral reef to leeward, and if he did not make the ship walk ahead, she would go ashore before eight bells. Presently he added, "I am afraid some of our sticks will carry away, for I don't believe the rigging has been set up for three years or more, and there is not a fathom of the running gear strong enough to tether a donkey. I wish I had never come in the old box.

Keep that pump going there, lads!" he shouted to the watch, who were stopping for a minute to light their pipes.

"Have you been mate of the *Bouncer* long, Mr. Doom?" I asked, in the hope of getting a crumb or two of comfort from his answer.

"No, by Jerry! I have not been in her long, nor I don't want to be, either. I joined her last Friday at Levuka, because I was hard up—dead beat, as the saying is. On the same day one of the hands was bending on the fore-top gallant sail, when the foot-rope of the yard carried away, and down the poor fellow came to the deck. We left him ashore at the mission-house with a lot of his bones cracked. After that I had an overhaul at the gear, and blest if every rope on board isn't rotten or stranded. I never sailed in such a parish-rigged old hooker before, and I shall clear out of her as soon as I get a chance. I'd as soon go to sea in a baker's trough or a brewer's vat."

"I wonder that you ventured to sea in her, Mr. Doom, or that you could get a crew to work her, knowing that she is unseaworthy."

"Shough! What's a fellow to do when he is out of luck? Did you ever know a ship go to sea without a crew to work her?"

"No, I don't think I ever did; but it seems marvellous to me that men willingly risk their lives. I can't make it out at all."

"Take a small pull on that lee-foretopsail brace!" shouted Mr. Doom to the watch on deck.

"Hoy, hoy! Hoo, hoy!" sang the men as they

T

pulled together at the brace. At their third pull, crash went the yard at the tie; and the sail flapped about till it split into shreds.

"Hang it all, lads! What did you go sagging away on the brace like that for? Do you think you are on board a frigate? Look sharp and snug the sail in, or it will shake the masts out of her. Haul on to the topsail buntlines and clewlines! Ease off the sheets, handsomely! Bear a hand, now! Call out the starboard watch, boy!"

Though I was somewhat scared, I had pluck enough to go and pull at the ropes to help the crew. When the sail was snugged in, as they called it, I went back to the quarter-deck. After awhile I remarked to the mate that the topsail-yard was not a very strong one.

"Strong! Didn't I tell you before that everything on board this old box is as rotten as stale turnip-tops?"

"It is a shame and disgrace to allow such a bad vessel to come to sea," I said, with honest indignation.

"You are right enough there, sir; but who is to stop rotten ships from going to sea if their owners are schemers? Well, it's a good job that the yard carried away just now; for I was going to reef topsails at eight bells, and then there would have been some broken necks on board, no doubt. Some of this after canvas must come off the ship now, and then she will sag to leeward like a haystack in a heavy flood."

"Do you think we shall weather the reef, Mr. Doom?" I asked with increasing uneasiness.

"Can't say, sir; I don't know where the reef is myself, for the skipper never gave me the bearings of it. He told me just before he turned in, to keep my luff, for there were gibbers to leeward. That's all I know about it at present. I must go and rouse him out of his berth, drunk or sober."

When the captain came on deck, I went below, for it was beginning to rain. It was a solemn season with me in that close, greasy cabin, and my mind was painfully active. I thought of my mother and father at home; but I confess that I thought more about myself and the probability of my being drowned; and I wished I had not left so much squaring-up work for my conscience, at a time when death seemed to be close alongside of us. It is a humiliating admission, but I candidly state the fact, that I require some powerful incentive, such as the fear of death or some other calamity, to keep me up to my religious duties. As far back as I can remember, I have always felt more devoutly inclined during a severe thunderstorm, than I have felt when the sun or the moon was shining in a clear sky. I should like to know if it is a constitutional peculiarity of mine, or whether it is common to humanity. Conscience tells me that it ought not to be so. That is all I shall say about it at present.

I made some very good resolutions that night. I did not sleep a wink, for I expected every minute to feel the ship bump on to a reef. Just about daybreak the captain roared down the skylight to me to come on deck and take a spell at the pump, for he wanted some of the men to fish the damaged topsail yard. I was going to stand on my rights and dignity as a passenger; but I thought it was risky to argue with a drunken man, who had so much temporary power, so I put on my gloves and went to the pump.

I set to work with my customary vigour, for I never could dawdle over a job. The sailor who was helping me at the pump-handle said drily, "You had better take it easy, mate. 'One hand for your owner and the other for yourself, to hold on by,' is a sailor's motto, always." I felt rather vexed with the fellow for trying to tempt me to skulk, and I pumped away more energetically to show my contempt for his lazy spirit. I have reason to believe that the man put but little of his strength to the handle, for it was very stiff in its downward action. Presently I grew short of breath, and I wanted to stop; but he said, "We *must* keep at it, mate. Pump or sink, that is our luck now. The ship is leaking like an old pig's trough." His remark stimulated me to go at it again; and I pumped like desperation itself, till my backbone seemed to give way in the centre joint, and I got as winded as a runaway horse. I sat down on the wet deck exhausted, and even the captain's savage threat to rouse me up with a handspike did not induce me to move. I think I shall never forget that wooden pump if I live to the age of Old Parr.

Many useful moral lessons on the penalties of fast life in general might be adduced from that simple experience of mine. I am loath to let slip the chance of making it benefit somebody, but I *must* get on with my story. If I should ever come out as a public lecturer on social reform or natural philosophy, the title of my first oration shall be, "The *Bouncer's* Pump-handle; or, Take it Easy."

For the next five days we made but slow progress towards Samoa, for the trade wind was strong and the *Bouncer* made much leeway. The pump was kept going until the sucker wore out; and then it was discovered that there was no pump-leather in the store locker. The captain cut up his sea boots, but they did not answer well for suckers, and we had to bale the water out of the hatchway with a tub and a whip from the main-yard. I continued to take my fair share of the hauling-up work; but I did not pull exhaustively. The pump was a caution to me that I could not forget.

Fortunately for us the weather continued moderately fine, or certainly we should have foundered. On the sixth day out we spoke a ship eastward bound. She hove to at our signal of distress, and Mr. Doom was ordered to go on board and beg some pump-leather and a bag or two of buscuit, for we were running short of provisions. When I asked the captain if I might go in the boat, he said I might go to Bungaree Nore, if I liked. I had no idea where that place was; but I went below for my portmanteau, and in a few minutes more I was off like an uncaged bird. Thankful, indeed, was I to escape with my life and property from that old registered coffin. That is a short "Tale of a Tub"; I might make it longer, but it would not be cheerful reading, and there is not much novelty in such a tale, as the short and simple daily newspaper reports of "Casualties at Sea" sadly testify.

The ship we boarded was the *May Queen*, bound for California with coal. I soon made a bargain with the captain for my passage, and he seemed glad of my company, for he had not any other passenger on board. It was a delightful change for me, for the accommodation was good. That voyage with the cheerful chatty American captain is amongst my pleasantest recollections of sea life. I was rather sorry when it ended, and I had to step on shore a stranger in the wonderful young city of San Francisco.

CHAPTER XXIV.

"Oh, 'tis the sun that maketh all things shine."—*Shakespeare*

A BRIGHT Australian boy, about five years of age, said one day, with childlike artlessness, "Mother, sometimes when I am sad, if I peep up to the sky I feel glad again, because I think Jesus is up there looking at me." I am thankful to that mother for telling me many of her precocious boy's sayings, which have done me more good than some long doctrinal sermons I have listened to. There is often more practical wisdom or heart comfort in a simple remark of an intelligent child, than there is in a whole volume of metaphysical abstrusities.

After leaving the *May Queen* to go on shore, I felt my constitutional depression creeping over me again like black spiders. It may seem childish of me to mention it, but just then little Sam's happy expedient occurred to my mind, and I thought I would try it. I looked upward for a second or two, and it made me sneeze; but I tried it again, and as I did so I mentally reasoned with myself thus: "High up in yon blue sky is the glorious sun, and it is shining upon half the world, warming everything it looks at, and making the whole face of nature bright and beautiful and lively. Now, if

I were to go and hide myself in the depths of a gold mine, or some other dark place when I get on shore, I should not see a glimpse of the sun's light, and should feel very little of its enlivening heat. The Almighty would not prevent me from burying myself like a mole if I were so inclined, but He does not decree or desire such seclusion. Nor does he wish me to be dreary while the heavens are declaring His glory, and when even these little mosquitoes are making music in the air, as if to trumpet forth their gratitude for life and freedom on this fine sunny morning. Why then should I not look with grateful eyes on the beauties of this new world around me, and bid my heart rejoice that I have escaped the perils and dangers of the sea,—that I sit here this morning safe and sound, a living man with a thankful heart?"

That quiet mental exercise seemed to calm my spirits wonderfully, and I presently got so lively that I began to sing part of a hymn of Dr. Watts', that my dear sister and I have often sung together long ago,—

"Why should the children of a king
Go mourning all their days?"

I think the sailors who were rowing me to shore were glad to hear me burst out singing, for they smiled and seemed to put more springiness into their strokes. I felt as happy as a bird.

I had often heard of ruffians with revolvers and bowie knives in their belts, who were always ready to slay a man for mere practice; I had also heard of other objectionable customs and pastimes of Californian society; still, I stepped ashore with a confident air. I feared no evil. I daresay if I had gone to look for rowdy company, I need not have walked far; but my tastes did not incline that way. Nobody molested me or showed any disposition to do so, that I observed. It is my opinion that a steady, honest man may find friends and congenial society in whatever part of the civilized world he may travel to; and in general he has not much to fear from foes, if he minds his own business, and does not intermeddle with other people's affairs.

Through the introduction of the captain of the *May Queen*, I got lodgings with a respectable family. A few days afterwards I went as assistant to one of the first druggist's shops in the city. My employer was a native of Boston. He had been established in San Francisco about five years, and had made money. There was as much difference between him and Mr. Cudbear, as there is between a blood horse and a donkey. Mr. Honeyman was a shrewd business man, but he did not make a slave of himself or of his helpers. He seemed to try to get as much happiness as he possibly could out of each day; but in doing so he did not neglect his shop. I soon grew fond of him, for he was more like a brother to me than an employer. His kindness of manner incited me always to strive to please him.

For six months I lived very contentedly. I had every Sunday to myself, so I joined a Church and took the Bible-class in a Sunday school. I grew increasingly partial to American institutions, as I became better acquainted with them and as my old silly prejudices wore away. I thought that America was the grandest country in the world; that everything seemed to be planned by nature on a gigantic scale, and that the Americans as a people were destined to be great—or perhaps the greatest among nations. I encouraged serious thoughts of becoming a naturalized citizen of the United States; and of thenceforward hailing the star-spangled banner as my national flag. How I came to change my mind again I will tell, as briefly as I can, for it is rather a delicate disclosure; but were I to omit it there would be an awkward gap in my story, like a hole in a bridge.

I will not allow anybody to dispute the fact that my voluntary search for unfortunate Morton was actuated by pure, unselfish kindness alone. That point is settled then. I confess that while I was following his mortal remains to the grave, a thought did once flash across my mind that his poor wife was now a widow; but I scouted the suggestion that followed, without a moment's parley. The same idea obtruded into my mind from time to time, but I would never entertain it while—to use a common phrase—the poor man's corpse was still warm. I hate meanness. After the lapse of six months, however, I ventured to believe that there was no moral wrong or indelicacy in my *thinking* of Ella in a tender way; and then my love for her soon began to glow again, and I longed to go and see her. That desire strengthened every day, until it grew stronger than patriotism, or love for my employer, or any other social or political virtue, and I was on the look out for a ship bound to Australia. What seemed to spur me on more earnestly was the idea, which came into my head all of a sudden, that Ella might possibly be wooed and won by some other suitor before I got back to the colony. I gave my employer a month's notice and prepared for a start. He seemed loath to lose me, and offered me a share in his business if I liked to stay; but I would not have stayed if I had been offered the Presidency of the United States. I took a cabin berth in a ship that was loading flour for Sydney.

Three days before I sailed a disastrous fire occurred, which destroyed fully a third of San Francisco city, including Mr. Honeyman's shop. I was exceedingly sorry for his loss, for he was not insured. The morning after the fire he remarked to me, in his usual off-hand way, "This is a bad turn for me, Roger; but it is worse for poor Boles, the chemist in the next block, he has lost every cent he was worth. I shall sell my little farm at Sacramento River, and that will start me off again." Mr. Honeyman owed me 160 dollars for two months' wages, which he offered to pay me; but I positively declined to take the money. That same afternoon he went to a lumber sale and bought materials for erecting a new shop; and I daresay he was doing business again in less than a month. If that man lives he will perhaps make a fortune. I hope he may, for he will do good with his money. He has the heart of a Peabody or a Stuart.

After a fair passage I arrived safely in Sydney. I went to stay at my old lodgings until the next boat sailed for Melbourne. Mrs. Dyke was glad to see me again; but her glad looks soon changed when I asked after her family.

She presently told me that Selina's husband had left her, and she was then occupying the front room, and trying to get a living for herself and infant by taking music pupils. It was a sad story that I had to listen to. The substance of it was, that Mr. Burney had deceived them all as to his pecuniary means. He had always lived beyond his income, and he was in debt when he married. He had managed to get further into debt, for he liked good living, and he would have luxuries so long as tradesmen would trust him. The end of it was that he was forced into the insolvent court; and as he had no assets save his furniture, his creditors took that, and poor Selina had to go back to her mother. Mr. Burney was dismissed from his situation; and after living for two months at Mrs. Dyke's expense, he started off to some new diggings, and had not since communicated with his wife.

Poor Selina! I pitied her. She was a nice girl, and would have made an excellent wife, if she had waited till the right man offered himself. But she was in too great haste to get married. Perhaps she was anxious to outmatch some of her young schoolfellows; at any rate she accepted a man without sufficiently scrutinizing his character, and now she has sorrowful reason to repent of her precipitancy. I thought Mrs. Dyke ought to have been more watchful over her young daughters; but of course I did not even hint my opinion to her, for I could see that the poor old lady was in great trouble.

She further told me that her son Bob was still in the broker's office, at the same low salary. Bob was not so steady as she could wish; but she hoped that as he grew older he would get more sense. It is a reasonable hope, and I trust it will be realized.

On the following Saturday I started for Melbourne in one of the inter-colonial steamers, and, as usual in those golden times, it was over-crowded with passengers. I had secured a sleeping berth on the previous day, otherwise I must have put up with a shakedown on deck, as scores of berthless passengers had to do. In addition to the ordinary rush of gold miners going to the rich Victorian diggings, there were a score or two of sporting men, who were returning to Melbourne after their annual visit to the Randwick Derby, besides the members of a travelling circus. It will therefore be judged that the saloon of the steamer was over full, and there was more excitement than any quiet man would like. I sat at the table that night reading, as well as I could for the distracting noise around me. At ten o'clock I put my book into my pocket and prepared to go to bed. A friend in Sydney had given me some homœopathic tincture, which was said to be a specific for sea-sickness; so I asked the steward for a tumbler, and carefully watching the roll of the ship, I managed to drop a single minim from a phial into the glass, then adding a teaspoonful of water, I sipped it and went to a small cabin off the saloon, which I had to share with three gentlemen of the circus troupe. The unusual call for an empty tumbler had attracted the attention of the passengers who sat at the long table, and I noticed that they left off card playing and watched me, with lively interest, as I dropped my infinitesimal dose into the glass. When inside my cabin I overheard one of them say, "That fellow has got some woefully strong stuff in his phial; I wonder what it is?"

"Iron tonic, perhaps, distilled from old steam hammers and thunderbolts," remarked another man, drily.

"It smells like potato whisky, or something of that bad sort," said a third joker. "I hope he hasn't taken a drop too much, for he is one of my cabin mates."

Some time after midnight, I was disturbed in my first nap by a tipsy man blundering into the cabin to go to his berth, and being only half awake, I muttered an exclamation of surprise, which I but indistinctly remember. I however heard the intruder go back into the saloon and laughingly say, "Ha, ha! the chap who swallowed that tremendous dose an hour or two ago is quite drunk, and he swears he'll blow up the ship with his little bottle, if we don't all go to bed directly."

The next afternoon we put into Twofold Bay, to land some gold miners who were going to the Kiandra diggings. I was hopeful that the ship would be more quiet after they left, for never before in my life, either in savage Fiji, or elsewhere, did I pass such a comfortless Sabbath. But to my disappointment there was a little crowd of miners on the wharf at Eden, who had come down from the Snowy River diggings, and were going to try their luck in Victoria. I might fairly have expected to see a sedate company embark from a town with such a happy name as Eden; but on the contrary, they were as prime a lot of rollicking "bhoys," as ever kicked up a shindy at Donnybrook fair, or any other lively place.

As we passed out of Twofold Bay in the dusk of the evening, an unfinished lighthouse on the southern shore attracted my notice. There stood a lofty circular tower on a rocky eminence, but with no lantern to it, and of course it showed no more light than the rock itself did. The sight of it had a gloomy influence on me, like gazing at an old mummy. I am not able just now to expatiate on the moral lessons or reproofs it seemed to aim at me; but any good pastor is welcome to reflect on the dark lighthouse, and use it in his pulpit as a solemn admonition to unprofitable professors. More than once on that cheerless Sunday evening I felt half impelled to stand up and show my gospel light or knowledge in the midst of that noisy company; but my courage failed me, and I slunk off, like another Jonah, into the most out-of-the-way nook I could find below, which was not much quieter than the 'tween decks of a cattle ship.

There stands the empty lighthouse to this day, as useless as one of the crumbling columns of ancient Sardis. But it often reminds old colonists of a romance in real life, which I will briefly notice in this chapter —"for auld lang syne."

Somewhere about forty years ago, a young Scotch gentleman arrived in Sydney with an abundance of money, partly his own and partly the capital of his friends at home, who evidently had unbounded confidence in his tact and ability to invest it for them in a profitable way. He was a remarkably fine-looking man, and of a highly-cultured mind—a fair type of "Tom Brown" after his schooldays were over. When he stood on the deck of his handsome schooner yacht, he looked the very *beau ideal* of a sailor; and if I add that he could handle his craft as smartly as any of the young Australian yachtsmen, it will be paying the highest tribute I can to his courage and skill on the water. He came to the colony at a time of severe depression, especially in pastoral affairs; so, as a buyer of stock and stations for ready cash, he was a welcome visitor to many an embarrassed man's homestead in the bush. Mr. Boyd went in for investments with a steady pluck, as well as with deliberate judgment, and he was not particular what he invested in, in an honest respectable way, so long as it gave promise of fair interest for his capital. He bought sheep and cattle and horses in tens of thousands; also town land and country land, and whaling ships and steam ships. He had warehouses and wharves and a bank; and a township was mapped out and named after himself, and the said lighthouse was built to guide vessels to safe anchorage off the site of the town. Boyd's superintendents were numerous, and some of them were as aristocratic as the old East India's Company's officers, and their orders passed current in bush or city as readily as Union Bank notes. Some colonial croakers used to say that Mr. Boyd had "too many irons in the fire"; but that is a rusty old saw, which has often jagged the credit of enterprising men. I will not try to explain the cause of the failure of Mr. Boyd's grand projects. They were not all successful, and many persons were sorry for it ; that is as much as I need say. No doubt he had much worry and anxiety with his very extensive investments; and to get away from business for awhile and to recruit his health, he sailed in his schooner for the South Seas. Sad to relate he was soon afterwards murdered by the natives on one of the savage islands—or so it was reported. The crew of his yacht were returning to Sydney with the mournful news, when they went on shore in a gale of wind near Port Macquarie, and the beautiful clipper, *Wanderer*, became a total wreck.

Many old colonists can remember Mr. Benjamin Boyd's tall athletic figure, and his cheery, sonorous voice. He was well-known and much respected in Australia ; and the non-success of his plans and his mournful fate caused a general regret. If he had lived to the present time, and retained his extensive pastoral possessions, he would be enormously wealthy; and then *who* would question his wisdom, or blame him for putting "too many irons in the fire"? No doubt there would, in that case, be a lantern on that deserted lighthouse, and perhaps the present bush-covered site of Boydtown would be a flourishing city.

> " Should auld acquaintance be forgot,
> And never brought to mind?"

CHAPTER XXV.

> "Save the love we pay to Heaven,
> None purer, holier than that
> A virtuous woman feels for him she'd cleave
> Through life to."—*Sheridan Knowles.*

On my arrival at Melbourne, I went direct to Rose Villa, and was just in time for tea. The Moss family were glad to see me, and welcomed me back as cordially as if I were a near relative. They listened with much interest while I gave them a summary of my adventures; and they said some pleasing things about my kindness in volunteering for such a troublesome undertaking. The children were also very demonstrative in their affection for me, especially my little favourite, Nelly, who had grown amazingly during my absence, and was a most interesting child.

After tea I went into the library with Mr. Moss, and there I opened my mind to him on the subject of my attachment to Ella; and I asked him if he thought there was any impropriety in my making proposals to her without delay.

"There can be no impropriety in your doing so, Roger; Morton has been dead ten months. It would, perhaps, be more delicate for you to wait a few months longer; but then you would run a risk of losing your prize, some man more bold and less scrupulous might forestall you."

"Do you think so, Mr. Moss?"

"Yes, I do; indeed, I have reason to believe that somebody is now looking at her with matrimonial desires. But do not be upset, Roger," he quickly added, as he perhaps observed that I was turning yellow. "I do not think she will accept Bushby, though he is rich and rather grand in his way; at any rate you stand a better chance than he if you make haste,—I have no doubt about that. It would be absurd to compare you with him."

"Who is Mr. Bushby?" I asked, with affected calmness.

"Don't you know old John Bushby? He is one of Mr. Benson's congregation, and M.P. for—for—I forget the place just now."

"Rich and grand, and a member of parliament! She will surely prefer him to poor Roger!" I thought; and I could not help sighing aloud.

"Tut! You need not be so uneasy, Roger," continued Mr. Moss. "I scarcely believe she will accept a little old shrimp of a fellow, who has two daughters as old as herself."

Those words revived me like smelling-salts. I had no fear for such a rival, if his money and title did not make Ella blind to his personal defects and heedless of his incumbrances. I drew myself up to my full height again.

"Now I advise you to go and see the widow at once, Roger; pop the question like a man, and don't mince matters, as you would have to do if she were a maiden and did not know anything about courting. I believe she will accept your offer without much pressing; anyway, if she prefers old Bushby to you, be sure that you will be better off without her, for it will be proof positive that she is a silly woman."

"I had intended to wait till I got a situation, sir. I could offer her my hand with more confidence, if I knew that I had the means or the prospect of providing a good home for her."

"Quite right, Roger. But now let me tell you that I have something in view for you, which will be much better than an assistant's berth. I did not mean to name it to you to-night, but perhaps I had better tell you in a few words something about it. I am building three shops, not far from the Town Hall at Prahran. One of them I shall fit up in good style for a chemist and druggist. Prahran is a rising suburb, you know, and there is a good opening for another chemist and druggist. A little fortune is to be made there in time, and you are a likely fellow to make it. I have been long anxious to show you some substantial token of my gratitude for your noble conduct in saving the life of my dear child, and I think I have now a good opportunity of doing so; in short, I mean to set you up in business, if you do not object. Thus I shall help you, and serve myself by securing a good tenant. Ha! ha! a lucky double hit of mine, you see. I hope you won't say nay to it, Roger, and upset all my plans."

I was quite taken aback by that unexpected stroke of good fortune. I was stammering my thanks to my generous friend, when he said jocosely, "You have not time to spare for compliments, for it is getting late, Roger. I am glad to see that you do not object to my scheme. Now hasten away directly and make it all right with the pretty widow; we can talk about the new shop some other time. The builders will not be out of it for a month, or perhaps five weeks."

I took a cab and went off to Ivy House. I expected to find Mr. Benson at home, for on Tuesday evening he was usually at leisure. To my surprise and concern, both Mr. and Mrs. Benson received me with a stately politeness, quite different to their former friendly bearing. I felt hurt; and if I had yielded to my first petty impulse, I should have taken my hat and bade them good-night. Happy for me that I was early taught to control my temper, or I should have made a sad mistake that night. By keeping cool and cautious, I soon found that Mr. and Mrs. Benson were under the impression that I had been wasting my time in Fiji ever since Morton's death. I have since learned that they got an unfavourable report of me from the captain of the *Ariel* on his return to Melbourne. I had offended the captain in some way when I was on board his vessel. I scarcely know how I did it; but it is not a very unusual thing for passengers, however careful they may be, to excite the feelings of some sea-captains, especially at times of protracted head winds or more tantalizing calms. Master mariners at such times are, perhaps, short of patience. But there is the excuse for them that they often have impatient, unreasonable owners, who seldom will look into the log book, to judge fairly of the cause of their ship having made a protracted voyage, until after they have discharged the captain as a drowsy man. Mortal man cannot make a sailing ship go head to wind, nor make it go ahead in a dead calm. When I told the Bensons about my involuntary voyage to California, and especially when I showed them the testimonials I had received from Mr. Honeyman and the Rev. William Taylor, their frigid manner waxed warmer, and they welcomed me back with a cordiality which touched my heart and sweetened my temper in a minute.

They had evidently resolved not to let me see Ella; and had I been too hasty I should have gone away sorrowing. But when the misunderstanding was removed, they rang the bell and in walked Ella in her widow's garb, looking mournfully beautiful. Her manner was reserved at first; but she grew more affable when Mrs. Benson had spoken a few words aside to her, of which I guessed the import. After awhile Mr. and Mrs. Benson left the room, and then I gave Ella a few particulars of poor Morton's death, which I had omitted in my written report. As she sat and wept over the memory of her deceased husband, I fancied it was a sort of sacrilege for me to foster thoughts of a new partnership with her, and my courting resolution was failing me. But she soon dried up her tears; and when I began to talk about her little pupils—by way of diverting her thoughts—she grew so fascinatingly lively, that I could no longer restrain my love from making itself heard and seen—and felt; so I stood up and said, with the manly boldness which Mr. Moss had prompted, "Ella! My darling Ella! let me tell you again that I love you ardently. I have never ceased to love you since I first saw your sweet face. I cannot live happily without you. I have the prospect of being able to support you comfortably, to provide a good home for you, and I will do my utmost to make you happy. Will you accept me? Will you consent to be my wife, at some early period? Say yes, my precious Ella! and make me the happiest man alive."

Without a minute's pause for consideration, she raised her head and looked at me with her beautiful truthful eyes, and there was a loving smile on her face which sent a rapturous thrill all through my system. She extended her right hand, and said in accents tenderly firm: "Take my hand, dear Roger! and with it take my heart. No man on earth has a truer claim to my life's affection than you have, and you shall have it all."

Oh, the ecstasy of that moment! The precious overflow of satisfaction! I can no more describe it all than I could paint a view of Jerusalem. While uttering my short declaration of love, I felt as cautious as I have since felt while lighting a fuse in a deep mining claim; but her prompt reply drove away all jealous fears for old rickety Bushby, and surcharged my heart with a sort of dancing rapture, which only a first-class poet could depict. Need I say that I kissed her soft, unresisting lips? But perhaps I had better not say any more about that true-love scene. I will only add, in plain prose, that dear Ella and I made an engagement that evening; and when Mr. and Mrs. Benson returned to the parlour, we told them of the happy fact, and they were glad.

The next morning, after breakfast, I went to tell Mr. Moss of my successful courting, and he warmly congratulated me. We then went to look at my new shop at Prahran; and, on the way thither, Mr. Moss told me that he intended to get me a cash-credit for £1000, at the Commercial Bank; so that I could buy my stock-in-trade and household effects with ready cash. I was thankful.

Many persons beside myself have been vexed at the tardiness of builders. My patience was almost worn out by them. Day after day I used to pay visits to the new shop, by way of spurring on the drowsy workmen; but they seemed to be insensible to my appeals, whether gentle or otherwise. Even the crown pieces, which I on four separate occasions gave the fellows, as a stimulus to their efforts to get out of the house soon, had a contrary effect to that which I anticipated; for each crown had just sufficed to buy beer enough to make them all tipsy and incapable of working for the day. The plasterers were the most tiresome fellows in the gang; they always seemed to be waiting for one coat of stuff to dry, before they began to daub over the walls and ceilings again. I would have gone into the house with the bare laths grinning at me, if the fellows would only have taken their dirty affairs out. Expectant bachelors can sympathize with my impatience, if nobody else will. Ten weeks elapsed from the night when Mr. Moss first spoke to me about the shop, before those dawdling workmen had finished and carried off their tools. Thus the happiness of dear Ella and myself was deferred for more than a month beyond our anticipated wedding-day; but she never uttered an impatient word or showed the least sign of disappointment.

At length the house was finished and furnished. The stock was also in the shop, and I had engaged a competent assistant. I never shall forget the pleasure and pride I felt in arranging the stock on my shelves and the show-bottles in my shop-window. When it was all finished, Mr. Moss paid me the compliment of saying that he did not think there was a neater little chemist's shop in Victoria than mine. Two days afterwards my devoted Ella and I were married by the Rev. Mr. Benson. Mr. Moss was my best man, and dear little Nelly was one of the bridesmaids, and remarkably pretty she looked. We took our wedding breakfast at Ivy House,—the nicest breakfast I ever partook of. Grandfather Moss threw an old slipper after us for luck, as we were leaving the hall door of the parsonage to get into the carriage that was to take us to the steamer, and loving congratulations sounded in our ears as pleasantly as silver bells.

Whether there was some kind of attractive influence

in the igneous rock upon which I was first bumped on the coast, I will not try to determine, but Queenscliff certainly had a peculiar charm for me. I proposed to spend our honeymoon there. Dear Ella said she could be happy anywhere with me; so to Queenscliff we went, and a precious fortnight we spent there. I shall never forget it. I would liked to have had a month of it, but remembered that I was only a young beginner in business; and I fancied, too, that we might live more economically in our own home than we could do at an hotel on honeymoon fare.

CHAPTER XXVI.

"Life's little stage is small eminence,
Inch high above the grave."—*Young*.

WHEN my wife and I returned home after our bridal tour, we found many valuable tokens of the kindness of our friends. In the drawing-room was a handsome new piano, the gift of dear little Nelly; on the mantel-shelf was an elegant clock, the gift of Mrs. Moss; and sundry smart cushions and mats and other drawing-room luxuries, presents from Mrs. Benson and her daughters, Ella's young pupils. On the dining-room mantel-piece was another clock of a more solid make, the gift of Mr. Moss; and on a little table, handy to my easy chair, was a family Bible, and on it a quaintly worded note from the donor,—Grandfather Moss,—giving his personal testimony to the value of the Bible as a guide-book for life's journey; and urging me to use his present, and not to keep it merely as a smart parlour ornament.

After tea I went into the shop, and received a cheering report from my assistant. Two physicians had already sent in prescriptions, and trade had otherwise been encouraging for a first start off. When the gas was lighted, I walked over to the opposite side of the street to get a fair view of the exterior of my shop and of the gorgeous coloured lamp, which showed my name over the door in large gilt letters. I felt proud, and wished my dear Uncle Jenner could take a peep at my new shop, which far outshone his own dusky establishment at Greenwich. Dear Ella was equally pleased with her house, which she had examined from bottom to top. It certainly was furnished with taste and economical judgment.

After the shop was closed that evening, and we were almost ready to retire to our chamber, Ella looked at me with a solemn meaning, and then glanced at the Bible on the little table. I understood what she meant, but a peculiar nervous fluttering in my breast seemed to master my resolution, and I whispered, to her, "I cannot perform that duty to-night, my darling; I have never been accustomed to it."

"Will you allow me to do it, love?" she asked, in such a gentle persuasive tone that I could not object; so she rang the bell, and in came the servant maid. Ella opened the Book and read the ninety-first Psalm; and then offered up a short prayer, with such fervour and simplicity of language, that every word touched my heart. I felt truly grateful to God for surrounding me with so many mercies and comforts, and especially for blessing me with such an exemplary wife.

When we arose from our knees and the servant had retired, I kissed Ella, and was going to tell her that her prayer had done me good, but I could not utter a word. She noticed my emotion, and passing her arm fondly around my waist, she said, "Come, dear, and hear me try my piano." We went into the drawing-room, and she sat down to the instrument and played "Ken's Evening Hymn," and sang it with exquisite pathos and feeling, reminding me tenderly of my early home and of my sainted sister, for it was a favourite hymn of hers. That night I promised dear Ella that I would henceforth conduct family prayers every evening, a duty which she had so reverently begun for me. I have kept my promise.

Why any man should be shy of conducting family devotion in his own household is somewhat puzzling to me now; but so it is with many good men whom I have met with. I confess that it was a dreaded task to me at first; but with Ella's encouragement I soon ceased to regard it as a task, and I used to look forward to that evening duty as a refreshing wind up to the business of the day.

The first year of my wedded life is a memorable part of my history, and the retrospect has a mournful sort of fascination for me. But I will make this part of my story as short as I possibly can, for I could not make it interesting reading to strangers, shape it how I might.

I do not think that any young couple could have been more loving than my wife and I were. It was all harmony and peace in our home. I am just reminded of a verse in a pretty little song that Ella used to sing sometimes, to please me; it aptly portrayed our domestic life,—

> "The summer has its heavy cloud, the rose leaf will fall;
> But in our home love wears no shroud, never does it pall.
> Each new morning's ray, brings no sigh for yesterday;
> No joy passed away would grief recall."

As I retrace the time I fail to remember a single jar in our social intercourse. Nothing occurred to mar our happiness; and our letters by each mail to my dear mother in England must have cheered and comforted her loving heart, for they were always full of good news. My business, too, was prosperous, almost beyond my expectations. Ella was not over fond of making new acquaintances, but our good friends Benson and Moss were always welcome visitors to our house, and they often called to see us in a homely, unceremonious way. Both Ella and I joined Mr. Benson's Church, and took classes in the Sunday-school, and I had the honour of being appointed leader of the choir in his church.

I may mention that one day I was rather startled by reading a paragraph, copied from one of the New South Wales provincial newspapers, giving an account of the death of Mrs. Cameron, Ella's mother, through the explosion of a spirit lamp. In consideration for Ella's delicate condition, I did not let her see the paragraph, nor did I mention the sad occurrence to her. I knew that she had rational views on the subject of mourning garments for deceased friends, and that it would not afterwards pain her to reflect that she had omitted to array herself in crape on the death of her mother. For my part I never did much reverence that dismal and costly custom of society. I certainly was shocked at the awfully sudden death of Mrs. Cameron; but I cannot honestly say that I felt much regret for the loss of a relative whom I had always dreaded, nor did I feel any compunction for neglecting to honour her memory by wearing a suit of black clothes in summer time.

About fifteen months after our marriage, dear Ella and I looked joyously forward to the advent of a "little stranger." As the critical period drew near, I confess that I sometimes felt an anxiety, but perhaps not more than is usually felt by fond young husbands on such domestic epochs. Ella's sweetly placid manner was unaltered; indeed, I never saw her ruffled save on one occasion which I have before noticed. I remember her saying to me one day, with tears of joy in her expressive eyes, "O Roger! I do feel very very happy this morning! I seem to be so near to heaven, that I can almost realize its peace."

Precious Ella! Her ecstatic words made me feel nearer to heaven than I had ever been before. I love to recall that memorable morning; for though it makes my heart sore, it seems to lift me out of the world for a time.

Soon after breakfast I heard that my trusty friend Dr. Bloom had been thrown from his horse and broken his leg. That was troublesome news, for almost at the same time our nurse intimated that the services of the doctor would soon be needed. It was an unexpected dilemma; but there was no time for deploring it. Another doctor lived close by, who was generally acknowledged to be a clever practitioner, when he was not tipsy. I hastened off to his surgery. He was at home, and apparently as sober as I was myself. I explained my errand, and he went with me to my house immediately.

It was a protracted case. Throughout that day and night, and until ten o'clock the next night, my anxiety was great. I kept in my shop, but I did my work as it were mechanically. At length I was told that I was blessed with a fine little daughter, and I almost danced for joy. Presently the doctor came downstairs, and after congratulating me in a few words he went away. I fancied he did not walk steadily, but I was too much excited to observe anything very carefully. Half an hour afterwards my servant maid ran into the shop, and said that the nurse wished me to go upstairs directly.

I almost flew up into the chamber, and my first glance at dear Ella alarmed me; but I made a desperate effort to appear calm, for her eyes were fixed upon me. As I stooped down to kiss her white lips, she feebly gasped, "Roger, dear! I am dying."

"O Ella! my precious wife! do not say that again. You are faint, love," I said in a tone of assumed cheerfulness, and I put my arm tenderly under her drooping head while I administered some medicine, which I hoped would be a restorative.

"Yes—dearest Roger! I am—go—ing to—heaven! Take care—of our dear babe—and—follow me—home!"

Those were her last words. They were uttered slowly,

but very distinctly, and there was an emphasis on the word *home* which has vibrated on my heart ever since.

I will not trust my pen even to hint, more than it has already done, at the cause of my beloved wife's untimely end, nor will I try to describe my gloomy home life for the ensuing nine months. Every room in my house seemed to be emptied of comfort. The declining state of my health at length became an anxiety to my friends, and Dr. Bloom gently insisted on my withdrawing from business, and taking a thorough change for awhile; so I resolved to go to Sydney. I had before placed my darling infant in charge of a respectable married couple at Toorak, and Mrs. Moss and Mrs. Benson kindly offered to see that she was well cared for. Nelly Moss said, that if her mamma would allow her, she would go out every Wednesday half-holiday during my absence, and nurse dear little Emma. It cost me a struggle to leave her, and I never till then knew what a strong natural tie binds an infant to a loving father's heart. I went to Sydney, and soon a marked improvement was noticeable in my haggard face, and I felt that my strength was returning.

One afternoon I went for a drive in a safety cab; some street noise frightened the young horse (which I dare say was fresh from the bush), and he ran away and upset the cab. I was severely hurt, and was carried to my lodgings insensible. In the next chapter I shall say a little about my peculiar experience during the wearisome time that I was again laid up with fractured

X

bones. After I recovered from the accident, I returned to Melbourne; and before resuming my business duties I went to stay a fortnight at Toorak, in the house of the young couple who had charge of my infant. Part of that time will always be green in my memory. I used to walk about the garden among the flowers with my precious daughter, who could run alone and was just able to lisp simple words. I would sit for hours together under the shade of a spreading acacia tree, nursing little Emma and fondly picturing days and years of future happiness when my darling grew up to womanhood. What a cheering companion she would be to me! How she would sooth and comfort me, and strive to supply the love of wife and sister, which I so sorely missed! What a delight it would be to me to watch the development of her personal charms, and the expanding of her precocious intellect! Ah me! none of those fond anticipations were to be realized; but I must hasten to the close of this sad chapter.

A lady came to the house one afternoon. She wore a French merino dress, and she carried the germs of death in its ample folds, for she had just before been on a visit to a house where some children were ill with scarlatina. I dare not repeat the plain words that Dr. Bloom vociferated against the lady for coming to the house and fondling my infant, nor tell how severely he condemned all the tribe of busybodies who go gossiping about the bedsides of fever-stricken patients, and then carry infection into other homes. I certainly think the said lady was thoughtless, but she was not unkind. Sadly I state that my precious child took scarlatina on the very evening of the lady's visit, and all Dr. Bloom's special skill in fever cases could not avert the fatal effects of the disease. My darling died in my arms, after a season of such intense suffering that I was thankful to see her released, though it was a double wrench to my heart which words cannot describe.

My late beloved wife and child are lying in one grave in the Melbourne General Cemetery. A white marble slab marks the place of their burial; but I should know it without such a landmark. It is a sacred spot, where I have spent many meditative hours, both by day and by night. The subjoined beautiful verse is the epitaph:

> "Yet these new rising from the tomb,
> In lustre brighter far shall shine;
> Revive, with ever during bloom,
> Safe from diseases and decline."

CHAPTER XXVII.

"One woe doth tread upon another's heels,
So fast they follow."—*Shakespeare.*

I CANNOT just now think of any way in which I might have aroused my Cousin Saul's feelings more quickly than I did the other night by innocently questioning his literary taste. He could not stand that, and we had a sad quarrel. I will soon explain all that it is necessary to say about the affair. Saul has several times lately complained that my story was getting too solemnly didactic to be popular, and he wished me to let him "spice it up," as he calls it, with some fanciful sketches from my diary of incidents of my travels. He said that such a collection of natural and sensational facts and scraps as I have in my note-book are as handy to an author as leather chips are to a cobbler, or as wooden skewers are to a butcher, and it is a sin to waste them. He was very cross because I declined to let him ransack my diary. It would be painful to me to see a chapter of his racy comments on things in general, just after my sad account of the death of my poor wife and child, and I told him so. He completely lost his temper; and after abusing me and my book in words which any conscientious reviewer would shudder at, he took himself off, and I think he has gone to the diggings again. I am not very sorry to part with him, for of late I have dreaded his censorian visits almost as much as if he were a surgeon coming to take out my weak eye. No doubt I shall miss his literary help, now that I have got used to it, but I shall be happily free from the peculiar worry which a nagging companion always causes to a sensitive mind. Peace I must have, or I cannot work at all.

Chesterfield says: "Wit is a very unpopular denomination, as it carries terror along with it; and people in general are as much afraid of a live wit in company as a woman is of a gun, which she thinks may go off of itself and do her mischief." My Cousin Saul is a wit, and I verily believe that he would not hesitate to scarify his own brother—let alone his cousin—for the sake of a new joke or a thrilling surprise. I told him on one occasion, when he was trying to show me the distinction between allowable hyperbole and wicked lies in a moral book, that I would never ignore truth, modesty, friendship, or any other virtue, for all the literary popularity in the world; on which he playfully remarked, "You have no more poetry in you, Roger, than a working bullock."

"I cannot help that, cousin," I said; "and I don't care much about my lack in that way, so long as I have honesty and common sense."

The salutary effect of change of air and change of scene on persons suffering from bodily or mental affliction has been gratefully acknowledged by hosts of patients besides myself. I do wish I could devise some happy plan of making my experience in that way helpful to poor invalids who are unable, from want of means, to try a change from their murky town or city homes to the pure air and enlivening peacefulness of the country. How glad I should feel this evening, as I sit writing, if I could be assured that some rich lady or gentleman will be influenced by this paragraph—when it is printed—to kindly furnish the means to a poor sick neighbour for a month's change into the green country!

From Melbourne to Sydney is about as striking a change as it would be from London to Colchester, or some other pretty inland borough in England. I do not mean to say that there is so great a difference in the size of Melbourne and Sydney, but the latter is more homelike to me, and there is less dash observable in its social life than there is in its handsome young sister city. Dr. Bloom showed his unselfish kindness, as well as his good judgment, when he recommended me to go to Sydney for a change. It was like throwing away his fees, but he knew that the trip would do me more good than all the physic he could prescribe. Blessings on the heads of doctors who study the weal of their patients more than they do their own pockets! I have met with some good men of that disposition in my travels.

I meant to have stayed in Sydney only a few weeks; but I was, as I before stated, upset in a runaway cab, and broke my left arm and my right leg, so I was obliged to lie in bed quietly for several months. I lodged all the time at Mrs. Dyke's house. There was a Miss Pikey staying there, who had lately come from England. She said she was visiting Australia for the purpose of studying the manners of colonial society—to write a book, I suppose. She was not young, and had evidently seen much of the world, for she was very shrewd. After my accident she showed so much sisterly sympathy for me, that I could not but feel thankful. Nothing perhaps stirs up a man's gratitude so much as kind attention from a woman in times of severe bodily and mental trial. An old song says, "The touch of a gentle hand sorrow will remove." I have no doubt it is true to a certain extent. Miss Pikey was very attentive to me. She often sat in my room for hours together and read to me, and tried to raise my drooping spirits by many other cheerful acts of kindness. By degrees she gained my confidence, and I told her all my troubles. She urged me to look upon her as a sister, and to use a brother's freedom with her. She was not prepossessing in her looks, but her manner towards me was soft and kind and soothing. It is no wonder that I enjoyed her company; for it is very monotonous for a man to lie flat on his back without moving an inch, for months on a stretch. I wish now that I had kept my tongue as still as I kept my broken limbs, or that I had been less communicative to Miss Pikey; but she had a peculiar way of drawing me out, and I thought she was honest and artless. I was as innocent as any brother on earth of a desire or intention to make love to her. How could I possibly think of such a thing, while my heart was still bleeding for the loss of my precious Ella?

I confess that I kissed Miss Pikey when I parted from her for good, but that was a mere formal salute. Soon after my return to Victoria I wrote to her, and gave her —in the fulness of my heart—an account of the death of my darling child. She sent me a tender, sympathising letter by return of post, and enclosed some verses of her own composition, on " My infant in heaven." It was only right and courteous for me to write and thank her for her poetry; and I did so with honest warmth. I subsequently received other letters from her; but having many troublesome matters to engage my thoughts, I omitted to write to her again; indeed, I never meant to keep up a correspondence with her. My astonishment and vexation may be imagined, when I received a letter rather sharply remonstrating with me on my neglect. I did not answer that letter; and soon afterwards I received another, imperatively calling upon me to fulfil my promise of marriage. Without taking time to coolly reflect on the danger of penning words that might be produced as evidence against me, I wrote her an indignant reply, hoping it would extinguish her love; and that shows how little I know about an over-warm woman's nature. The next letter I received was from her lawyer, informing me that he intended to commence an action against me for breach of promise of marriage, unless I chose to pay his client, Maud Pikey, two thousand pounds, and professional costs.

I was very much upset. How could I be otherwise? I felt a delicacy in speaking to any of my friends about it; so I carried the dead weight, I may say, of my fresh trouble in my own breast. I soon had another unexpected trouble on top of it, and that was the last straw, or faggot, that broke me down; and as a business man I have never got up again. I will explain it all as well as I can; but it is not a pleasant retrospect.

I before stated that I had a competent assistant. John Sams was his name. I got him direct from the ship that he arrived in from London, so I felt assured that he had no colonial nonsense about him. His testimonials were flattering. He was a remarkably quiet young man; indeed, no one would have supposed that he was a chemist's assistant, he was so placid. I thought he was the most unselfish man I had ever met with in trade; for he was always willing to stay in the shop and take the work off my hands, and he was most attentive and conciliating to customers. When I told him that I hoped to be able to increase his salary next year, he said he was quite satisfied with what I paid him. I never met with a man who seemed to care less for money than he did, or one who spent so little on himself. Besides, he was very sympathising—or at least I thought so, for I have often noticed tears in his eyes when he saw me sorrowing over my bereavement. I placed unbounded confidence in him.

It was just at the period for my second annual stock-taking, that I received the harassing letter from Miss Pikey's lawyer. Mr. Sams saw that something was troubling me, and he said he was willing to take stock without my help; he would work day and night at it. I thought it was generous of him to make the offer, but I would not agree to it; for I considered it would be imposing on his good nature. We took stock; and after summing up carefully, I found, to my surprise and chagrin, that I was not much better off than when I first opened shop. Mr. Sams seemed astonished, and said he could not account for it. Perplexed beyond measure, I went off to tell my new trouble to Mr. Moss. He looked carefully over the balance sheet, which I carried with me, and then he said emphatically, and with a look of real pity,—

"I will give you my opinion in a few plain words, Roger. That shopman of yours has been robbing you."

"Do you think so, sir?"

"Yes, I certainly do, and I believe you think so. The truth is, I have suspected, for some months past, that the fellow was a schemer; but I had no means of testing his honesty. The first time I mistrusted him, was soon after you left for Sydney. When he was telling me how deeply he felt for your sorrows, there was a roguishly cunning look in his eyes which I was afraid of; and I thought to myself, If you are not a thief, Mr. Sams, your looks just now belie you. Now I advise you, Roger, to go and start him off at once. Get rid of the robber before he murders you."

"But I think it is my bounden duty to bring him to justice. It is not fair to let a thief loose on society."

"How can you prove that he is one?"

"This miserable balance-sheet is enough to prove it, sir. I am positive that my business has incressed rather than fallen off for the last twelve months."

"True; but all that does not amount to *legal* proof that Sams has robbed you. You cannot touch him, and he knows it, the wily rogue. Go home and discharge him directly. That is the best thing you can do; and mind you do it quietly, quarrelling with such a fellow would only injure yourself."

I went home, and by a strong effort I managed to say calmly to Mr. Sams, "I shall not require your services any more. You must leave my house immediately."

"Very good, sir," he replied, in his usual snivelling tone; and without another word he left the shop, and went to his room to pack up his effects.

I sent an advertisement to the newspapers for another assistant; and the next forenoon I had several applicants. I engaged the smartest-looking young man in the lot. He had a strong recommendation for ability from some chemist at Ballarat.

Two days afterwards, Mr. Sams walked demurely into the shop, and asked me to give him a written certificate of character. In an instant my indignation bubbled over, and I shouted to him, as I pointed to the door, " Walk out of my shop instantly, or I'll thump the life out of you, you abominable rogue!"

That was all I said, but it was more than I could afford to say, for each hard word cost me nearly fifty pounds. I was very much excited, and I did not reflect until it was half a minute too late. Sams shuffled off at once, no doubt pleased at the success of his speculation.

I then put on my hat and went off to Rose Villa. I stopped there several hours, for I wished to see Mr. Moss to tell him what had just occurred; but he did not come home that evening. When I returned to my shop at nine o'clock, I found my new assistant lying down behind the counter, drunk. I went for a policeman and had him carried away to the lock-up.

Because I unfortunately happened to get two bad specimens of the genus, I by no means wish to underrate chemists' assistants in general. My third was one of the right sort—a young man of principle, and thoroughly trustworthy. I am sure he would say that I was not a bad master; at all events, he would give me credit for lightening his Sunday work as much as I possibly could. I have no doubt that with his talented co-operation, my trade would have revived again; but I seemed to have lost all heart and energy for business. I longed to get into some pleasant nook in the country, where I could be quiet for awhile and rest my heart.

Mr. Sams soon brought an action for defamation against me. He had my late sottish assistant as a witness, and he swore terribly hard. No doubt he was paid for it; besides, it gave him a nice chance of paying me the grudge he owed me for putting him in the lock-up. Sams got a verdict and £150 damages. The law costs were nearly £100 more. It will be a lifelong warning to me, to "hold my tongue."

About the same time I got notice of action, at suit

Pikey *versus* Larksway. In a desperate spirit of resistance, I vowed that I would not let all my honest creditors' money go into the pockets of swindlers; so first of all I sold my business to a ready-money purchaser. I made the more haste over that bargain, because I heard that Mr. Sams was going to open a shop in the neighbourhood. I sold the section of land which had belonged to poor Ella, for ready cash, and I paid Mr. Moss, and every other creditor in full; then I went to Sydney to defend the lawsuit. Some friends of the plaintiff came to me on the evening that I landed from the steamer, and proposed that I should settle the case amicably, namely, by paying all law costs and giving the plaintiff a moderate compensation; but I sternly replied that I would be skinned alive before I would pay Miss Pikey even the price of a brass bodkin.

It was a vexatious suit for me, though it afforded much amusement to the crowded court, and some nice sensational stuff for the newspapers. Miss Pikey lost her case; and I should guess from her miserable appearance in court, that she was very sorry she had been persuaded to sue me for damages, and make a show of herself.

I have heard some talkative persons say that "they never did anything they were ashamed of." I should be ashamed to say as much as that for myself, because it would be untrue; but I can honestly affirm that I never did half as many wickedly mischievous tricks as the counsel for the plaintiff tried, in his cross-examination, to make me confess to. He ransacked my history down to my school-days; and any simple-minded person in the court might have concluded that I was a suspicious character, if not a downright rogue; for I could not possibly help getting confused sometimes, and making mistakes in my answers to the many very cross questions that were put to me. Miss Pikey's antecedents too, came in for a searching investigation by the learned counsel for the defence. Her virtues got a thorough sifting; and vexed enough I was to see her subjected to the humiliating ordeal; for though I consider that she acted foolishly and unkindly, and caused me no end of worry, yet in all fairness I will say I do not believe that she was such a depraved woman as my barrister emphatically declared her to be. His address to the jury grated on poor Miss Pikey's virgin fame, like a baker's rasp on a French roll; and I really blushed for the seeming lack of gallantry in my learned counsel. But he did not seem to care what he said, and there was no more signs of blushing about *his* face than there is in a plaster bust of Napoleon Buonaparte. I have reason to believe that Miss Pikey was the dupe of a plausible mischief-making fellow, at that time well known in the colony, and who was notorious for instigating simple folks to go to law and fool away their money.

CHAPTER XXVIII.

"Round our path and round our bed
Angels ever watch and wait."—*Anon.*

ON my return from Sydney, after the harassing law proceedings which I have briefly noticed, I was in a weak state of health, and my doctor said it was necessary for me to rest awhile to recruit my strength. He advised me to get into some suburban locality, away from the whirl of business affairs, but where I could see a little pleasant society occasionally. At the recommendation of a friend, I went to lodge for a month or two in the house of a homely, respectable family, near Emerald Hill. Mr. and Mrs. Robinson were from the north of Scotland, and had been several years in Australia. They had an interesting family of young children, whom they were "training up in the way they should go." Both Mr. Robinson and his wife had seen much trouble and sorrow, so they knew how to sympathise with me in my varied afflictions; and I have often been cheered and helped by their intelligent, Christian counsel. They had also several relatives in the neighbourhood—exemplary people—to whom I was introduced; and I rightly estimated the honour.

It is indeed a privilege to me to have some nice

friends with whom I can occasionally spend an hour pleasantly and profitably. I have an unconquerable dislike to domestic gossip, which often means scandal; and I think I would almost as soon be out on a common in a moderate snowstorm, as be sitting by the fire indoors, if I were obliged to listen to a company of confirmed newsmongers. But I do dearly love a little easy chit-chat about things in general, or the social and religious news of the world. One way that I like to spend a fine leisure day, is to start out soon after breakfast for a day's ramble in the bush or by the sea-side. If I can get two genial companions, so much the better; for then the talking, if fairly divided, comes easier to one whose lungs are not over strong. But if I cannot get two companions, I am glad to get one, of the right sort. I am always willing to carry my own share of the day's provisions, and also to do my fair share of the talking. Many a day's real enjoyment I have had in that way in Australia, with valued friends, some of whom have ceased their earthly rambling, and others are now living in distant lands, and perhaps have nearly forgotten me and "the days when we went gipsying."

During my resting time at Emerald Hill, it was not always practicable to find a nice companion who had a day to spare; so I often took a stroll by myself. One of my favourite haunts was the Melbourne cemetery. There are many "sermons in stones" in that secluded retreat; and the solemn quietude of the place was always soothing to my wearied spirit. Another favourite resort of mine was the Melbourne Botanic

Gardens. I usually returned homeward by way of Richmond Bridge, and along the northern bank of the charming Yarra to Princes Bridge, and then took a car to Emerald Hill. But there are many other walks in the suburbs of Melbourne that were delightsome to me for their rural quietude, and also for the English-like appearance of some of the gardens and hedges about the many ornate homesteads.

One afternoon I returned to my lodgings, after a prolonged visit to the cemetery; and on entering the parlour my hostess and a lady friend of hers were sitting there, and I thought they were discussing some tender subject, for they were both shedding tears. I apologised for intruding, and was about to retire to my bedroom; but Mrs. Robinson begged me to stay, and she introduced me to her friend, Mrs. Foster.

"We were just then talking of my darling child in heaven, Mr. Larksway," said my hostess; "you will remember I told you a little about her the other day. This lady was dear Eva's governess; and she could tell you that I have not overstated my sweet child's amiable qualities."

Any reference to a child in heaven was attractive to me, for it reminded me of my own sainted infant, whom I had parted with just as her innocent blue eyes were beginning to look at me with loving intelligence. So I sat and listened with real interest, while Mrs. Foster descanted affectionately on the precocious virtues of her late favourite pupil, Eva; who I judged was about five years of age.

Y

"You know, Mrs. Foster, I once told you of the presentiment I had, that my darling Eva was not long for this world," said Mrs. Robinson, with increasing emotion. "I never saw a child of her age of such an uniformly gentle, heaven-like disposition."

"She was, indeed, a most amiable little girl; and I can truthfully say that I never had her equal in my school," responded Mrs. Foster.

For ten minutes or so, poor Eva's mother and her late governess exchanged tender memories of the dear departed one; and while I sat and listened to them, I was trying to recall the loving features of my own precious infant, whose grave I had recently visited. Presently an allusion to a mysterious occurrence at Eva's death so excited my curiosity, that I asked Mrs. Robinson to give me the particulars of it. (I may here state that I am giving assumed names, and my memory will not serve me to relate the incident precisely as it was told to me; but allowing for those variations, it is substantially true.)

After partially recovering her usual composure of manner, Mrs. Robinson said, "My dear Eva was coming home from school one afternoon, when she was met by a boy leading a fierce dog by a chain. The boy behaved in a rude way to her; and upon her resisting him as well as she was able, he threatened to make his dog bite her. Poor Eva ran away very much frightened, and did not cease running until she reached home. Her father immediately went out in search of the boy, but could not find him. Eva did not go to school again for a day or two, and then I took her there. I meant to have fetched her home, but some other duty prevented me. At the usual time in the afternoon Eva came home, looking excited but not alarmed; on the contrary, there was a peculiarly joyous expression on her face which strangely impressed me. As soon as she entered the house, she said to me, 'O mamma! I have seen such a beautiful man!'

"'Have you, my dear? Who was he?' I asked, and I took her up in my arms and kissed her.

"'Oh, I don't know who he was, ma! He had such very bright eyes, and he looked at me all the way home.'

"'Where did you first see him, my dear?'

"'I saw him at the corner, opposite the school. I was running home, for I was afraid of the boy with the big dog, and I saw the beautiful man. I don't know which way he came, ma.'

"'What did he say to you, Eva?'

"'I didn't hear him speak, ma; but he looked so very, very kind at me. Oh, I wish you had seen him, ma! He was so beautiful!'

"'Was he walking beside you, my love?'

"'Yes, ma; and he wore a long dress. Very, very white it was!'

"'But you know, my dear, that clouds are sometimes white, and they look something like men and women? Don't you remember you have told me that you often fancy you see pictures in the clouds?'

"'Yes, mamma, I know I have; but the beautiful man was not up in the clouds. He was almost close to me, and he was near me till I came inside our front gate.'

"'Did you not feel afraid of him, dear?'

"'No, mamma; I did not feel afraid. I thought he would not let the big dog bite me.'

"Question the dear girl as I would, her testimony was not in the least degree shaken," continued Mrs. Robinson. "After that she did not seem timid of going to school alone; still, I thought it was better to send some one with her, and I always took that precaution. A few months after the strange event she was taken ill. Despite all our care, and the best medical skill we could get, her disease baffled our efforts; and at length all hope of saving her life was gone. Our darling Eva—the light of our home and the idol of our heart—was to be taken from us. On the night she died, I was watching beside her cot in this very room. Every little event of that mournful time I remember as distinctly as if it were but yesterday. The gas was turned down low, and the venetian shutters outside were closed. It was near midnight, when Eva opened her eyes and gazed towards that window. I shall never forget the sweet expression of her face when she whispered to me with her dying breath, 'Oh, mamma! Look! look! There is the beautiful man again at the window!' Those were the last words my sainted child uttered in this world. Soon afterwards she died in my arms."

I freely confess that I know comparatively nothing about modern spiritualist mysteries; and I believe poor

Eva's mother knew no more about them than I do; so I can confidently say, there is nothing of that sort of philosophy connected with her touching little story. I am equally certain that good Mrs. Robinson did not invent it with a sensational object (sedate Presbyterians are not often that way inclined), and if it was only a delusion of dear Eva's excited brain, I must say it was one of the most happy delusions that I ever heard of a child experiencing. I have ventured to put the incident into my book, because I feel sure it cannot do any harm; and it may, perhaps, help to point some bereaved mother's drooping spirit to the home where her darling child has gone before.

"There is a special Providence watching over children." I have heard that axiom quoted with a sort of playful composure by parents who are not over-careful in looking after their young families. Of course I believe the axiom is true; for if it were not for a kind, protecting Providence, there would be sudden deaths and mutilations every minute of the day among the hosts of young children who are allowed to stray and play about the streets everywhere. We certainly do hear now and then of a child being accidentally killed or maimed in some way, but such disasters are wonderfully rare considering the number of poor children who have no attendant nurses and no playgrounds but the public highways.

I remember some years ago seeing a picture in a shop window in Sydney which much interested me. It represented a pretty little infant boy of two or three years old, who had strayed to the verge of a mountain precipice. He was stretching his hand out to pluck a flower that was growing over a chasm; and it would have made one shudder to see the awfully dangerous position of the child; but there was an angelic form floating, as it were, on the air, with its hands spread out to catch the child if it fell, or to bear it up and save it from falling. "He shall give His angels charge over thee, to keep thee in all thy ways. They shall bear thee up in their hands." Those Divine promises came to my mind as I gazed at the picture. I wish now that I had bought it.

A child belonging to a family that I knew fell from an upper window on to a paved yard, and she was not seriously injured; and a little girl, the daughter of a missionary from the South Sea Islands, fell from the balcony of a house a few doors from where I lived in Sydney, and she was not hurt in the least. I have often looked at the lofty balcony, and asked myself the question, "If it were not a special interposition of Providence which saved that child from being killed or seriously injured, what was it that did save her?" I could give many other examples of a providential guardianship over children, if my testimony were needed. I firmly believe in the doctrine. But while I would gladly try to cheer and encourage parents who are doing their best to keep their children out of harm's way, and to train them up in the way they should go, I should be sorry to pen a single line that might induce careless parents to leave to a "special Providence" what is manifestly their duty to do themselves.

CHAPTER XXIX.

"Gold ! gold ! gold ! gold !
Bright and yellow and hard and cold."—*Hood.*

IT is about seven weeks since I finished the preceding chapter. In the meantime a change has taken place in my circumstances which will put a stop to my literary work for awhile. No one will suppose that I regret it when they know of my rare good fortune. I am almost too excited to explain it all in a common-sense way. I could more easily write about my ill luck for years past, for I am so well acquainted with it.

In my first chapter I alluded to a chancery suit that I had then pending. I have always been rather chary of mentioning it, for poor persons who have chancery suits are continually hearing annoying old jokes about "Paddy's rope," and other queer things that are supposed to have no end to them. But I have no dread of stale jokes of that sort now, for my long-pending case has come to a satisfactory close.

About three years after dear Ella's death I was at the Castlemaine diggings. I had a share in a deep claim with several other young men. One day I came up the shaft at about dinner-time, and was sitting in a hut with my mates, when my eyes accidentally caught sight of an advertisement in an old copy of the *Age* newspaper, in which half a Dutch cheese was wrapped. I took up the paper and read as follows: "John Cameron Campbell. If the above-named gentleman, who left Scotland for Australia about the year 1838, be still living, he will hear of something greatly to his advantage by communicating with Messrs. McPhee and Co., Edinburgh. Any person who can give authentic proofs of the decease of the said John Cameron Campbell will please communicate with Mr. John Coke, solicitor, Collins Street, Melbourne."

It was impossible for me to avoid showing excitement, but I did not explain to my mates what had affected me so suddenly, and I allowed them to conclude that I had some bodily ailment. Instead of going below to work again, I told them I was going to Melbourne to get some advice. They did not demur to my going, so I dressed in my best clothes and off I started.

The next morning I went to see Mr. Coke. I told him in a plain, straightforward way what I knew about the late John Cameron, and that I had married his only daughter, who was deceased. Mr. Coke said he would like to see documentary proofs of the facts I had stated; so I ran off to Mr. Benson's house and got my writing desk (the one that had belonged to Cameron) and carried it to Mr. Coke's office. He seemed pleased at my honest trustfulness, and asked me to leave the desk just as it was, and call again to-morrow. When I called again he received me very pleasantly, and said that my proofs seemed satisfactory so far as they extended, but that the certificate of Mr. Campbell's marriage with Miss Clara Bond, and the proofs of her decease, were wanting. Those were the missing links; and if they were supplied, he thought the evidence would be conclusive, and my heirship would be acknowledged.

I will not give the details of my troublesome journey, the second time, to Mr. Jerry Badkin's house, nor of my tedious and expensive negotiation with him and his tricky wife. I will simply state that after the exercise of much tact and patience, I got Clara's marriage certificate, and the district coroner's certificate of her death. I hastened back to Melbourne, and handed the papers to Mr. Coke. He then said he would forward all my documentary evidence to Scotland, and would communicate with me as soon as he received a reply to his budget. I left him my address, and then went back to the diggings, after two months' absence, and resumed my groping labour in the bowels of the earth. By the way, what a chilling difference there was between my hard, daily routine as a gold digger, and the enticing picture my fancy had conjured up of the work before I had even seen a deep mining shaft! It was almost as striking as the difference between the real drudgery of writing my book, and the poetical ideas I indulged in about authorship before I tried to compose my first page.

"Things are not what they seem."

About a year after I had returned to Castlemaine, I received a letter from Mr. Coke requesting an interview with me. I hastened to Melbourne again, and then I was told that the paper I received from Mr. Badkin was the certificate of marriage of a John Cameron to Clara Bond; in short, the proofs had been disputed by the executors of the will of the testator, Mr. Angus Campbell, and his estate had been thrown into chancery. I did not then quite understand the meaning of that significant legal term; but I have since had leisure to study the thing more than enough, for my estate has remained in chancery nearly twelve years.

In the meantime I have had numberless interviews with Mr. Coke; and I have explained the whole particulars of Cameron's motive for dropping his patronymic. Nothing could be logically clearer than I made that simple circumstance to appear on paper; still, the Master in Chancery could not see it. His lordship's obtuseness was really marvellous to my honest senses. Relying on the justness of my claim, I have secretly clung to the hope that I should one day get my rights; but the day of decision seemed to be intolerably slow in its approach, and I own that I sometimes encouraged heathenish opinions of British law. I once made up my mind to go to Scotland and plead my own cause in person; but I was dissuaded from the step by Mr. Coke, who moreover had possession of my papers, and politely declined to part with them until his costs were paid. For years I have been battling with poverty, and the fight seemed doubly hard to me, knowing that I was the rightful heir to a lot of money, which the law, through its lazy, tortoise-like movements, was keeping me from enjoying. It is no wonder if I have grown rather fretful of late.

That was the tantalizing state of my affairs until the arrival of the last Suez Mail, on Tuesday week. I shall not forget that day in a hurry. While I was in the act of writing a conciliatory letter to Saul, and urging him to come and help me to finish off my long story, so that I might raise a little money on the manuscript, I received a note from Mr. Coke asking me to call on him without delay, as he had some pleasing news to communicate. I was very soon at his office, and there I learnt that my chancery suit had been decided the right way, and I was the acknowledged heir to the real and personal estates of the late Mr. Angus Campbell, of Ayrshire. Furthermore, Mr. Coke informed me that he had authority to furnish me with any ready money I required.

The good news nearly knocked my legs from under me. On that morning I had not a shilling in my pocket, nor had I left any money at my lodgings; moreover I was faint for want of a good meal. I timidly asked Mr. Coke if he could let me have ten pounds. I thought I had asked for too much, and I was just going to say five pounds would do, if he could not spare any more, when he said, "You may have ten thousand pounds, if you like, Mr. Larksway; or twice that sum if you really wish for it to-day."

I was so thoroughly stunned that I burst out crying. But it was only a temporary outgush of feeling, the next minute I was laughing at the idea of my crying over a princely fortune.

Mr. Coke smiled at me pleasantly, and said, " I think

you had better let me pay a little money—say a thousand pounds or so—to your account for immediate use. Where do you bank, sir?"

"Oh, my dumps! Ha! ha! bank indeed! I have had nothing to do with bankers for many years past. But say the 'Commercial,' I like to encourage colonial institutions. Perhaps you would not mind giving me fifty pounds at once, Mr. Coke?"

"Oh, certainly—by all means!" said the obliging lawyer. He took up his pen and wrote a cheque in a minute, and then told the clerk to run across to the bank and get the cash for me.

"Please to get gold, will you, Mr. Gill?" I said to the young man. "Notes have a musty smell—like cat's meat."

Mr. Coke smiled again at me. I dare say he thought I was soon getting fastidious. Presently the clerk returned with fifty new sovereigns in a small linen bag, which I put into my pocket. I then shook hands very heartily with Mr. Coke and his clerk, and away I went to my humble lodgings in a state of wild excitement, which perhaps was mistaken by some strangers who passed me for the influence of drink. My dinner was waiting for me when I got home; and my landlady said she feared it was cold.

"How much do I owe you, Mrs. Goody?" I asked, stopping her apology for the cold sheep's tail and pumpkin on the table.

"Let us see, sir. Two pounds for a month's rent, and eighteen pence for your coals, and ninepence for—"

"Never mind totting up any more items; hold your apron up," I said, and I shot out about half the contents of the linen bag, without counting it. "There, take that to begin with, ma'am."

The dear old lady staggered back for a pace or two, and looked as scared as if the sovereigns were live cockroaches.

"Don't drop it, Mrs. Goody. It is all honest money, never fear! I have got my fortune at last, and I mean to spend it like a man. Hurrah!—

'Oh, hard times, come again no more!'"

"Bless my soul!" exclaimed the kind old creature, who seemed to be quite mystified at my strange behaviour, it was so unusual for me to shout and sing; for years past I had hardly spirit enough to sneeze.

"Don't be frightened, ma'am! Let me explain everything in a few words. I have been long waiting for a chancery suit to end. It is ended at last, and I am a rich man. That's all about it. I am a little bit excited over it just now; but I shall cool down presently."

"I am very thankful indeed to hear it, sir," she replied, warmly. "I am sure you deserve something rich, for you know what it is to want."

"Indeed I do know it, Mrs. Goody; and I should have known worse straits if it had not been for your kindness. You have often made shifts, rather than dun me for money when you knew I was very poor. Now I promise that you shall never know what poverty is again. Don't weep, my dear old friend! You have been almost as kind as a mother to me, and I will never forget you, so cheer up! Go and spend all that money this afternoon. Buy yourself a lot of new clothes and some blankets. Don't be afraid to spend the money; I'll give you plenty more, to-morrow. You shall have a new carpet for your parlour, and everything else you want to make you snug and comfortable for life. Never mind thanking me any more to-day; I shall have some time to spare next week."

I was too much excited to eat my dinner, so I sat down and finished the letter I had half written to Saul, and begged him to come to me immediately. I gave the little boy next door a shilling to run with the letter to Saul's lodgings. I meant to have a bit of fun with my crusty cousin before I told him of my good fortune. In less than an hour Saul entered my room. I knew he would be glad enough to come to me if I asked him; still, it was not in his disposition to look pleasant after a long sulk, without a deal of coaxing. He first lighted his pipe, and then he asked me what I wanted with him in such a scalding hot hurry.

"Ha, ha! look at this, Saul," I said, and I shook the little bag and made the new sovereigns tinkle like fairy music. I thought that the sound of the best kind of current coin would put him in a good humour in a minute; but, to my surprise, he got almost as excited as if I had thrown a mulful of Scotch snuff into his eyes, and he exclaimed fiercely, "By Jemmy! if you have sold that manuscript, Roger, I'll summons you to court for swindling. One-third of it belongs to me, and I'll have it out of you too."

"Tut tut! bother the manuscript!" I said, and I took the packet out of a closet and tossed it to him. He caught it, and then sat down looking as puzzled as a boy at some clever conjuring trick. It was so strange for me to exhibit a bagful of sovereigns that it fairly staggered him. I could not keep my spirits down any longer, so I said, "Saul, my boy! What do you think? My precious chancery suit is ended, and I am a wealthy man. Ha, ha! I am as rich as old—what's-his-name, of Carlton. Mr. Coke sent for me this morning to tell me the news. I told you it would come to pass."

I think I would sooner have a full-length portrait of Saul (if it were possible to get it), as he appeared at that moment, than I would have the second best picture in the Melbourne Gallery of Art. It would be one of the most striking exemplifications of the subduing influence of wealth that was ever seen in real life,—a glimpse of him was as impressive as it would be to see a mounted policeman shedding tears. In an instant the bullying scowl slipped off Saul's face, and a lamb-like or rather a sheepish shyness came over him. He instinctively took his hat off, and pushed his pipe all alight into his waistcoat pocket, as if he were ashamed of his impudence in smoking before a rich man, with his dinner on the table. I was not calm enough to reflect on the curious subject just then, neither have I time to write much about it now, but it will be a nice study for me by-and-by. I dare say I shall soon develop into a philosopher. Rich men often do that, for they have so much encouragement.

In figurative words, I may say Saul was struck dumb for a minute or two, and he seemed as humble as a blind beggar. I could not enjoy the sight of his embarrassment, though he had so often worried me; so I extended my hand to him, and said, "Saul, my dear fellow! Let us bury all past grievances. Now, not another word about them," I added, stopping his stammering apology. "Let us love one another for the future, and forget that we have not always done so in the past. We are blood relations, you know—the only pair of our kin on this side of the world. How are you off for money?"

"I have not a single penny, Roger. Downright hard up."

"I guessed as much; but never mind, I have plenty. Here is a sovereign for the present. I hope you won't get drunk with it. I shall want your sober advice presently."

"I promise you on the word of a man, that I will not touch a drop of grog this blessed day, cousin."

"That's right. Be a man and keep your promise, and then I shall be encouraged to trust you further. I must go now to see my good friends the Mosses and the Bensons, but I shall be back this evening. Will you come here at eight o'clock?"

"Oh yes, cousin; I will be here at that time. But do you mean to stop in this dingy cottage now you can afford to hire a mansion?"

"I would not pain kind old Mrs. Goody by leaving

her suddenly; but as soon as I have seen her house put in comfortable trim, I shall take a suite of apartments at Menzie's or Scott's."

I went in a cab to Mr. Benson's, and afterwards to Mr. Moss's. I need not say that those staunch friends were really glad to hear of my good fortune. I had a long chat with them all. In the evening I returned to my lodgings; and just as the clock was striking eight Saul arrived. I can hardly tell whether I was more astonished at his extreme punctuality, or at his meek style of handling the knocker. Formerly he used to hammer at the door like a tipsy boiler-maker, and make Mrs. Goody jump. I never before heard him give such a modest rat tat. He was quite sober, and was not smoking. His manner was nervously deferential at first, but he soon regained confidence as he saw I was not lofty. After a little talk about town news, I said, "You will not be surprised to hear that I am soon going to Scotland, to look after my property?"

"I hope you will not go away and leave your new book unfinished," he replied in a pleading tone, which sounded very strange to me after my long experience of his rough censorship. I remember that he once told me my manuscript was not worth a bunch of carrots.

"Never mind the book, Saul. I am tired of it."

"I daresay you are, cousin; but it would be a sad pity to waste so much labour of your clever brain. Will you allow me to suggest that you publish the manuscript, and state, in a nice modest preface, that the raw material for another book, and a much more spirited one, is on the literary anvil, and only wants hammering into correct shape. And you may safely say the primest parts of your interesting experience are to be written; for as your very sad subjects are done with, there will be full scope or run for fun and fancy, eh, Roger? There is always a comical side to poverty, you know; and there is poetry in an empty pocket."

"If so I surely ought to have seen or felt some of its charms. I will think over your suggestion, Saul, when my brain calms down a little. I have ample material for some useful books, and I shall perhaps write them when I have leisure."

"As I have often said before, I have no doubt the present book will sell well; and it is more likely to be remunerative now that you are independent of it; that is usually the case. But I am going to suggest, Roger, that if you will trust me with your diary or note-book, I will do all the work of the second book while you are away. You shall have no trouble at all."

"It is kind of you to make the offer, Saul; but perhaps I may want to take my diary with me. Will you allow me to offer you a little friendly advice?"

"Oh, certainly, cousin. I shall be proud and thankful."

"Well, then, I hope that while I am away you will settle down into some useful occupation—turn steady, you know, and try to do good in the world. Only think what an influence you might exert among some of the wild young men of Melbourne, if you would henceforward live soberly and religiously. It would delight me exceedingly to see you make a fresh start off in the right way, from this very night."

"There is not much use in trying to make an old crooked tree grow up straight," remarked Saul gloomily.

"That is true, cousin; you cannot bend an old tree, and there is perhaps not much prospect of turning the course of life-long habits in an old man, though even that is not a hopeless work to attempt. But you are a young man yet, just in your prime; and suppose you were to live till you are 'threescore years and ten,' what a vast amount of good you might do in the world in forty years!"

Saul sighed again, and looked uncommonly thoughtful; so I gave him a little more advice of an encouraging sort, and he listened as submissively as if he were one of the little boys in my Sunday-school class. I need not tell all I said to him; but I am glad to state that before he went away he promised me that he would try to follow out my good counsel. He said he would make a beginning in the right way by being moderate in the use of intoxicants; and he thought that was one grand step towards a thorough reformation of his whole character.

I have not much faith in his moderation scheme; still, I am willing to accept of any instalment of good from him. When I have more time to spare I will talk to him again, and advise him to try total abstinence.

I hope I shall not prejudice any one against my cousin by the somewhat pettish remarks I have made about him in the course of my story. Poor fellow!

though he certainly is wild, I do not think he is wholly lacking in good principle, and under other circumstances, perhaps, his virtues might have nobly developed. Unluckily for him, he brought his capital to Victoria in ready money, and he was an easy prey to the sharpers who are always on the look out for "new chums" of his class. Of course he soon lost his money; and worse still, he lost his character for sobriety and industry—at any rate, no mercantile firm would venture to give him employment, although he was a very competent clerk, and I think he would have stuck well to his duties if he had got a situation with a considerate master. For the last two years or more he has divided his time between "fossicking," as he calls it, at the diggings, and living at my expense at Melbourne. Surely he has suffered enough for his folly in "letting his best friend creep out of his pocket." That is the expressive way he speaks of losing his money.

I have heard many persons ask in a reproachful tone, "Why does not your cousin get something to do?" I was tempted to say to one of those complainers, "It would be a real kindness if you would help him to get employment, sir; and I am sure he would be thankful, for he is not a lazy man." I think that suggestion of mine, mildly as I put it, offended the gentleman, who was one of the fault-finding genius, and not a helper of the helpless. I daresay other persons have privately grumbled at me in a similar way for years past, as they have seen me going about threadbare and dejected, earning a precarious livelihood as an itinerant dentist;

but not one man in this large city has come to me and kindly inquired into my circumstances, or asked me if he could assist me in any way. Oh! what a luxury and comfort it would have been to me if a sympathizing friend had kindly put his arm in mine some day and said, "Come and take a walk for half an hour, Larksway, and tell me what makes you look so dispirited, and show me how I can help you." Any one might have said as much as that to me without fear of my asking him for a loan of money, or of my troubling him very much in any way; the sympathy was what I wanted—it would have been like balm of Gilead to my sad spirits. But those days of hardship and neglect are gone and past; perhaps I shall not be slighted now that I am rich. I do trust that the dreary experience I have had may be put to practical use in the world, and that I may be instrumental in leading many poor, downcast, sensitive fellows off the bleak common of poverty, and putting them into a happy way of helping themselves and earning an honest livelihood. If I keep in this Christian-like disposition—if my wealth does not make me unmerciful, selfish, and proud—I hope I may have a very long life; and though I may not put the world wholly to rights, I will do something towards it.

There is no denying the fact that Saul has been very cross with me occasionally; but no doubt he has had much to worry him besides my literary dulness. An insufficiency of wholesome food is naturally irritating to a young man with a strong appetite. Besides, I think I am in a measure to blame for submitting to his constant nagging, till he has got to believe that I would not go along without it.

In a retired country place, where I lived a sort of hermit's life for more than four years, a man used to pass my house almost every day with a donkey and cart. The man invariably walked about two yards in front of the donkey, with his hands behind him and his head bent down, as if he were thinking out some abstruse point in mental philosophy. There was something so uncommon about the man and the animal, that I was curious enough to observe them carefully, as opportunity offered. I found that punctually every three minutes the man would turn half round and shout, "Come up!" But the gruff command did not seem to influence the donkey, except to make it wag its ears now and then; it moved on its own even way, and the driver kept his position in front. He was not a surly man, I judged, for he was usually singing in a low minor key, but he stopped his tune at measured intervals, to growl out, "Come up!" to the donkey. After studying the two characters for several months, I came to the conclusion that the man systematically shouted to his patient companion from mere habit, more than from any idea that it was necessary to do so; and the donkey had got so used to the stern appeal, that he did not mind it any more than he did the noise of the wheels behind him. Perhaps the poor beast knew that it was hopeless to attempt to run away, for the cart was usually laden with vegetables, and he thought his best policy was to bear his owner's gruffness quietly. Some unlucky Benedicts that I have met with were equally patient under the constant home naggings they received, knowing that they could not run away with their load of family responsibilities behind them. I have usually been silent under Saul's rhetorical rasping, and perhaps that has encouraged him to give me more than I deserved. But the poor fellow is sorry enough for it now, I can see; so if that were any compensation to me, my virtue of patience would be amply rewarded; and after all, as good Jeremy Taylor says, "Harsh words never broke a man's back."

"The smallest dog that e'er bow-wow'd will surely have his day,
For that *all* canines are allowed—or so the poets say."

Saul is extremely anxious for me to leave him my diary. He says that he is sure he can find real sensational plots in it, and facts and fancy enough to make a lot of books, which will sell like paper collars or canned Swiss milk, or any other pure and useful production of nature or art. I daresay he might find subjects for his active fancy to stretch to any tragical or ludicrous length; but I know my loving cousin too well to trust him with my private jottings in his present state of mind. If I can help it, my diary shall never go into the hands of any man who is not conscientious and prudent; for I do not want anything that I have penned to do mischief, or to cause pain to any one in the world, after I have gone hence. I know that a famous phrenologist once examined Saul's head, and found some monstrous bumps or organs, which give him a natural aptness for humorous composition and fanciful mental colouring.

I would not undervalue such gifts, for they may be made very useful if kept under good moral control, and guided by religious principle. In this age, when cheap literature of an awfully pernicious character is being extensively circulated, I think it is wise to encourage any man or woman who has the skill and the goodwill to write wholesome, readable books, of an amusing or entertaining kind, which may in some degree counteract the mischief which those positively wicked books are doing to the minds and bodies of millions of young persons all the world over. If the happy change that I am hoping for takes place in Cousin Saul, I shall be delighted to take him into my full confidence, and to let him do as he pleases with some of my voluminous notes of travel and observations on things in general. In the meantime, I must act with proper caution. I mean to entrust this MS. with an old friend, who will see it through the press; and I shall leave it to his judgment how far to allow Saul to help him in the editorial work.

The Rev. Mr. Benson has kindly promised to look after Saul during my absence, and to supply him with funds on my account. I shall be very glad if the good advice and example of that gentleman should induce a thorough reform in my clever but wayward cousin, and help him to properly estimate the value of a good character.

CHAPTER XXX.

"Glories, like glowworms, afar off shine bright,
But seen too near, give neither heat nor light."
—*Webster*.

I AM now preparing for my voyage to Europe, and am rather flurried, which is perhaps natural enough under the circumstances. Many congratulatory letters have reached me from old nodding acquaintances, who have heard of my good fortune; and a few of the letters contained requests for loans of money. I have been wondering how much either of the bold applicants would have lent me a fortnight ago. But I never did ask any one for a loan of money, so I have not thoroughly tested my neighbours, and it is not exactly fair to conclude that they would not have helped me, if I had applied to them.

The Bensons and the Mosses have always been true friends to me, money or no money, and their children are almost as dear to my heart as my own young cousins. It is nearly sixteen years since I pulled little Nelly Moss out of the sea, and I think our friendship has been growing firmer every year. Nelly has developed into a very fine young woman; and it is a remarkable fact that she strikingly reminds me of my sainted Ella, for she has the same lovely blue eyes, and the same gentle, confiding disposition. A few years ago she used to run up to me, whenever I called at Rose Villa, and throw her arms round my neck like a little sister; but she is now too old for that tender sort of greeting. I remember when she was growing up a tall child, or about stretching out of her childhood and her short frocks, she used to blush and look rather funny when she first came into a room to receive me, and I felt somewhat embarrassed on her account. Of course I liked to kiss the little darling, but I could see that her maidenly modesty was beginning to feel gently shocked at the idea of kissing a man, now that she was entering her "teens." It is hard to break off early-formed habits, as I have found in that simple instance, but it was needful to make the effort; so I studied my part carefully, and one day when I went to Rose Villa, I put on a good resolution, and said, as if it were a sudden idea, "Why, Nelly, my dear girl! you seem to have grown quite a woman, since I was here a month ago. I am half afraid to kiss you now; and I think you must, in future, only shake hands with me at meeting and parting, as you do with other gentleman friends." I could see that dear Nelly was relieved, and I was glad I had been self-denying enough to adopt the sensible expedient.

I have reason to believe, from what Mr. Coke told me yesterday, that my Scottish tenants are making preparations for giving me a grand reception on my arrival at Ayrby Park. For my part I had rather they would let me go there quietly. I have not been used to grand ovations or glorifications. It strikes me I shall not stay long in that cold country; it will not suit my nature after so long a residence in this genial climate. I believe that Australia will be my home.

My dear mother is still living, and I wish she were able to return with me and share my home and fortune. I have kept up a regular correspondence with her ever since I left England, and it is a comfort to me to know that I have not neglected my filial duty in that respect. In the course of my wanderings, at the gold-diggings and elsewhere, I have met with men who have confessed to me that they had not written to their parents for years. One young fellow told me that he knew his dear old widowed mother was very poor, and yet he had often spent more money in one night's drinking spree than would keep her for a month. I got him to promise me that he would send some money to his mother in England by the next mail, and I have reason to hope that he kept his word; anyway, I don't think he will soon forget the few kindly words I said to him on that subject. As a set-off to those cases of filial neglect, I have much pleasure in telling something of an opposite character. I was one day the guest of a gentleman who has risen to wealth and honour in Australia, and who is specially useful in his own immediate neighbourhood. When walking with my host over a part of his estate after dinner, we came to a fine stone monument, which he told me was erected by him to the memory of his late beloved parents. He added, with reverential feeling, "I believe that I owe my great success in temporal affairs mainly to my careful observance of the Divine injunction to honour my father and my mother." I think my friend had not inherited money or property from his parents, for they were dependent on him during the latter part of their lives. If I were at liberty to state the circumstances which he told me, confidentially, it would be as clear to the reader as it is to me, that he has not over-estimated the direct advantages he has gained by obeying that Divine law. He is an Australian by birth, and I am proud to claim him as one of my most trusty friends.

There is a small estate on the banks of the beautiful Yarra Yarra, a few miles above Melbourne, which has often delighted my fancy. For landscape beauties, on a limited view, I have not seen anything to surpass it since I left Suffolk. I daresay the owner will want a fancy price for his pretty homestead; but if he can be persuaded to sell it, it shall be mine, and I will exercise my taste in laying out my grounds, and building my house, when I return to Victoria.

I remember when passing Sunbury a few years ago, on my way to Sandhurst, I was struck with the natural and artistic beauties of a spot, which I was told belonged to a young millionaire. I remarked to my informant, "The gentleman has shown extremely good taste in laying out his grounds, and in the architectural style of his mansion." I have not seen the place since it was finished, for it was dark when I last rode past it; but I daresay it is very beautiful, a residence fit for the Queen.

I should like something after the same style, but on a much smaller scale. I think it will afford me infinitely more satisfaction to beautify some nice rural nook, that I can call my home, with my superfluous capital, than it would do to lock it up in bank stock or foreign securities. I want to do something towards making the world look better.

If I can secure that choice little estate at Hawthorn, and can carry out all the designs that are now pleasantly floating in my brain and glowing in my heart, I hope I shall be happy. But still I seem to have more doubts on that subject than I was ever troubled with before. It is a curious fact, that though I am rich—I may say very rich—I do not feel wholly satisfied with my lot. Two or three weeks ago, I should have had a difficulty in raising ten pounds, if I had sold or pawned every article of personal property that I owned; to-day I daresay I could raise two hundred thousand pounds by merely signing, " Roger Larksway," Mr. Coke told me as much yesterday; and yet I felt more composure of mind in the days of my poverty, and I could then sleep more soundly at night than I can do now, for I often lie awake for hours together, planning what I shall do with all my houses and farms, or puzzling my brain to compose replies (that will look well in print) to the forthcoming addresses of my dutiful tenants. I do not mean to say that I am sorry I have come in for a large fortune—by no means—and perhaps I should feel sorely troubled if I were to lose it all again; still, I do solemnly declare, that the possession of wealth does not yield me a fifth part of the delight or satisfaction that I anticipated from it before it was mine, and when I was afraid that the chancery lawyers would eat it all up. But after all, perhaps this is only morbid feeling, which will soon wear off amongst the gay and festive society I may expect to meet with on board the mail steamer. I shall travel first class, of course; and if any one on board should suspect that I ever travelled second class, he will not be likely to let me know it, consequently I shall not feel my pride wounded at all. Ill-natured thoughts are as powerless to hurt as stuffed snakes.

I have bought a variety of nice presents for my most valued friends in Melbourne; but I have instructed my agent not to deliver the articles until I have started. The diamond necklace for dear Nelly is the richest one I could get in the city, and it is a really splendid ornament. I should like to see her wear it on her approaching birthday; but I shall be at sea. I trust the rumour I heard, last week, that Nelly is engaged to Mr. Jolly, is not correct, for I do not like the young man. I think he is rather too bold. I should wish to see her marry some one who is thoroughly worthy of her. My good friend, Mr. Benson, has promised to keep me posted up in news of interest while I am away; so no doubt he will tell me occasionally how dear Nelly is getting on.

I have purchased a comfortable little annuity for Mrs. Goody. Now she will have no more anxiety about her ways and means. Poor old soul! she has had more than enough of that sort of worry in her lifetime. I feel it is pleasant to have money to spare to give nice presents to deserving friends, and to help the poor and afflicted. I pray that I may not grow miserly; and that I may be ever ready to distribute.

I had almost forgotten to mention, that a few days ago three electors of a small suburb of Melbourne waited on me at this hotel, with a request that I would allow myself to be nominated as a member of Parliament for their electorate, at the forthcoming general election. The leading spokesman, in a few studied sentences, expressed his admiration for my principles, and hoped that I would honour the constituency of ——— by consenting to represent its interests in the Legislative Assembly.

I had not the least idea of the object of the visitors when they were ushered into my private sitting-room, so my astonishment may be imagined when they stated their errand. How they became so well acquainted with my political principles was a mystery to me, for I had never seen either of the gentlemen before to my knowledge, and I have lived very secluded of late years; besides, I never did show any disposition to come out as a public man. I replied, "Gentlemen, this is an unexpected requisition. I have no alternative but to decline it; and I ask you to kindly forgive me if the abruptness of my answer should seem to indicate a want of due appreciation of the honour you would confer upon me. You have certainly made a mistake in your estimate of my fitness for the duties of your representative; but your mistake is excusable considering that I am quite unknown to you."

"I beg your pardon, sir," said a second speaker. "I knew you years ago, when you kept a drug shop at Prahran; and sorry enough I was when you shut up, for I never could get any physic that agreed with me and my missus, like the liver pills you used to sell us at a shilling a box. Perhaps you remember my name, sir, John Fisher? It is in your books."

I said, "I know that my vegetable pills were really good, for they were carefully prepared from a recipe which I got from my worthy uncle; but, Mr. Fisher, you surely do not consider that——"

The third man interrupted my pointed question by saying, "We consider that you are an honest man, sir; and we know that you are rich and have a great stake in the country. We believe that you are a fit and proper person to represent our town in Parliament, and we respectfully request that you consent to do so."

"My good friends," I replied solemnly, "you are in error in supposing that I have a great stake in the country, for all my property is at present on the opposite side of the world. Whether or not, I know that I am not qualified for the post you kindly wish me to fill, and on that account I could not conscientiously undertake it; indeed, I would as soon think of setting up as a physician with my bare skill to make liver pills. I quite agree with you that it is the duty of every man to do what he can to serve his country and his fellow-men; but it is clear to my mind, that going into Parliament would not be the best way that I could make myself useful to the community. Your present member, Mr.

Mason, is an honest man, and an experienced politician; will he not consent to be nominated for re-election?"

"Oh, no doubt he will be willing enough, sir," said Mr. Fisher, who was the most fluent speaker. "But we think that a little opposition, or fresh blood, as the saying is, will be good for our electorate."

"And perhaps be good for certain trades during the contest," I suggested; whereupon the deputation winked.

"Well, gentlemen, I thank you for the honour you would confer upon me; but when I tell you that I am preparing to go to Europe by the next mail steamer, you will see that I cannot possibly accept your invitation. If I am spared to return to Victoria, and I then feel assured that it is my duty to offer myself as a member of Parliament, I promise you that I will not shrink from it; but I shall decidedly not aspire to the honour and responsibility, until I have, by a course of diligent study, in some degree qualified myself for the important duty."

I daresay the decided tone in which I spoke convinced the gentlemen that they need not stay any longer; so they wished me good day and departed, looking rather dissatisfied that they had not succeeded in luring a rich simpleton into an expensive electioneering contest.

Most heartily do I wish that I had the power to express in convincing words my opinion on a subject of vital importance, which the foregoing incident suggests. I wish that before I leave these shores I could appeal to the colonists in general, from Cape Leewin to Cape Melville, and all the way round again, and persuade them to use their honest judgment in electing thoroughly competent men as their representatives in the Parliament of their respective colonies. This is indeed a great and a good land, teeming with richness and fair promise; and it is a sad pity that its young growth should suffer from careless or inefficient legislation. There is certainly no lack of able men in the country, and I do wish they would all wake up to their duty. I state as a grim fact (and it is far from being a personal compliment), that many men who are even less qualified than myself, have been deluded into offering themselves as members of our colonial legislature. Surely that is not the way to " Advance Australia!"

* * * * *

I will now shut up my writing-desk, for it is near midnight, and I have yet to finish packing a portmanteau. Mr. Moss is coming in the morning, to drive me in his carriage to the boat jetty, at Sandridge. The mail steamer will start from her moorings punctually at nine o'clock. Dear, patient reader! good-bye, for the present.

Yours truly,
ROGER LARKSWAY.

Scott's Hotel.

CHAPTER XXXI.

> " Here, at the dead of night,
> By the pale candlelight,
> Weary and sad, I write—
>   Sitting alone.
>
> Write, though my feeble pen
> Nearly drops, now and then,
> As my heart faints again—
>   Always alone."—*Desart.*

I, SAUL JACKSON, have been politely invited by the editor to add a sort of postscript to the foregoing narrative, written by my respected cousin, Roger Larksway, Esquire, of Ayrby Park, Ayrshire. It would be about as easy for me to get a church bell into my leathern hat box, as to compress what I would like to say into a few pages, and that is all the space I am offered. I must be brief this time.

I have had the honour of receiving several letters from my cousin since his departure from Victoria, a year ago; and if I had space enough for it, I should be proud to give a description of his enthusiastic reception by his Scottish tenantry, and other interesting particulars of his brilliant career in his own native land. It seems almost marvellous to me, that the general respect for my cousin should have increased so immensely within the last fifteen months; but so it is, and he merits it all, "for he is a jolly good fellow," as the song says. In his last letter to me he expressed regret for having written a few sentences in his narrative which somewhat reflect on my virtue, and he wishes me to ask the editor to erase every damaging word from the manuscript. It is kind of Roger to be so careful for my feelings, but I am sure I deserve all his strictures, so I modestly decline to allow a syllable to be altered. I have been a sad tease to him, I know, but I hope soon to let him see that I am a reformed man. One of my quondam sporting friends jocosely remarked, yesterday, that I was looking as serious as the owner of a blown-up powder mill; so I coolly told him that I had been a grinning fool long enough.

I would not venture to put into print the delicate disclosure I am now about to make, did I not know that it is almost certain that before this volume can be issued from the press, the marriage of my honoured cousin with Miss Nelly Moss will be announced in the Australian papers, and of course will go all over the world. There is great preparation for the solemn event going on at Rose Villa, and the fortunate bridegroom elect is expected to arrive in Melbourne by the next Suez mail steamer. I daresay he is at this moment wishing the screw propeller was being driven by electricity, and that the *Bombay* was going ahead twice as fast, or twenty-four knots an hour. Young bridegrooms usually are rather impatient.

As I now look at it with neutral calmness, it does strike me as being the most sensational affair of the kind that ever happened in real life—that my cousin should have been close at hand at the identical minute, years ago, when little Nelly Moss slipped off that old, rusty steam-boiler into the sea! Nobody can reasonably doubt that it was an accidental slip of Nelly's, and her screams were as natural as the quacking of a little duck. Had she been twenty years older, it might be an open question, for some full-grown women will try any sort of startling expedient when a nice young man is within hail. But dear Nelly was an innocent baby, and my cousin's act was one of unselfish kindness—pure and genuine as virgin honey in white wax. I should not like Roger to hear me laugh, but I cannot help a little sly merriment at the serio-comical idea, that the dripping, squealing morsel of humanity—not much bigger than a lobster—that he was carrying on shore under his arm, was his future wife and the sharer of his immense fortune! Ha! ha! it certainly is wonderfully funny! And I say with hearty meaning, though in trite, unpoetical terms, I wish I had been in Roger's shoes, wet as they were; but shoes or no shoes, I wish I had a nice affectionate wife of my own, for I am tired of living a lonely Robinson Crusoe sort of life—it isn't natural.

By the way, the other day I read in a London newspaper of a fellow—not a savage islander, but an Englishman—who saw a young child drowning, and he did not pull it out of the water because he was afraid of wetting his feet. That cowardly booby will never fish up an amiable young wife, as my cousin did; indeed, I hope he may never find a girl silly enough to marry him, for it might be a calamity to our race. Roger Larksway did not scruple to wet his feet nor his waist, and he will soon have a substantial reward for his manliness—a pretty young wife, who will love, honour, and cherish him all the days of her life. Oh dear! I cannot explain my feelings exactly, but I do think that if I could fish up such a precious jewel of a girl, I would dive, head first, into a hot spring after her at this present moment —that is if the water was not quite boiling. But alas! there is no such luck for poor Saul! I shall never get such an opportunity of distinguishing myself, though I am always on the look out.

There is a difference of about sixteen years in the ages of Nelly Moss and my happy cousin, and some tame folks that I have heard speak of it think the disparity is too great; but I should certainly not make it an insuperable objection if the chance were mine, and Roger evidently takes the same yielding, affectionate view of it that I do. There is no use in taking notice of what young Dick Jolly says about the match, though it is natural enough for him to object to it.

A paragraph in a Scotch paper that I saw a few weeks ago, stated that the fortunate young heir to the Ayrby estate was beginning to pull down a long range of brick buildings which had been used, half a century ago, by some sporting members of the Campbell family, as stud stabling, dog kennels, etc. The materials of the buildings were to be used in the erection of thirty cottages for aged men and women. And an old brewery, also detached from the family mansion, was to be taken down, and the materials used for a school of art in the village close by. It further stated that Mr. Larksway had promised to give a thousand volumes of books, and some valuable oil paintings, from his picture gallery and library. The same newspaper also gave a report of some Highland sports at Ayrby park, on Mr. Larksway's birthday; when two unlucky Scotchmen sprained their backs in tossing the caber. Both the sufferers and their families had been provided for by Mr. Larksway. I hope he won't have too many capersome pensioners.

I cannot yet make out if my cousin is going to sell his estates and settle down as a Victorian colonist, or whether he will return to Scotland and take his young bride with him. If he should go back, I shall try to induce him to take me with him as his private secretary. That little billet would suit me better than trying to get into "the house," as member for the new Rampant Rush diggings, though the £300 a year is not to be sneezed at by a poor fellow like myself, to say nothing of the honour of the thing.

It would not seem modest of me to write much about my own virtues, so I will merely remark that I have kept the promise I made to my cousin, like a man. I have never been drunk since he left Melbourne, though I confess I have had some hard struggles to conquer my obstinate old habits, and I have very often longed for a fortnight's spree. Good Mr. Benson has watched over me with a father's care, and I shall ever feel grateful to him. He urges me to be a teetotaler, and says that I shall find it much less trouble to do without grog entirely, than to tease my appetite with what I call my sober allowance of three or four glasses a day. I told him the other evening that I would consider over his kind proposal. I am still considering over it, with the sort of shivery indecision that I felt when I was about to take my first dive into the sea from the top of a bathing machine at Brighton. I want some good sober fellow behind me to give me a friendly push off. I think I will wait till my cousin returns to Melbourne; he is the soberest man I was ever closely intimate with; and if he advises me to take the teetotal pledge, I'll take it, and I'll stick to it too, like John Gough or Father Matthew.

Sunday Library for Young People.

Each Volume Illustrated and Handsomely Bound.

PRICE ONE SHILLING EACH.

I.
THE STORY OF A RED VELVET BIBLE.
By M. H.

II.
MARY MANSFIELD;
Or, the Time to be a Christian.
By the SAME AUTHOR.

III.
ARTHUR FORTESCUE;
Or, the Schoolboy Hero.
By ROBERT HOPE MONCRIEFF.

IV.
THE SANGREAL; Or, the Hidden Treasure.
By M. H.

V.
WITLESS WILLIE, THE IDIOT BOY.
By the Author of "Mary Matheson," etc.

VI.
HENRY MORGAN; Or, the Sower and the Seed.
By M. H.

PRICE ONE SHILLING AND SIXPENCE EACH.

I.
AUNT MARGARY'S MAXIMS:
Work, Watch, Wait.
By SOPHIA TANDY.

II.
MARY BRUNTON AND HER ONE TALENT.
By E. A. D. R.

III.
TALES FROM THE HOLLY-TREE FARM.
By Mrs. CHARLES BRENT.

LONDON: HODDER AND STOUGHTON, 27, PATERNOSTER ROW.

Sunday Library for Young People.

Each Volume Illustrated and Handsomely Bound.

PRICE TWO SHILLINGS AND SIXPENCE EACH.

I.
NEWLYN HOUSE, THE HOME OF THE DAVENPORTS.
By A. E. W.

II.
LABOURERS IN THE VINEYARD.
By M. H.

III.
LITTLE HARRY'S TROUBLES.
By the Author of "Gottfried."

IV.
THE HARLEYS OF CHELSEA PLACE.
By Sophia Tandy.

V.
ORPHAN LOTTIE;
Or, Honesty Brings its Own Reward.
By Kathleen.

VI.
THE CHILDREN OF THE GREAT KING.
By M. H.

PRICE THREE SHILLINGS AND SIXPENCE EACH.

I.
LILY HOPE AND HER FRIENDS.
By Hetty Bowman.

II.
AUNT MARGARET'S VISIT;
Or, the False and the Real.
By Jane M. Kippen.

LONDON: HODDER AND STOUGHTON, 27, Paternoster Row.

27, PATERNOSTER ROW, LONDON.

HODDER AND STOUGHTON'S
LIST OF
Gift Books for the Young.

BY DR. MACAULAY, Editor of "The Leisure Hour."

I.

Crown 8vo, cloth, 5s. With Thirteen Illustrations.

TRUE TALES OF TRAVEL AND ADVENTURE, VALOUR AND VIRTUE.

"Dr. Macaulay's name is a voucher for spirited work, and 'True Tales' are instructive as well as interesting."—*Times.*

" Full of stirring incident."—*Daily News.*

"The book, we need hardly say, is full of very interesting reading."—*Spectator.*

"With no little vigour and power of condensation he tells of such achievements, and such perils, and suffering as fell to the lot of the early Australian explorers, of the Garibaldians, and of the Arctic navigators; relieved by tales of such victories as those of Trafalgar and the Nile. Suitable biographies are skilfully introduced."—*British Quarterly Review.*

II.

GREY HAWK: Life and Adventures among the Red Indians. An Old Story Retold.
Eleven Illustrations. Handsomely bound, gilt edges, 5s.

"The editor of the *Leisure Hour* having come across a romantic story of real life, has worked it up into a genuinely interesting Indian story. The illustrations and handsome style in which the book is got up make it very suitable for presentation."—*Sheffield Independent.*

"We cannot better testify to its absorbing interest than by saying that we have read every word of it. It is a unique picture of Indian life and customs—of a state of things which already has well-nigh passed away. It is as instructive as it is romantic. As a book for boys, and not for them only, it can scarcely be surpassed."—*British Quarterly Review.*

BY DR. MACAULAY, Editor of "The Leisure Hour."

III.

ALL TRUE. Records of Peril and Adventure

by Sea and Land—Remarkable Escapes and Deliverances—Missionary Enterprises and Travels—Wonders of Nature and Providence — Incidents of Christian History and Biography. With Twelve Illustrations. Crown 8vo, cloth gilt, 5s.

"'All True' contains records of adventures by sea and land, remarkable escapes and deliverances, missionary enterprises, etc.; is as entertaining as the majority of such books are depressing, and may be welcomed as a welcome present for children. The illustrations are above the average of those vouchsafed to us in children's books."—*Spectator.*

IV.

ACROSS THE FERRY: First Impressions

of America and its People. With Nine Illustrations. Crown 8vo, cloth, price 5s.

"Dr. Macaulay not only records his own impressions, but he incorporates with them much of the useful and interesting information which an intelligent traveller not only picks up, but takes special pains to furnish himself with. The volume is a series of Photographs of America as it was in 1870, and is full, therefore, of practical interest."—*British Quarterly Review.*

THE BOY IN THE BUSH. A Tale of

Australian Life. By RICHARD ROWE. Crown 8vo, with Illustrations, 3s. 6d.

THE POSTMAN'S BAG. By JOHN DE

LIEFDE. With Illustrations. Crown 8vo, 2s. 6d.

"Commend us to Mr. de Liefde for a pleasant story, whether in the parlour or on the printed page. He is himself a story-book, full of infectious humour, racy anecdote, youthful freshness, and warm-hearted religion. In this pretty volume we do not get any of his more elaborate tales; it is professedly a book 'for boys and girls,' and is made up of short stories and fables, the very things to win children's hearts."—*The Patriot.*

BY MRS. ROBERT O'REILLY.

"Mrs. O'Reilly possesses the art which Miss Mitford exhibited so remarkably in 'Our Village.' To make a short tale attractive has baffled the art of some of the greatest of our novelists. It is a special gift, and she may be congratulated on its possession."—*Pall Mall Gazette.*

I.
THE RED HOUSE IN THE SUBURBS.
With Twenty-six Illustrations by F. A. FRASER. Cloth gilt, 3s. 6d.

II.
REED FARM.
With Thirteen Illustrations by TOWNLEY GREEN. Crown 8vo, cloth gilt extra, 3s. 6d.

"One of Mrs. O'Reilly's best and happiest efforts."—*Christian Age.*

III.
MEG'S MISTAKE, and other Sussex Stories.
With Twenty Illustrations by FRED. BARNARD. Crown 8vo, cloth, 5s.

"The humour and pathos of these stories are beyond all praise."—*Standard.*

"We have never seen better stories of their kind."—*Academy.*

THE CHILDREN OF CHINA: Written for the Children of England.
By the Author of "The Children of India." With Numerous Illustrations. Handsomely bound, fcap. 4to, gilt edges, 5s.

"Miss Marston's beautiful book comes to us in all the glory that gold, turquoise, and black can give to its binding. The fortunate children who get this book as a present will be pleased with its outward appearance, they will be delighted with its interior. The paper is good, the printing is good, the illustrations are good, and what is of greater importance the writing is good. The author knows well how to talk interestingly to children, and her style is so clear and simple that she contrives to convey an immense amount of information in her 320 pages."—*Illustrated Missionary News.*

"Will be joyfully welcomed. Well written, very elegantly bound, and profusely illustrated, with a good map at the beginning. We have seldom seen a book for children which we liked better, or could more heartily recommend as a prize or present.—*Record.*

BY THE LATE W. H. G. KINGSTON.

"Mr. Kingston's inimitable stories."—*British Quarterly Review.*

I.
FROM POWDER MONKEY TO ADMIRAL. A Story of Naval Adventure. Eight Illustrations. Handsomely bound, 5s. Gilt edges.

"Kingston's tales require no commendation. They are full of go. All lads enjoy them, and many men. This is one of his best stories—a youthful critic assures us his very best."—*Sheffield Independent.*

II.
JAMES BRAITHWAITE, THE SUPERCARGO. The Story of his Adventures Ashore and Afloat. With Eight Illustrations, Portrait, and Short Account of the Author. Crown 8vo, gilt edges, handsomely bound, 5s.

"'The supercargo's exploits at sea during the early part of this century appear as fresh and vigorous as though they were described yesterday. It is a healthy, hearty, enjoyable story."—*Daily Chronicle.*

III.
JOVINIAN. A Tale of Early Papal Rome. With Eight Illustrations. Cheap Edition. Fcap. 8vo, 2s. 6d.

"It is a powerful and thrilling story."—*Methodist Recorder.*

IV.
HENDRICKS THE HUNTER; or, The Border Farm. A Tale of Zululand. With Five Illustrations. Crown 8vo. Handsomely bound in cloth, gilt edges, price 5s.

"A delightful book of travel and adventure in Zululand."—*Athenæum.*

"A boy may be happy all day with Mr. Kingston's 'Hendricks the Hunter.'"—*Saturday Review.*

"HENDRICKS THE HUNTER."

Specimen of the Illustrations.

BY THE LATE W. H. G. KINGSTON (Continued).

V.
CLARA MAYNARD; or, The True and the False. A Tale for the Times. Ninth Thousand. Crown 8vo, 3s. 6d.

"An admirable story, in which the mischievous results of Ritualistic teaching are effectively shown."—*Rock*.

VI.
PETER TRAWL; or, The Adventures of a Whaler. With Eight Illustrations. Handsomely bound in cloth. Crown 8vo, gilt edges, price 5s.

"Here will be found shipwrecks and desert islands, and hair-breadth escapes of every kind, all delightful and spirit-stirring."—*Court Journal.*

"It is a manly sort of book, with a good deal of information in it, as well as the adventures which boys love."—*Athenæum.*

KATE'S MOTHER. By ELLEN HODGSON. Crown 8vo, 3s. 6d.

"A brightly told simple domestic story."—*European Mail.*

"A homely tale, very charmingly told of humble family life, with its trials, and sorrows, and loves; its disappointments and compensations. It is a thoroughly natural story, and one that will help to elevate and purify the life of the household.—*Christian.*

POOR PAPA. By MARY W. PORTER. With Four Illustrations. Crown 8vo, sewed, 1s.

"His troubles are very comic."—*British Quarterly.*
"Intensely amusing."—*City Press.*
"Admirably told."—*Liverpool Albion.*

STORY AFTER STORY of Land and Sea, Man and Beast. By the Author of "Sunday Evenings with my Children," etc. With 130 Illustrations. Square crown 8vo, cloth, 3s. 6d.

"The pages contain engravings in abundance, each one serving to illustrate a pleasant little story."—*Sunday School Times.*

"For young people this volume must prove quite an attractive mine of amusement. It will make an excellent prize."—*Schoolmaster.*

"A most attractive and useful volume for young readers."—*Rock.*

BY MISS DOUDNEY.

I.
A LONG LANE WITH A TURNING.
A Story. With Sixteen Illustrations by M. E. EDWARDS. Handsomely bound, crown 8vo, cloth, 5s.

"Miss Doudney is a charming writer of good stories without being goody, and this ought to be a favourite amongst her numerous works."—*Academy.*

"A charming story for girls."—*Record.*

"I consider it not only one of the best of her stories but one of the best stories of its kind."—*Truth.*

II.
WHAT'S IN A NAME? With Eight Illustrations. Crown 8vo, handsomely bound, 5s.

"One of Sarah Doudney's most charming idylls. The story is very sweet, full of charming surprises and soft emotions."—*Court Journal.*

"One of the most charming stories it is possible to conceive."—*Whitehall Review.*

III.
NELLY CHANNELL. With Four Illustrations. Cloth, 3s. 6d.

"A quiet and wholesome story well told."—*Daily News.*

"A clever tale, inculcating noble principles."—*Christian.*

IV.
NOTHING BUT LEAVES. With Frontispiece. New and Cheaper Edition. Eleventh Thousand. 3s. 6d.

"A pretty and well-written story."—*Athenæum.*

"One of the most charming and exquisitely-told tales that we ever had the pleasure of perusing."—*Literary World.*

THE CHILDREN'S PASTIME: Pictures and Stories. By L. G. SÉGUIN, Author of "Walks in Algiers," etc. With 200 Illustrations. Square crown 8vo, 3s. 6d.

"It contains many excellent stories. They are well illustrated by many woodcuts. A treasure for those who have to amuse young folk."—*Scotsman.*

"A capital gift-book for a good boy or girl."—*Literary World.*

"A welcome gift in any nursery of young children."—*Literary Churchman.*

CHEERFUL SUNDAYS: Stories, Parables, and Poems for Children. With 150 Illustrations. By the Author of "Story after Story," etc. Square crown 8vo, 3s. 6d.

"'Cheerful Sundays' is the title of another volume of religious stories and verses for children. It is well done, and is excellently illustrated.—*Scotsman.*

"A good book for Sunday reading for little ones."—*Standard.*

SEPPEL; or, The Burning of the Synagogue at Munich. By GUSTAV NIERITZ. With Frontispiece. 1s. 6d.

"The narrative is of thrilling interest."—*Edinburgh Daily Review.*

BUSY HANDS AND PATIENT HEARTS; or, the Blind Boy of Dresden and his Friends. By the same Author. Eighth Edition. Crown 8vo, illustrated, 1s. 6d.

"One of the most beautiful stories ever written for children."—

"A real and genuine Christmas story."—*Times.*   [*Nonconformist.*

THE "PRIZE" ILLUSTRATED EDITION OF

FROM LOG CABIN TO WHITE HOUSE. The Story of President Garfield's Life. By W. M. THAYER, Author of "George Washington," "The Pioneer Boy," etc., etc. Handsomely bound, large paper, gilt edges, price 5s.

THIS EDITION, containing Twenty full-page Illustrations, and Two Steel Portraits, completes the issue of 135,000 copies of this extraordinarily popular work. Its subject, its style, and its appearance combine to render the book pre-eminently suitable for presents, prizes, and school libraries.

CHEAPER EDITIONS at 1s., 1s. 6d., and 3s. 6d. may also be had, containing a fine portrait of President Garfield.

"One of the most romantic stories of our time."—*British Quarterly Review.*

"The boyhood of Garfield, his struggles with poverty and other difficulties, his self-education, his strong religious sense, are all depicted in a way that brings out very strikingly the great character of the man."—*Guardian.*

"There could not possibly be a better or more useful gift-book for Christmas-tide, New Year, birthday, or indeed any 'tide,' year, or day than this thrilling story of one who from his earliest boyhood to the hour of his martyrdom, was every inch a king."—*Golden Hours.*

"FROM LOG CABIN TO WHITE HOUSE."

Specimen of the Illustrations.

BY L. T. MEADE, Author of "Scamp and I," etc., etc.

I.
THE AUTOCRAT OF THE NURSERY.
With Forty Illustrations by T. PYM. Fcap. 4to, handsomely bound, 5s.

"We have seldom seen a more spirited and delightful story for little children."—*Guardian.*

"A most charming children's story, exquisitely illustrated."—*Truth.*

"First of all, make way for his majesty, an imperious, courageous, delightful infant of three years, who calls himself 'Tarhe.' The lady, L. T. Meade, authoress of 'Scamp and I,' who tells us and her younger readers all about him, is assisted by T. Pym, an artist scarcely behind Miss Kate Greenaway in drawing children, with forty charming illustrations of this delightful nursery history."—*Illustrated London News.*

"T. Pym, who has illustrated this book, has drawn some capital and natural studies of child-life. The story itself is agreeably told, its author evidently understanding and appreciating the little ways of children. The nursery tale has all the naturalness of children's conversations, and will forcibly appeal to the young minds for whose amusement it has been written. The illuminated binding is exceedingly beautiful."—*Whitehall Review.*

II.
HOW IT ALL CAME ROUND.
With Six Illustrations. Handsomely bound, price 5s.

"A charming story. The characters are excellently drawn."—*Standard.*

"The story is worthy of the highest praise. Altogether, this is one of the best stories of the season."—*Pall Mall Gazette.*

III.
HERMIE'S ROSEBUDS, and other Stories.
With Illustrations. Handsomely bound, price 3s. 6d.

"A collection of short pieces by this gifted authoress, illustrative of the quickening and ennobling influence exerted even on the worst of men by children. The whole series is a powerful and pathetic illustration of the text, 'A little child shall lead them.' 'The Least of These' is a capital sketch, so is 'Jack Darling's Conqueror.'"—*Freeman.*

THE AUTOCRAT OF THE NURSERY.

Specimen of the Illustrations.

BY L. T. MEADE, Author of "Scamp and I," etc., etc. (Continued.)

IV.

SCARLET ANEMONES. With Frontispiece.
Fcap. 8vo, cloth, 1s.

"Two delightful tales."—*Sheffield Independent.*

"Two pretty little shilling books. The former tells of a child who was lost through a careless act of deception, and found again by the sense and prayerfulness of a young girl. 'The Two Sisters' is a story of the love and devotion of a twin for her frailer sister. Both tales are good beyond the average."—*Christian World.*

V.

ELLIE AND ESTHER; or, The Two Sisters. With Frontispiece. Fcap. 8vo, cloth, 1s.

THE ORIENT BOYS: A Tale of School Life. Crown 8vo, cloth, 3s. 6d.

"A healthy story, of American origin, well told, and pointing some good morals that boys will do well to learn."—*Christian.*

"'The Orient Boys, a Tale of School Life,' will find favour among the boys, who will be more than interested in Carlos Chrysostomo Colimo. It is out of the ordinary and somewhat monotonous style on which school tales are constructed."—*Sheffield Independent.*

CHARITY MOORE. A Story. By LINA ORMAN-COOPER. With Illustrations by T. PYM. Crown 8vo, cloth, 1s. 6d.

"A tale of the brave deeds and unselfish life of a workhouse girl. It is romantic without being improbable, and altogether a very pretty story, prettily written, prettily illustrated, and prettily bound. With its covers decorated with holly and robins, it will be a welcome Christmas gift for many a little maiden."—*Christian.*

BY MISS M. A. PAULL, *Author of "Tim's Troubles," etc.*

I.
FRIAR HILDEBRAND'S CROSS; or, The Monk of Tavystoke Abbaye.
With Frontispiece. Crown 8vo, cloth, 5s.

"The volume is beautifully written, and never were the struggles of a true and faithful heart more touchingly depicted. The tenderness of the sentiment which binds the friar to Cicely is depicted with such exquisite refinement and delicacy that many a bright eye will be dimmed with tears in the perusal."—*Court Journal.*

II.
THE FLOWER OF THE GRASS-MARKET.
With Five Illustrations. Cheap Edition. Crown 8vo, cloth, 3s. 6d.

"There is a healthy moral tone of a very high order sustained throughout the work, and an easy grace and diction, which make it highly commendable."—*Edinburgh Daily Review.*

"A handsomely got-up volume. The story is admirably written. The reader never loses interest in the fortunes of the various characters in it."—*Sheffield Independent.*

THE STORY OF THE LIFE OF JESUS
Told in Words Easy to Read and Understand. By the Author of "The Story of the Bible," etc. With Forty Illustrations. Handsomely bound, fcap. 4to, cloth, 3s. 6d.

"An excellent Sunday book for children; the story is tenderly and brightly told, the pictures of Eastern life and Jewish manners form an effective running commentary on the text, which is interspersed besides with graphic views of the sacred cities, sites and scenery."—*Times.*

"A noteworthy book for the children. The forty or more engravings are fresh and true designs, fitly representing Oriental costumes and scenery. We have so often seen the regular conventional drawing, that it did us good to set our eyes upon these original sketches. The binding is attractive, and the form and type of the book are all we can desire. The language is suitable for children, and it tells the wondrous story so that it may be understood of the little ones."—*Sword and Trowel.*

BY DR. GORDON STABLES, R.N.

I.

STANLEY GRAHAME. A Tale of the Dark Continent. With Eighteen Illustrations. Crown 8vo, cloth, gilt edges, 5s.

"The story never flags from beginning to end, and there can be no shadow of doubt that it will be received with delight by every healthy-minded lad. The illustrations are very good."—*Scotsman.*

"A fine book for boys, full of admirably vigorous and picturesque writing, and of wholesome manly form."—*Society.*

II.

ADVENTURES ROUND THE POLE; or, The Cruise of the "Snowbird" Crew in the "Arrandoon." Eight Illustrations. Handsomely bound, gilt edges, 5s.

"It is a story of thrilling interest, the essence of a dozen Arctic voyages, lighted up by a good deal of fun and frolic, and chastened by manly religious feeling. It has excited us as we have read."—*British Quarterly Review.*

"The illustrations are excellent. Healthy-minded boys will find in the volume a source of great pleasure. It is brightly written, it is full of adventure, and it is thoroughly wholesome."—*Scotsman.*

III.

THE CRUISE OF THE SNOWBIRD. A Story of Arctic Adventure. With Nine Full-page Illustrations. Handsomely bound, gilt edges, 5s.

"This is a capital story of adventure of the sort that all true boys delight in. Every page teems with wonderful stories 'of moving accidents by flood and field, of hair-breadth 'scapes'; and perhaps the greatest charm about these 'yarns' is that they are so true to nature that they read like actual experiences. A story which is full of 'go,' and will, we venture to predict, be one of the most popular 'boys' books' of the season."—*Academy.*

BY MRS. PRENTISS.

I.
THE STORY LIZZIE TOLD. By MRS. E. PRENTISS, Author of "Stepping Heavenward." Illustrated. Fcap. 8vo, cloth. 1s.

"One of the most charmingly delicate tales of an invalid child's life that we have ever read."—*Nonconformist.*

II.
THE LITTLE PREACHER. With Frontispiece. Fcap. 8vo, cloth, 1s. 6d.

"Of the 'Little Preacher,' the scene of which is laid in the Black Forest, a German gentleman, talking to a friend about the authoress, exclaimed enthusiastically, 'I wish I knew her! I would so like to thank her for her perfect picture. It is a miracle of genius,' he added, 'to be able thus to portray the life of a *foreign* people.'"—*Congregationalist.*

SLYBOOTS, and other Farmyard Chronicles. By BEATA FRANCIS, Author of "Fables and Fancies." Handsomely bound, with Numerous Illustrations, 2s. 6d.

"Delightfully simple and natural, and lighted up with gleams of fun and humour."—*Literary World.*

"We have thoroughly enjoyed and heartily laughed over these chronicles."—*Bath Journal.*

"There is a subtle moral in each of these chronicles, and the style is extremely humorous. A most enjoyable volume."—*Derby Mercury.*

CLUNY MACPHERSON. A Tale of Brotherly Love. By A. E. BARR. With Six Illustrations. Crown 8vo, 5s.

"The story is of thrilling interest."—*Literary World.*

"The book, which is splendidly got up, is throughout exceedingly readable."—*Perthshire Constitutional.*

"This singularly beautiful story."—*Daily Review.*

THORNTON HALL; or, Old Questions in Young Lives. By PHŒBE J. MCKEEN. Crown 8vo, nicely bound, price 3s. 6d.

"An interesting and well-written story. The characters of the girls are well drawn, and the tone of the book excellent throughout."—*Church Sunday School Magazine.*

b

MRS. REANEY'S SHILLING SERIES.

Tastefully bound in cloth, price 1s. each.

Found at Last.
Little Glory's Mission.
Unspoken Addresses.

Number Four, and Other Chippings. [Stories.
Not Alone in the World.

"Written with all the author's well-known sweetness and persuasiveness of style."—*The Outlook.*

"Good little books in Mrs. Reaney's very best style. We hope they will sell by hundreds of thousands."—*Sword and Trowel.*

CAPITAL FOR WORKING BOYS.
Chapters on Character Building. By J. E. M'CONAUGHY. Crown 8vo, cloth, price 3s. 6d.

"We should like every working boy to read it. It is full of wise saws and modern instances, pithy quotations, and taking anecdotes. The spirit of persevering industry and independence will be fostered by such reading, while neatness, promptness, truthfulness, economy and true religion are not forgotten. Every wise father who has sons about to leave the home fireside should give each one of them a copy of this capital book."—*Sword and Trowel.*

THE WINTHROP FAMILY. A Story of New England Life Fifty Years Ago. By the Author of "May Chester," etc. Crown 8vo, cloth, 3s. 6d.

"A very dainty, winsome volume."—*Freeman.*

"Primitive New England life, hospitality, and home-heartedness are finely wrought out in it. There is a quiet, easy grace, a pleasant sparkle, and a genial attractiveness in the style which exactly suits the life, manner, and personages of the narrative. A most admirable one for home interest and delight."—*Golden Hours.*

"THERE'S A FRIEND FOR LITTLE CHILDREN." By JULIA F. ARMSTRONG. With Twelve Illustrations. Handsomely bound, crown 8vo, cloth, 2s. 6d.

"Very well told. The illustrations in it are well done."—*Scotsman.*

"A truly delightful story."—*Ecclesiastical Gazette.*

"There is no child who will not be charmed with the story."—*British Messenger.*

"THERE'S A FRIEND FOR LITTLE CHILDREN."

Specimen of the Illustrations.

WORKS BY MRS. G. S. REANEY.

I.

JUST IN TIME; or, Howard Clarion's Rescue. Handsomely bound, crown 8vo, cloth, 5s.

"It is really one of her very best books, and that is high praise indeed. She always writes with a purpose, and her stories clearly indicate both culture and a wide knowledge of the world and its needs. The secret of her success doubtless lies in the fact that her pictures of life are real, and consequently true to the experience of the reader. The present story, which is gracefully told, is likely to have many appreciative readers."—*Christian Commonwealth.*

II.

DAISY SNOWFLAKE'S SECRET. A Story of English Home Life. New and Cheaper Edition. Elegantly bound, 3s. 6d.

"Winning in style, pure and earnest in tone, and of commanding interest."—*Daily Review.*

III.

OUR DAUGHTERS: Their Lives Here and Hereafter. Eighth Thousand, cloth, 3s. 6d.

"A thoroughly wise and helpful book."—*Christian.*

IV.

OUR BROTHERS AND SONS. Fourth Thousand. Elegantly bound, 3s. 6d.

"One of her best books, written in excellent English, and with a racy, earnest pen."—*Evangelical Magazine.*

THEODORA CAMERON. A Home Story. By PHŒBE J. McKEEN. With Five Full-page Illustrations. Seventh Thousand. Crown 8vo, cloth, price 5s.

"A pretty story of the great civil war, which, though issued in a single volume, comprises not less matter than an ordinary novel, and introduces the reader to many varieties of character, and numerous stirring scenes in the home and on the battle-field."—*Daily News.*

BY ISAAC PLEYDELL.

IN A CORNER OF THE VINEYARD.
A Village Story. With Frontispiece. Crown 8vo, 5s.

"The hard, rough life of the men is vigorously drawn."—*Athenæum.*
"The characters are drawn with graphic skill, and the story is one of absorbing interest."—*Derby Mercury.*
"A touching and stimulating story."—*Christian World.*

BELL'S LADIES' READER. A Class
Book of Poetry for Schools and Families. With an Introduction on the Principles of Elocution. By D. C. BELL, Joint Author of "Bell's Standard Elocutionist." Crown 8vo, cloth, 2s. 6d.

BELL'S STANDARD ELOCUTIONIST.
Principles and Exercises. Followed by a copious Selection of Extracts in Prose and Poetry, Classified and Adapted for Reading and Recitation. By D. C. and A. M. BELL. New and greatly Enlarged Edition. Containing over 500 of the choicest Extracts in the English Language, with the Principles of Elocution fully stated. Strongly half-bound in roan, 544 pages, 3s. 6d.

"This is the best book of the kind."—*Bookseller.*

FERN GLEN FARM. By HELEN PINKERTON
REDDEN. With Illustrations by the Author. In crown 8vo, cloth, handsomely bound, 3s. 6d.

"It is a singularly simple and sweet picture of child-life framed in the the fairest imaginable setting of natural scenery and domestic affection. Th story is fragrant with the breath of trees and flowers, and pervaded with a healthy enjoyment of the delights of rural life that is charming and contagious. Were anything needed to increase our interest in the persons of her youthful heroes and heroines, it is supplied in the delicate grace and airy fancy that illumine the illustrations with which she has beautified her little book."—*Presbyterian.*

BY J. R. H. HAWTHORN.

I.

LAUNCHING AWAY; or, Roger Larks-
way's Strange Mission. With Frontispiece. Crown
8vo, cloth, gilt edges, 5s.

"An excellently written book of incident and adventure mainly in Australia. The author knows how to make such a book interesting, and he has in this one eminently succeeded."—*Scotsman.*

II.

THE PIONEER OF A FAMILY; or,
Adventures of a Young Governess. Second Edition.
With Frontispiece. 5s.

"Few stories have such an air of reality about them. Mr. Hawthorn has the faculty of drawing his characters in such graphic fashion, that we seem to have known them, and are forced to sympathise with their joys and sorrows."—*Aberdeen Free Press.*

"Full of terse and powerful sketches of colonial life."—*Freeman.*

OLIVER WYNDHAM. A Tale of the
Great Plague. By the Author of "Naomi; or, The
Last Days of Jerusalem," etc. Sixteenth Thousand. Crown
8vo, cloth, 3s. 6d.

"The chief merit of the book is the exquisite delicacy with which it illustrates Christian feeling and Christian principle in circumstances the most trying and varied."—*Weekly Review.*

DAVID EASTERBROOK. An Oxford
Story. By TREGELLES POLKINGHORNE. With Frontispiece. Handsomely bound, 5s.

"An exceedingly interesting story."—*Rock.*
"A bright, vigorous, and useful work."—*Freeman.*

BY MARIE HALL née SIBREE.

I.
NOBLE, BUT NOT THE NOBLEST.
Crown 8vo, 3s. 6d.

"The picture is skilfully drawn, with tender touches and with artistic lights. We heartily commend it. To those who have read the author's previous stories of 'The Dying Saviour and the Gipsy Girl,' 'Andrew Marvel,' etc., this is scarcely necessary."—*British Quarterly Review.*

"A more elegantly written, graceful, and powerful story the present story season has not yielded us."—*Freeman.*

II.
ANDREW MARVEL AND HIS FRIENDS. A Story of the Siege of Hull. Fourth Thousand. With Four Illustrations. Crown 8vo, cloth, 5s.

"Mrs. Hall's knowledge of the historical details is as exact as her imagination is fertile and faithful. The pictures are good, and the beautiful photograph of the statue of Marvel at Hull well deserves to be noted. Messrs. Hodder and Stoughton have certainly made it a beautiful and attractive book."—*British Quarterly Review.*

III.
THE DYING SAVIOUR AND THE GIPSY GIRL, and other Tales. Fifteenth Thousand. Crown 8vo, cloth, 3s. 6d.

"The stories are gracefully written: they are marked by good feeling and refined taste, and the moral conveyed by them is unexceptionable."—*Spectator.*

IV.
THE DYING SAVIOUR AND THE GIPSY GIRL, and THE LIGHT OF THE WORLD. Two Stories. Eighteenth Thousand. Fcap. 8vo, price 1s.

"A literary gem not less admirable for the beauty of its diction, and the artistic finish of its details than for its lucid exhibition of the gospel. The 'Old, Old Story' was seldom told in sweeter words."—*S. S. World.*

CHEAP ILLUSTRATED EDITIONS OF J. B. DE LIEFDE'S STORIES.

I.

A BRAVE RESOLVE; or, the Siege of Stralsund. A Story of Heroism and Adventure.
With Eight Full-page Illustrations. Crown 8vo, handsomely bound, 3s. 6d.

"Gives a capital picture of the Siege of Stralsund in the Thirty Years War. It is an excellent historical novel."—*The Guardian.*

"A highly interesting romance. The exciting events of the Thirty Years War are depicted with much fidelity, and the love story lends an additional charm to a thoroughly readable book."—*Court Journal.*

"It is admirably done—we have not read a better historical story for a long time."—*British Quarterly Review.*

II.

THE BEGGARS; or, the Founders of the Dutch Republic.
With Four Illustrations. Crown 8vo, handsomely bound in cloth, 3s. 6d.

"Mr. de Liefde's 'Beggars' is a piece of genuine historical romance, fu of incident, and not wanting in colour and lesson. The book is a good and lively one, and we cordially recommend it."—*Argosy.*

"This is an interesting and animated story, the scene of which is laid in the Netherlands at a time with which Mr. Motley's works have made us familiar. The hero of Mr. de Liefde's tale engages in an attempt to rescue Count Egmont the night before his execution, and afterwards takes service in the fleet of Sea Beggars, which was so troublesome to Spain, and of such service to the young Dutch Republic. There is no lack of adventure in the book."—*Athenæum.*

DAVID LIVINGSTONE. The Story of his Life and Labours; or, The Weaver Boy who became a Missionary.
By H. G. ADAMS. With Steel Portrait and Thirty Illustrations. Fifty-seventh Thousand. Crown 8vo, cloth, 3s. 6d.

"An admirable condensation of 'The Story of the Life and Labours of Dr. Livingstone.' Comprehensive in range, abounding in detail, and vividly presenting the graphic description of the great explorer himself."—*Record.*

Specimen of the Illustrations.

RE-ISSUE OF JACOB ABBOTT'S STORIES.

I. **JUNO & GEORGIE.**
II. **MARY OSBORNE.**
III. **JUNO on a JOURNEY.**
IV. **HUBERT.**

With Frontispiece. Fcap. 8vo, cloth, price 1s. 6d. each.

"Well printed and elegantly bound, will surely meet with a hearty welcome. We remember the delight we took in them years ago, and how lessons which they inculcated have left their traces until this day. Dr. Arnold, of Rugby, was one of the warmest admirers of the author of 'The Young Christian,' and recognized in him a man of congenial spirit. For strong common sense, knowledge of child nature, and deep religious fervour, we have had nothing superior to these four delightful stories."—*Freeman.*

"The author of 'The Young Christian' is really an English classic. One of his little books exerted such an influence on Frederick Robertson of Brighton, that its perusal formed a turning-point in the life of that great preacher; and there have probably been thousands on both sides of the Atlantic similarly affected by the writings of the same author. We therefore welcome with peculiar satisfaction the elegant edition of four of his best stories."—*Christian Leader.*

SHORE AND SEA. Stories of Great Vikings and Sea Captains. By W. H. DAVENPORT ADAMS. Ten Illustrations. Handsomely bound, gilt edges, 5s.

"A book which is as thrilling as any romance."—*Scotsman.*

"An interesting book for adventure-loving boys. It contains a capital description of the life, customs, and manners of the Norsemen, together with much pleasantly-told information concerning 'Sebastian Cabot,' 'De Soto,' 'The Early Colonizers of Virginia,' 'Drake,' 'Hudson,' and 'Henry Morgan.' This collection will be deservedly popular."—*Pall Mall Gazette.*

"This is a carefully written and thoroughly good book. Mr. Adams has tried to sketch the lives of famous sea captains with fidelity as well as with graphic power. . . . It is the romance of the sea as it has been actually realized, and boys will find it as instructive as it is interesting."—*British Quarterly Review.*

JACOB ABBOTT'S STORIES.

Specimen of the Illustrations.

BY MARY PRYOR HACK.

I.
CHRISTIAN WOMANHOOD. Uniform with
"Consecrated Women" and "Self-Surrender." Elegantly bound, 5s.

"We know no more suitable present for a young lady than this charming book, with its sketches of Mary Fletcher, Elizabeth, last Duchess of Gordon, Ann Blackhouse, Frances Ridley Havergal, and others. It will be a very fountain of inspiration and encouragement to other good women."—*Sheffield Independent.*

II.
CONSECRATED WOMEN. Fourth
Thousand. 5s. Handsomely bound.

"The memorials are all deeply interesting, bright, and vivid."—*Freeman.*

"Some of these brief biographies are deeply interesting."—*Record.*

"The stories of such philanthropic women are profoundly touching."—*Spectator.*

III.
SELF-SURRENDER. A Second Series of
"Consecrated Women." Second Thousand. 5s. cloth elegant.

"A most delightful book, written by a woman, about women, and for women though it may be read by men with equal pleasure and profit. Each of the eleven chapters contains in brief, the life, history, and work of some sister who was made perfect either through service or suffering."—*Christian.*

THE SISTERS OF GLENCOE; or,
Letitia's Choice. By EVA WYNNE. Twentieth Thousand. Crown 8vo, cloth elegant, price 5s.

"Its life pictures are skilfully drawn, and the most wholesome lessons are enforced with fidelity and power."—*Temperance Record.*

"An admirable story, illustrating in a most effective manner the mischief arising from the use of intoxicating liquors."—*Rock.*

BY ALEXANDER MACLEOD, D.D.

I.
THE CHILDREN'S PORTION. Crown 8vo, cloth, 5s.

"As a preacher to children, Dr. Macleod has perhaps no living equal In these delightful chapters he seems to us to be at his best."—*Christian.*

"Sunday school teachers will be glad of the very numerous illustrations and anecdote contained in it."—*Literary World.*

"Admirable specimen of what such addresses should be, thoughtful, earnest, simple, full of affectionate appeal, and freely illustrated."—*Sunday School Chronicle.*

"This is a collection of short sermons addressed to children. They are well adapted to strike the fancy and touch the heart of the young."—*Record.*

II.
TALKING TO THE CHILDREN. Tenth Edition. 3s. 6d.

"An exquisite work. Divine truths are here presented in simple language, illustrated by parable and anecdote at once apt and beautiful."—*Evangelical Magazine.*

III.
THE GENTLE HEART. A Second Series of "Talking to the Children." Fifth Thousand. Crown 8vo, 3s. 6d.

Mr. SPURGEON says: "We have been fascinated with the originality and beauty of its thought, charmed with the simplicity and elegance of its language, enriched with the store of its illustrations, and blest in spirit through its abundant manifestation of 'the truth as it is in Jesus.'"

LINKS IN REBECCA'S LIFE. An American Story. By PANSY. With Frontispiece. Handsomely bound in cloth, 5s.

"By one of the ablest and sprightliest of American story-tellers."—*Christian.*

"We should like to see every young lady of our acquaintance fully engrossed in the reading of this book. It is an admirable five shillings' worth."—*Sword and Trowel.*

BY THE AUTHOR OF "CHRISTIE REDFERN'S TROUBLES," etc.

I.

THE BAIRNS; or, Janet's Love and Service. With Five Illustrations. Thirteenth Thousand. Crown 8vo, cloth elegant, 5s.

"A special interest attaches to 'The Bairns.' The characters are forcibly delineated, and the touches of homeliness which seem almost peculiar to our northern kinsfolk impart a peculiar charm."—*Record.*

II.

FREDERICA AND HER GUARDIANS; or, The Perils of Orphanhood. Cheaper Edition. Crown 8vo, cloth, 3s. 6d.

"An exceedingly well-told story, full of incidents of an attractive character. The story will be admired by all thoughtful girls."—*Public Opinion.*

"A sweet, pure, and beautiful story, such as may be put with confidence into the hands of any English girl."—*Sheffield Independent.*

III.

THE TWA MISS DAWSONS. Crown 8vo, cloth, price 5s.

"We gladly welcome a new book by the author of 'The Bairns.' That charming Canadian story opened a new field for readers of fiction. The present story is limited to Eastern Scotland. It is a family picture, settling down chiefly to the experiences of a charming old maiden aunt—a most admirable delineation—and an equally charming niece."—*British Quarterly Review.*

YENSIE WALTON. An American Story. By J. R. GRAHAM CLARK. With Frontispiece. Crown 8vo, cloth, 5s.

"In tone and spirit, plan and execution, this is a superb story. Rich in delineation of character, and in descriptions of real experience. A more fascinating and inspiring picture of a school-mistress, in one prolonged, prayerful, and sustained endeavour to lead an orphan pupil to Christ, was never drawn."—*General Baptist Magazine.*

BY EDWIN HODDER.

I.

EPHRAIM AND HELAH. A Story of the Exodus. Eighth Thousand. Crown 8vo, cloth elegant, 5s.

"Mr. Hodder gives a vivid description of the daily life of the Hebrews immediately at and before the time of the coming of Moses. The picture is full of interest."—*The Queen.*

II.

TOSSED ON THE WAVES. A Story of Young Life. Fifteenth Thousand. Fcap. 8vo, cloth, 3s. 6d.

"We cannot think that a boy could take up the book without feeling its fascination, or without rising a better lad from its perusal. The scenes of life on the sea and in the colonies are peculiarly attractive."—*British Quarterly Review.*

III.

THE JUNIOR CLERK. A Tale of City Life. Fourteenth Edition. Crown 8vo, cloth, 2s. 6d.

"Mr. Shipton observes that the author described this tale to him as a fiction. He remarks: 'It may be so to him, but for every one of his statements I could supply a fact. It is not merely true to nature as a narration of the means by which young men may be—it is a true record of the ways in which many have been, and many still are being—led to dishonour and ruin.' Such a recommendation as this will be sufficient to ensure for this little book a hearty welcome from many readers."—*Christian World.*

THE WHITE CROSS AND DOVE OF PEARLS. A Biography of Light and Shade. By SARSON C. INGHAM. Sixth Thousand. Crown 8vo, cloth, 5s.

"'The White Cross and Dove of Pearls' will not disappoint the expectations of those who may already have formed justly high opinions of this strikingly original and sympathetic writer's ability to interest, to amuse, and to elevate her readers. It is a fiction without false sentiment, without unhealthy imagination, and without a single vulgar or frivolous idea."—*Daily Telegraph.*

WORKS BY W. M. THAYER.

A Shilling Edition of

FROM LOG CABIN TO WHITE HOUSE.
The Story of President Garfield's Life. Now Ready. 140th Thousand. In Paper Boards, Illustrated Cover, with Fine Steel Portrait. Cloth Edition, 1s. 6d.; Cloth gilt, 3s. 6d.; Illustrated Edition, gilt edges, 5s. Suitable for Presents, Prizes, and School Libraries.

II.

GEORGE WASHINGTON: His Boyhood
and Manhood. With Steel Portrait. Fifth Thousand. Handsomely bound, 5s.

"The character of Washington was a very noble one, and his life may well be taken as an example by boys. The biography is writted in a lively and pleasant tone, and without any of the dryness which is too often the accompaniment of this form of literature. While the details are all strictly historical, the characters are made to live and breathe."—*Standard*.

III.

TACT, PUSH, AND PRINCIPLE. A
Book for those who wish to Succeed in Life. Crown 8vo, cloth, handsomely bound, 3s. 6d.

IV.

THE PIONEER BOY, AND HOW HE
BECAME PRESIDENT. The Story of the Life of Abraham Lincoln. Tenth Thousand. With Portrait. Handsomely bound, 5s.

Many of the details of this work were furnished by PRESIDENT LINCOLN himself, and by his early associates and friends.

"Mr. Thayer is not merely a biographer, a compiler of dry details, but he invests his subject with a halo of delightful romance, and the result is as pleasing as the most imaginative book of fiction. So cleverly has the author done his work, that the result is a combination of pictures from the life of this great man, with humorous anecdote and stirring narrative."—*Society*.

"The author has done his work thoroughly well, and the result is a book of exciting narrative, of humorous anecdote, and of lifelike portraiture."—*Daily Telegraph*.

LONDON: HODDER AND STOUGHTON, 27, PATERNOSTER ROW.

www.ingramcontent.com/pod-product-compliance
Lightning Source LLC
Chambersburg PA
CBHW032013220426
43664CB00006B/232